RETRIBUTION

RETRIBUTION

A US Marine's Fight for Justice, from the Russian Gulag to Ukraine's Front Lines

TREVOR REED
WITH JIM DeFELICE

wm
WILLIAM MORROW
An Imprint of HarperCollins*Publishers*

HarperCollins books may be purchased for educational, business, or sales promotional use. For information, please email the Special Markets Department at SPsales@harpercollins.com.

hc.com

FIRST EDITION

Designed by Michele Cameron
Map designed by Mapping Specialists, Ltd.

Grateful acknowledgment is made to the following for the use of the images that appear in the photo insert: courtesy of Trevor Reed (page 1; page 2, top; page 7, middle right; page 8, middle right); courtesy of Joey Reed (page 2, middle; page 3, bottom); RU24 handout (page 3, middle; page 6, middle); courtesy of Jon Franks (page 4, top; page 7, middle left); Undisclosed (page 4, bottom); courtesy of Reed Family (page 5, bottom; page 6, top; page 7, top); courtesy of Guy Nance (page 7, bottom); and courtesy of Austria (page 8, top; page 8, bottom left).

Library of Congress Cataloging-in-Publication Data has been applied for.

ISBN 978-0-06-342854-6

25 26 27 28 29 LBC 5 4 3 2 1

To all American wrongful detainees and hostages, as well as the loved ones who fight alongside them, though oceans away;

and

to the fallen heroes of Rogue Team, especially my friends Bradley Carl "Super Dave" Jennison, Simon Petrik "Rauta" Rajakisto, Richard "Austria" Schermann, and Corey John "Rocky" Nawrocki, and to all foreign volunteers in Ukraine who gave their lives to protect the innocent;

and

most of all, to my family, without whom I would not be here.

I know not what course others may take; but as for me, give me liberty or give me death!

—PATRICK HENRY

CONTENTS

PART ONE
GULAG

Map of Eastern Ukraine
Yavoriv
Lviv
Kyiv
Kharkiv
Dnipro
RUSSIA
Kharkiv
Approximate line of Russian occupation in May 2023. The occupation line has moved west since the events of this book occurred.
KHARKIV
UKRAINE
LUHANSK
DONETSK
Kramatorsk
Druzhkivka
Bakhmut
Klishchiivka
Andriivka
Kurdyumivka
Ozarianivka
40 mi
40 km
Lviv, Kyiv, Dnipro, and Kharkiv: Major cities.
Yavoriv: A small town in western Ukraine where we completed the GUR special operations training course.
Kramatorsk: The largest city controlled by friendly forces near where we were fighting. We occasionally traveled to bases there for logistics.
Druzhkivka: A small city where our safe house was located.
Klishchiivka and Andriivka: Occupied cities north of where we were fighting, which were recaptured as a result of our operations. Klishchiivka was completely destroyed.
Bakhmut: The epicenter of the hundreds of battles raging in the region. It was completely destroyed.
Kurdyumivka and Ozarianivka: Small towns that held enemy armor, including tanks. Both were destroyed.

AUTHORS' NOTE

This book is a personal account, based largely on memory. We have endeavored to make it as accurate as possible.

In some instances, we have changed names and identifying characteristics for privacy, or to make it more difficult for the individuals to be identified and retaliated against.

Dialogue in quotes, including translations from Russian, is meant to *suggest* what was said, while staying true to the meaning. While in some instances the precise wording has been lost to time, we believe the sense is accurate.

We have endeavored to use the spellings of Ukrainian cities, towns, etc., preferred by Ukrainians.

RETRIBUTION

PROLOGUE

There were better days in Ukraine, days with more action, days with less suck. Days I fought hard against the Russians, paying them back for unfairly imprisoning me. For beating and starving me in solitary confinement.

Days of revenge. Days tinged with remorse, though not for the enemy.

Great days.

This wasn't one of those. This was the day I was going to die.

It hadn't started that way. I was supposed to be in Kyiv, on "vacation," ultimately heading home after months of fighting with a special commando unit as a paid volunteer. We'd done a lot of good work, fighting against an imperialistic enemy who had tried to roll back decades of progress against fascism and dictatorship. In a battle of David versus Goliath, we were David, and David was winning.

For the Ukrainians, it was a fight of good versus evil. For me, it was something even more primitive. It was payback.

I had come to Ukraine for revenge. Russians had imprisoned and mistreated me for three years, locking me into small, dank cells barely big enough to turn around in, feeding me starvation rations of stale bread and salty fish and bones. I'd lost fifty pounds in that time, and barely kept my sanity. The Russian government had lied about me, about who I was, and about who they were. They had persecuted me and stolen my dignity. They'd pushed me from the woman I loved, and driven a wedge between myself and my parents. Their president had mocked and slandered me. When at last I escaped, the need for revenge burned deep in my soul. Not only did I want it; I knew I would have it, even at the cost of my life.

This isn't a metaphor. I had become a different human in the gulag. My friends and family saw it, even before I was released. It was an ugly thing, but beautiful in its intensity. The drive for revenge overrode everything. My parents had spent tens of thousands of dollars and three years getting me out of Russia. They had done everything within their power to get me home safe. But the man they brought home was not the same one they had raised.

When I told my father I was going back to kill Russians, he looked at me in shock and bewilderment, utterly confused.

In the next moment, he understood.

That moment killed him.

Not literally, thank God, but his perception of what I had become broke something inside of him.

I hurt him as deeply as a child can hurt a parent. I regretted it immediately; I regret it to this day. But regret didn't change my mind. Payback was not an option; it was a necessity.

I am a free man. I am Trevor Reed. You did not crush me with your lies and injustice. I will spend every pulse of my blood proving it. And I will prove it with your blood. You took three years of my life; now I am going to take some of yours.

There were other reasons I volunteered to go to Ukraine to fight. Having experienced Russian cruelty up close, I knew what the Ukrainians were experiencing, and I wanted to help them. It was an act of sympathy and comradeship, a need to help other humans in a parallel position to mine.

There is also an undeniable thrill to war. I felt it. I wanted to feel it. Fighting for the right cause, alongside people you trust, even if against the odds, focuses the mind and spirit like no other human activity.

There is great purpose in righteousness. There is a reason we honor heroes.

But mostly, I wanted the Russians to know they hadn't won. I wanted them to find out that they had failed to break me. I wanted them to understand that I had come back and I had hit them harder than they had hit me. They'd taken me hostage and persecuted me, but I was the one who had won.

And so I went to Ukraine to fight.

We'd spent that day near and around a canal in the Donetsk region of Ukraine. Not far from the embattled city of Bakhmut, the region was thick with seesaw battles and some of the bloodiest fighting in the war. While typically our role was to conduct reconnaissance or advise and assist Ukrainian troops, on this mission we helped spearhead an attack. Russian troops in the sector had begun a haphazard retreat. Guided through a minefield by blue tape on the ground left by Ukrainian sappers, we had harassed the Russian positions with grenades, machine guns, and rifles. We'd withstood several artillery barrages, and sweated out an encounter with a Russian tank. Our team leader had been wounded, either by shrapnel or small-arms fire. But we'd achieved our objectives, and then some.

Unlike in the movies, though, there was no crescendo of victory as night approached, not even a "job well done" from headquarters.

We didn't expect one. We had completed our assignment, done what we came to do.

Having pushed beyond our objectives, we were ordered to rest up and prepare to withdraw in the morning.

Plans changed. The man tasked to lead us back came in the middle of the night, hours earlier than expected. Rather than exfiltrating the battlefield in the ample morning light, we had to walk in pitch-black darkness.

Even with night vision—and sometimes by day—seeing Russian mines in the heavy woods or overgrown fields was difficult. But we'd done it many times before, and were fairly confident, though tired, as we set out. We moved in "Ranger file"—one behind the other, spread out to lessen the possibility of collateral injuries if a mine exploded or a bomb struck—treading across a path behind our guide.

The first sign of trouble came when the guide suddenly stopped and made us backtrack to a split in the trail. He had set off confidently, as if he could walk the territory in his sleep. Now he seemed not so sure. A mistake at a turn may seem a small thing, but small things in war are often fatal. You want to feel confident in times of danger. Indecision and second-guessing are like acid, eroding the foundation of your self-assurance. Focus is lost. Mistakes come easier, and become more dangerous.

We hadn't gone too far when I heard a sharp, cracking boom some meters ahead, followed swiftly by a stream of curses and agonized screams.

Belka, a Belarussian attached to our team, had stepped on a mine.

A half-dozen things happened immediately. A team member got to Belka and started applying first aid. I called HQ on our radio, asking for a medical evacuation—a "casevac" or casualty evacuation in military slang. We regrouped, getting our bearings, figuring out next steps.

Belka's leg had been shredded. The heel of his foot was gone. Everything below his knee hung loose, attached by a few strands of muscle and tendon. A tourniquet stopped the worst of the blood loss from his leg, but he had other wounds throughout his body. He needed to get help quickly. We arranged a rendezvous point for the evacuation.

Pele and Austria, the two biggest members of the team, came up to carry Belka. Pele was an infantryman who'd worked as a contractor in Afghanistan and had earned a reputation for making jerk-ass comments at the worst possible time. He kept his mouth shut now; this was too serious a situation for even his shenanigans. Austria, quieter, more circumspect, got into place quickly.

Another comrade, Greek, went to hand me something, probably the radio. Pele started to go off the trail to pass by.

The next thing I knew, another mine exploded.

The explosion blew much of Pele's leg off. Greek, next to me, was struck with fragments in the face and groin so hard he thought he lost his family jewels.

The same explosion took me down. Blood streamed from my legs. I pulled my tourniquet out and managed to get it around my right leg as I fell. I tightened it; worried that I hadn't gotten it over the wound, I had a teammate tie another.

Rescuers rallied toward us. Greek recovered from his initial shock. His wounds, though serious, would turn out not to be life-threatening. Pele muttered about seeing his dead mother. He, too, would survive the explosion, though without his leg.

For a while I thought I was going to be okay. But then things began to go numb. I felt like I was sinking into the earth. My arms, which hadn't been hit, stopped working. I realized I was very likely going to die.

Lying on the ground, I told Greek that I wanted him to give a message to my family.

"I think you're being a little dramatic," Greek snapped. Then he got a good look at me. "What do you want me to say?"

"Tell my family—"

"Tell them you died doing what you love," he interrupted.

"No. Shut up. Tell my family I died a free man."

"You died a free man?"

"Yes," I insisted.

It was the most important thing I could tell them, the most important fact of my existence. It thanked them for helping free me from the Russians, and at the same time embodied the greatest truth of my life.

I am a free man.

I didn't die, as you can tell since I'm writing this book. There is more to that story, and to my story, and to my parents'. But that is the bottom line: When I *do* die, I will die a free man.

In spite of everything the Russians did to me, in spite of all their hatred and their injustice, I will not be broken. I was not broken. And in my own way, I have paid them back for everything they did to me.

In the process, I have learned that the greatest revenge is to survive and be free.

PART ONE

GULAG

ONE

SEMPER FI

I've had strange and traumatic experiences I wouldn't wish on anyone, but before all of those, I was a pretty normal guy. And for the record, I still feel I'm a normal guy, except for those experiences.

I can't honestly say what I've lived through hasn't changed me. I've hardened—yet softened as well. I better understand violence, but also love. Some things haven't changed. Stubbornness, for good and bad. Patriotism. The sense of right and wrong. An appreciation of the past. A hope that the future is worth the trials and sometimes torture of the present.

I was born in 1991 in Texas, eighth generation. My family is more Texan than most, with a great-great times four or five Scotts-Irish grandfather and mother named Reed. In 1831 or thereabouts, the Reeds got a land grant to settle in the area around present-day Temple, a bit south of Waco. We have a copy of the original land grant, now in the University of Texas archive, signed by Santa Anna—Mexican president Antonio de Padua María Severino López de Santa Anna y

Pérez de Lebrón. That means that my ancestors were in Texas before it was Texas.

According to papers my family has found, some of our ancestors received pensions from the Republic of Texas Army. So whenever the revolution against Mexico started, they must have joined up. They don't seem to have actually fought, though. As the story goes, they met Sam Houston's army after he'd captured Santa Anna, which effectively ended hostilities, but were still considered veterans.

My mom Paula's roots in the US aren't quite as deep. Her ancestors emigrated from Mexico to Texas in 1900. Her father came from Costa Rica, serving in the American army in Vietnam before becoming a citizen.

Service to our country runs deep in my family. My uncle Jerry on my mom's side was a paratrooper in the 82nd Airborne and fought in Desert Storm. My other uncle on my mom's side, Charlie, was medically discharged from the Corps when he snapped both femurs in Marine Boot Camp. Back on my dad's side, my grandpa Reed was in the Navy; my great-grandfather William Jolley served in the US Army 82nd Field Artillery (horse drawn) and later was a sailor in World War II and saw action in the Pacific.

I myself was born in Fort Worth in 1991 and lived in the area as an infant and young child. In 1994, soon after my sister Taylor was born, my dad got a job as a fireman in California. We moved to Bear Valley Springs in Kern County, just outside of Tehachapi. There were a number of firefighters and police officers who had homes in the valley where we lived, making for a close-knit community.

The name "Tehachapi" is said to come from a word for "hard climb" used by the Kawaiisu Native Americans who lived in the area. That makes a lot of sense: the town itself is mostly flat, but it's nearly four thousand feet above sea level. The highest peaks in the local Tehachapi Mountains rise roughly eight thousand feet. The center of town is some forty miles southeast of Bakersfield. It's grown a bit since I lived there, but still has a small-town feel, very different certainly than Los Angeles, which is roughly a hundred miles farther south.

It was a beautiful place to grow up. With two lakes, a bunch of trails zagging through the mountainous hills, plenty of room for horses, a golf course—if you love the outdoors, this was the life. The area has its share of animals, including bears and coyotes. Every year there was a competition to see who had the best llamas. One year a mountain lion got the winner.

A small community means you get to know a lot of your neighbors pretty well, especially at school. My dad had us try out just about all the available sports to see what we liked. I played soccer, roller hockey, basketball, and baseball. I took judo lessons and went out for wrestling. About the only thing I didn't try—at least not much—was music. I played guitar for like five minutes before deciding I wasn't musical.

Boy Scouts was special. Later on I realized just how much I learned there, from knots to first aid and navigating in the wilderness. We'd go out for a couple of days hiking, dealing with cold and heat in the wild. It turned out to be good prep for the military, but that was the furthest thing from my mind at that point. I zoomed through the ranks to First Class, then earned merit badges and engineered a community service project to make Eagle Scout.

Wrestling prepared me in another way. I went out for the team as a freshman because I'd heard it was hard, and I wanted to prove myself. I still remember the assistant coach telling us on day one to do a hundred push-ups after they had us run several miles.

"Are you serious?" someone gasped.

"Do I look like I'm fooling around, son?" the coach shot back.

We dropped and didn't stop.

Things got tougher from there. Wind sprints, crab walks, bear crawls, monkey rolls . . . I can't describe the exercises without my body getting sore.

Kids quit in droves. By the start of the season there were just enough wrestlers to fill out the twelve weight classes in varsity, with four kids, including me, left for jayvee. We had three-hour practices that were nothing but running, calisthenics, and some very basic wrestling drills. The head coach might bark, he might smile, once in a great while laugh, but the one constant in preseason was grinding pain.

There was, however, a method to his madness. See, because we were a small school and community, we didn't have a feeder program like a lot of our competitors did. The schools in Bakersfield and Antelope Valley, below us in the desert, had the benefit of kids who'd learned to wrestle at four or five, progressing through stages. We didn't even have a junior high program. You didn't learn basic techniques until you got to high school. So our wrestlers competed at an immediate disadvantage.

Or would have, if they weren't generally in better shape than their opponents. Rather than trying to cram the fine points of wrestling technique into a few weeks ahead of the meets, our coaches beat the living bejesus out of us so we could last longer and wrestle stronger.

I would go out on the mat for the first two periods (high school matches have three two-minute periods) and get my ass kicked, just trying to keep from being pinned. And then it was like my opponent hit a wall. They were tired. I never would feel fatigue. That last period was mine, primitive moves or not. In my freshman year, I think I got MVP for the JV team. I won almost every match I entered.

Endurance was the big thing, but the throws I'd learned in judo played a part, too. My coach didn't like that—usually.

"Stop using that judo shit!" he'd yell.

But . . . I remember a match where I was getting my butt kicked. In the third period I looked at the clock and there were like twenty seconds left.

"Throw him!" said the coach.

So I did. As soon as my opponent landed, I went in for the pin.

"You're scaring me, son," said the coach afterward. "I thought you were going to lose that."

"You told me not to use judo."

"Well, don't lose!"

Lesson learned: use whatever you've got when the chips are down.

With that first season over, I realized I'd accomplished what I set out to do. I had done what 95 percent of the people who tried out that first day couldn't. My friend and I agreed, mission accomplished. Time for something else.

But my dad was like, no, you're staying in there. You don't quit something once you've started.

So it turned out I wasn't just learning about whether I was tough enough to take on a hard task. I was learning about commitment. It was another valuable lesson—and I learned it in a fun way, I guess, because I really loved wrestling as the years went by. I went all in, learning advanced techniques. My takedowns improved. I never did totally banish the "judo bit" completely—it might be the last thing a senior class wrestler was expecting—but I learned to rely mostly on proven technique, strength, endurance.

Wrestlers compete in different weight classes; "making weight" is an ordeal for many. I wrestled in the 125-pound weight class my senior year. Given that I weighed like 145 in the off-season and had, oh, maybe something like 6 percent body fat, I had to dial in really hard to make weight. I didn't use diuretics, but I absolutely monitored what went into my mouth. Four days before the weigh-in, I wouldn't eat anything. The last day, I'd have half an orange. Meanwhile, I'd be working out three hours every day, which meant three hours of cardio. From sprints to wrestling, I'd burn off serious calories. If the weight was still high, a sauna suit would take off even more.

I did pretty well overall, generally placing in the top three in our league each year. I competed at the regional level, but never made it to the finals. Still, wrestling was an important experience, teaching me things you can't learn in classrooms, a lot of them about myself.

The most valuable lesson?

It came after I was named team captain. As a leader, never show weakness or hesitation. If you appear invulnerable, your teammates or the people you lead will believe you are and will keep going until you quit.

I won't say I let my classes slide, but schoolwork wasn't my highest priority. As graduation neared in the spring of 2010, I planned on the military, aiming for the Marines. Though I'd proved to myself I could handle difficult tasks, I wanted to take myself to the next level.

The biggest obstacle turned out to be my parents. They didn't want me to go into the service at all, let alone become a Marine.

The irony was, my father had been a Marine. He kept trying to talk me out of joining, warning me that it would be harder than I imagined. I probably should have put more store in what he was saying. Face it, if someone who's achieved a goal tells you the goal isn't worth it—well, you're foolish not to give that goal some very serious scrutiny. But when you're a teenager, and the advice is coming from your dad . . .

Yeah, what did he know?

I can't say I won him over to the idea, but he did eventually help me prepare, thanks to my mom. Possibly the most important thing he did was show me the "Marine way" of marching, along with how to handle and shoot a rifle as Marines do. That gave me a bit of an advantage later on.

But it took a while to get there. My parents managed to convince me that I should try going to college before joining the service, probably believing that I'd like school so much I'd choose to continue with it. Except I hated community college. My job, part-time stock guy in a clothing store, wasn't much better. I wasn't even partying, and that's half the reason most people go to college.

I told myself, as soon as the semester ends, I'm going into the military. I don't give a hoot what my father says.

He wasn't happy. But I told him one day I was going to the recruiter, and I did. And that was that.

I love my dad now and I loved him then. That's bedrock. But we didn't get along when I was a teenager. He's really a type A personality. Worse, from his point of view, there's only one right way of doing things: *his way*. Even if there are other right ways and they're more efficient, if those are not *his* way, they're not the right way, so don't do them.

Looking back, I probably was just as stubborn as he was. Or almost. I'm sure I was disrespectful and probably added a lot of worry to my parents' lives. But we all did what we had to do, and in the end, it kind of worked out.

Though it could have gone a lot more smoothly.

I'd been leaning toward the Marines for years. I remember seeing a movie set in the Pacific theater of World War II and thinking the Leathernecks were pretty badass. They fought hand to hand, using flamethrowers and all kinds of weapons.

Hollywood. But with a grain of truth.

More contemporary things, like news reports and video from the wars in Afghanistan and Iraq, convinced me I should serve my country. I wanted action. Besides the Marines, I thought about aiming for elite units, like the SEALs or Army Special Forces. I almost signed on with the Army for a chance to go through Ranger training, hoping to serve in the famous 75th Ranger Regiment. I was equal opportunity military, as long as it looked badass.

But the Army recruiters turned me off when I went to meet them—they looked a bit sloppy in their cammies, unlike the Marines. The funny thing is, the Marine recruiters acted like they didn't really want me. The Army offered an enlistment bonus and guaranteed I'd be able to become an Airborne forward observer with the Rangers.

The Marines, on the other hand, told me I might get one of my three top assignments, without a real guarantee. I had to insist on infantry, and it wasn't until the CO of the recruiting office personally met me and signed off that I got a contract specifying that, a rarity at the time.

For the record, infantry is usually not considered a plum assignment, even in the Marines. It doesn't prepare you for a job in civilian life, and it's often not a place where you can quickly win promotions (and pay raises). The recruiters couldn't understand why I wanted it when I had test scores that could have gotten me into jobs they considered better.

If you want to prove yourself in combat, though, there's no better place than infantry. And Marine infantry is badass, my main requirement.

Your introduction to the Corps is an introduction to trauma. You get there, they strip you out of all your clothes, send you to medical. You get a zillion shots; you bleed out of both your arms; they shave your head. Exaggerations? Maybe, but it feels like I'm making it sound easier than it was. My head was bleeding and I had a uniform that didn't fit. Someone wrote a number on my arm and sent me down the line, like I was a cow on my way to the slaughterhouse. But instead of being chopped into hamburger meat, I was shunted to a row of pay phones.

I think there were five drill instructors barking in my ear. "Hurry the fuck up! Come on! Dial it! Say exactly what's on the wall and hang up."

I called home. My dad answered.

"Good evening, sir. This recruit has reached Marine Corps Recruit Depot, San Diego. I will call you in three and a half months. Goodbye, sir!"

I hung up the phone and joined the other recruits, sprinting into the dark jaws of hell on earth, otherwise known as Marine Corps boot camp.

Back home, my father turned to my mother. "I've never heard his voice in that pitch before," he said, shaking his head and fighting flashbacks of his own boot camp.

I have to admit, as hard as the experience is, when you look back at it, you laugh at a lot of things that happen in boot camp. You accept why a lot of things are done the way they're done; you realize that the process not only prepared you to be a Marine, but also helped you be a better person.

Usually.

But while you're going through it, especially as an eighteen- or nineteen-year-old kid, you're likely to be thinking, *Holy shit! I wanted to be here???? Why did I sign that paper?!?*

I couldn't have been there more than an hour when I realized, *Oh shit, this is exactly as bad as my dad said it was!*

Not only did boot camp suck, not only were the Marines psycho, but *my father* was actually right.

A lot to handle at eighteen.

I wrote a letter to my parents. *Hey guys,* I told them, *I'm sorry that I was a bad kid. I understand everything that you told me as my parents now was true. I was disrespectful and I didn't understand any of that, but I understand now and so I'm sorry and I hope you'll forgive me.*

The effect of the letter was the opposite of what I intended. They really worried about me now: *It must be really bad if he's saying that.* But my relationship with my parents, my father especially, improved dramatically. My dad wrote me every day. He had received very few letters when he was in boot camp and knew how important it was to get information from the outside world. Besides talking about what was going on with the rest of the family, he'd often include inspirational stories about famous people who had been Marines. Every letter was a morale booster.

There's a saying that every Marine is a rifleman. While there are many jobs in the Corps that don't require you to use a rifle, let alone fight as an infantryman, there is a lot of emphasis on basic rifle skills and justifiable pride in the average Marine's shooting ability. The instructors aren't just good at the physical aspects of handling a rifle; they incorporate psychology to push you further.

Case in point: Our senior drill instructor had (allegedly) just finished requalifying on the range and "bragged" that he'd been nearly perfect. Further, he said he was from Texas, and therefore was obviously very good. So good, in fact, that no one in our platoon could beat him.

And if by some miracle they happened to do that, they would be awarded a phone call home.

Getting a phone call home during boot camp *is* a reward. Most recruits are missing their folks and families by the time rifle training comes around. But the potential bragging rights of beating your instructor? Off the charts.

I did pretty well on the test, but I thought the promise of the call home was bs. So when he called me into his office, I thought I was in trouble.

"Recruit! What was your score?"

"This recruit scored 239 out of 250, senior drill instructor." That was on the long-range portion of the test, with iron sights.

He told me his score, which was lower, and asked if I knew what that meant.

I could feel my muscles already starting to tighten. *Drop and don't stop?*

He handed over his cell phone.

I nervously punched in my father's number, still unsure if I was about to be thrashed—Marine jargon for doing push-ups until your arms fall off.

"Hello?" said my dad, obviously wondering who the strange number belonged to.

"Dad?"

"Trevor?"

"Yeah."

"Is everything okay?"

"Yes. This recruit outshot the senior drill instructor at the range. So he got a phone call."

"Uh, oh. How are you?"

"Good."

"What are you doing this week?"

"I don't know. I gotta go. I love you. Bye."

I hung up. The instructor looked at me like, *That's all you're going to say?*

I managed to get out of the office with both my dignity and my arms intact . . . at least until the next set of exercises.

I was doing reasonably well in boot camp when recruits who had signed up for infantry were taken to an auditorium. The NCOs in charge began asking questions about our backgrounds to winnow down the group.

Over the next few weeks, there was more screening, more questions. We didn't know it, but the instructors were also reviewing things like our performance at PT and on the rifle range. Kind of like double-super-secret-probation: No one explained why any of this was going on. I had no idea what was up until finally, with the screening process almost over, one of the recruiters said we were being screened for Presidential Support Duty.

Marines are assigned to some of the most difficult and important guard duties in the world. We protect embassies, property, and officials. We also guard the White House and Camp David, the facility traditionally used by presidents outside of Washington, DC. Marines there have been protecting the president and the city of Washington since before the War of 1812. The DC facility contains one of the oldest buildings in the city, and among other things houses the Commandant.

By the end of screening and selection in boot camp, I think maybe there were four of us left, or maybe only two. Then, after all that work, they told us that if we wanted to be in the program, we would have to extend our enlistments for a year.

Oh, hell, no.

Serving more than my contracted four years wasn't something I'd been planning on, and to be honest, at that I point I didn't realize how much of an honor it was to be selected. But then I got a letter from my father, saying something like *You might want to consider this.* And I was like, *Man, my dad was really down on my being in the Marine Corps. So if he said, do an extra year, it must be something important.*

So I decided to go for it.

There were still some hurdles. I had to get through Infantry School, pass a clearance check, undergo additional training, and then be assigned to the unit.

Wait. Did I forget to mention the Crucible, at the end of boot camp?

To become a Marine, you have to survive boot *and* the Crucible, which is fifty-four hours of forced marches, combat exercises, obstacle courses, teamwork, sweat, more sweat, and pain in places of your body that have never felt pain before.

I got through it okay, earning the privilege of calling myself a Marine. But I was still pretty far from being a *useful* Marine. The next step in that process was Infantry School.

There was a lot of yelling there, and some of the instructors were so hard on their men that they were disciplined by Command, a rarity in the Corps even then. I got my face smashed into the gun rack for grabbing the wrong rifle out of the armory, and kicked in the face for shooting my rifle after its laser died, even though I'd been ordered to do just that.

You can't win, really.

We were at Camp Pendleton, a massive complex that dates to World War II. This is in Southern California, and the weather can be as brutal as some of the training. You freeze in the morning and roast in the afternoon. I think we lost about 33 percent of our class to injuries, along with a handful of guys who decided to go to the brig rather than continue with training, and a few who went out for the weekend and never came back—at least until they were arrested.

Long "humps" were part of the routine. We would go out with packs so heavy you needed help to get them on your back. I got blisters on the fifteen-kilometer hump, which messed me up for everything that followed. My leg hurt like crazy, but I knew that if I reported a possible injury or went to the medical personnel on base, I'd very likely be recycled—meaning I'd have to relive the entire ordeal. So instead, I arranged with my father's help to see a doctor off base.

The diagnosis: possible stress fractures, center of the femur, both legs.

Both legs, though the right felt worse.

The doctor advised me not to do any physical activity for twelve weeks. Instead, I marched twenty kilometers a day or two later. That's how much I wanted to avoid going through infantry training again.

It was my dad who really saved me. We had weekends off. He was in Tehachapi, and would drive down every weekend to see me. That's a four-hour drive. He'd patch up my blistered feet, treat the beginnings of trench foot and other nasties, then shove as much food and liquids into my body as possible. Without that, I wouldn't have been able to crawl a kilometer, let alone march twenty with a heavy pack.

Done with Infantry School and additional training, I was assigned to Guard Company, stationed in Washington, DC, and often called 8th & I, after the unit location. Besides training and waiting for clearances, Marines at 8th & I guard the Commandant, the Corps' highest ranked officer.

The city was not exactly crime free at the time, and while we didn't necessarily go out looking for trouble, it did occasionally find us. Especially since our barracks were in southeast DC, not the safest part of town.

One weekend some friends—Cody, Taron, and a fellow I'll call Johnny Utah—and I were on the Metro coming back to the barracks when a group of young men about our age entered the train car and tried to shake down the passengers for valuables. Marines are not known for taking that sort of thing with grace, and I was on the Metro more than once when would-be robbers spotted a group of us and canceled their plans. We tend to stand out, even in civilian clothes. But for some reason, on this night these guys were oblivious. One of them made the mistake of asking us for "donations."

"We don't want to demand money," they said, or something similar. "Because that would be robbing you. We don't want to do that. We just want your money."

Charity for a good cause, no doubt.

Taron stood up and began taking off his jacket.

"Why you taking off your jacket?" asked one of the thugs. "You getting ready for a UFC fight or something? I'm not going to fight you. I'll stab you."

"Really?" Johnny pulled out his own knife.

The thug stepped back. By the time he recovered his breath, his friends were in the next car. He decided he should follow, donations be damned.

We had a brief debate about whether or not to aggressively end their charity work. We decided instead to alert the police officer we saw on the platform as the train pulled to a stop.

I never did get around to seeing if their charity was registered with the IRS.

There were other adventures, a few of which may or may not have involved drinking, which of course none of us did as we were under twenty-one. Mostly we were stereotypical Marines, always on our best behavior in and out of uniform.

Guarding Camp David was pretty much like guarding any facility . . . except it was Camp David.

The president's country house.

Every Marine has a strong sense of mission, but I think it's fair to say that Marines guarding the president and his family have an *extremely* strong sense of mission. You don't go around saying you have an important job; you just know you do. And you DO NOT screw it up.

Most of the time, what we do isn't all that interesting. About the only potential invader I encountered in the eighteen months I was there was a timber rattlesnake, who had the audacity to slither out in front of a friend and me one night as we drove to the gate. After securing the potential intruder, I brought him into the camp proper for an interrogation, or maybe show-and-tell. Even our Gunny was impressed. At least that's how I interpret his remark: "I don't care what Reed catches, as long as it doesn't bite anyone."

"Gunny" is Marine Corps lingo for Gunnery Sergeant, an E7 in the military ranking system. Gunnys are typically the unit's operations chief, working with officers on training, operations, and tactics. The rank is highly respected.

Some of our NCOs—noncommissioned officers, sergeants or an occasional corporal—had seen serious action in Iraq, Afghanistan, or both. Marines had been in some of the heaviest fighting in the war, at Fallujah, Ramadi, the provinces out west. They were badasses. One staff sergeant at the Marine Barracks in Washington, Corey Nawrocki, had two Purple Hearts and a Bronze Star with V, meaning he had earned one of the nation's highest medals in combat. Our First Sergeant had done tours with MARSOC, the Corps' special operations units, before coming to us. He had a stack of ribbons on his dress uniform bigger than I've ever seen. The NCOs didn't share their stories too often, but when they gave you advice, you tried to soak it up.

And while a lot of enlisted Marines tend to complain about their officers—my dad certainly did—ours at Camp David were uniformly excellent. They had us training all the time.

The word "easygoing" has never in history been applied to *any* Marine officer ever, but the major in charge of our unit had a balanced approach to discipline and mission. He made it clear that if you screwed up, you were out. But there was none of the pettiness you sometimes found elsewhere in the service.

The highlight of my assignment at Camp David was meeting President Obama. On one of his visits, he came out to meet us and take some pictures for us in formation. He actually shook hands and spoke to each one of us. Now, when a general did that, or even a colonel, I was a little nervous. But with the president—I don't know, he just seemed really kind of chill. I was not really nervous at all. I was like, wow, that's the president. Nice.

"Good morning, Mr. President," I said, as if I were greeting a celebrity, or even the father of a friend I hadn't seen since childhood, not the COMMANDER IN CHIEF.

The president looked at me kind of funny, probably wondering why this one Marine was grinning while everyone else was grim-faced and practically shaking.

"Where are you from, son?" he asked.

"I'm from Fort Worth, Mr. President."

I don't remember the rest of the conversation. It didn't last much longer than what the photographer needed to get a picture, but I'm sure I grinned the whole time.

After the president met all of the Marines, we lined up to take a group shot. At the time, I was one of the shortest guys, if not *the* shortest guy, at the base. And when we lined up, I was in the back, leaning over to try to get into the shot.

"Can you see everyone?" Obama asked the photographer.

"I can see everyone," she answered.

The president—not a short fellow—turned around and spotted me. "I know you can't see this guy," he said, grabbing me by the shoulder and yanking me next to him.

And so in the group photo, the president has his hand on my shoulder like we're old buddies.

Here's something to know about my father:

It was arranged that each Marine and a family member could have a picture with the president in the Oval Office. I had to choose between my mom and my dad. I chose my dad, figuring it would mean a lot more to him than to her. He's big on photos; she frankly couldn't care less.

Plus I felt like I owed it to him, because without him I wouldn't have made it through Infantry School.

I also thought he'd be, you know, stoic. He being a Marine and all.

My mom called for a report afterward.

"I really do wish I brought you, Mom," I had to confess. "Dad cried the whole time."

All right, he says he didn't actually cry, though in my mom's version of the story, he was bawling. But his eyes definitely welled up, and he was really close. My father truly wears his emotions on the outside. You never have to guess what he's feeling, even when he's overwhelmed.

That photo, by the way, would play an important part in my life a few years later.

I was at Camp David for roughly eighteen months, making corporal along the way. A lot of guys at the end of their tours go on to Marine Recon, MARSOC, or look for other prestigious assignments to advance their career. I wasn't looking to stay in the Corps long term, though. I managed to wangle an assignment to 3/1—Third Battalion, First Marine Regiment—which is part of the 1st Marine Division. I got the post by saying my father had served in the unit, which was true enough. But I really wanted to go to the West Coast because that's where all the good beaches and hot women were.

Or so I heard.

I did get 3/1, if not the women. I'd also hoped to be assigned to a boat or helicopter assault company, figuring there'd be a lot less marching. Unfortunately, I ended up in a Trak company—a unit that moves in amphibious vehicles, unaffectionately known as amtracs. I'm exaggerating when I call them tractors with grenade launchers and fifty cals—but I'm exaggerating just a little. Thinly armored, the Assault Amphibious Vehicle or AAV-design dates from the late

1960s and early '70s. Propelled on land by tracks similar to what you would find on a tank, the crew compartment feels claustrophobic and lacks adequate protection against contemporary IEDs, let alone large-caliber weapons. It also sucks in exhaust and leaks in the water.

Amtracs are carried and launched from the well deck of a landing ship, in our case, the USS *Rushmore* (LSD-47). If Marines packed into every nook and cranny, the ship could accommodate something like five hundred of them. We had less than that, but it often felt like more.

As a team leader and later heading a squad, I learned there are times when you have to be a hard-ass. Even in the Corps, there are a few Marines who are out of shape and, to be honest, lazy—at least from a Marine perspective. I had one or two like that . . . at first. We did a lot of remedial PT to get things straightened out. At the same time, I did my best to share my training with them and the rest of the team. I also became a Marine Corps Martial Arts Instructor, and helped train the platoon and company in hand-to-hand combat.

My squad may not have been the best looking on a parade field, but when it came to the things you had to know and do in combat, they kicked butt. The big lesson for me: the important thing isn't that your troops like you, it's that they know how to do their job. If they respect you because of that, it's a bonus.

We embarked on a long tour with the 15th Expeditionary Unit, sailing with the Seventh Fleet to Southeast Asia, Indonesia, and other countries in that area. We did some time in the Persian Gulf, and landed our amtracs in the Kuwait desert—about the last place you want to drive an amphibious vehicle around. We spent a little time on the Kuwait border with Iraq without seeing more than a Bedouin and thirty camels, then floated off to Africa to support an operation I still don't know the details of.

On the way back, I made sergeant. I'd gotten extra points as a Presidential Guard, had good ratings and awards for my shooting and

PT. I'd been a squad leader for about eight months, and I suppose if I'd reenlisted I might have looked toward leading a platoon of my own and more promotions. But that had never been my intention. While the Marines had helped me mature, I didn't want to make a career out of the Corps.

My one regret at the time was that I hadn't seen any combat. I'd joined the Marines to prove to myself what I could do. Like those Army commercials: "Be all you can be." Except tougher, because it was the Marines. But I'd come so far that I felt I didn't need the last step of combat to prove to myself that I could endure. I appreciated the training I'd gotten. I better understood and respected how my father had pushed me growing up to be self-reliant, how my mom had inspired me to help others.

Would I be courageous under combat? You never really know until you're there, but I had a sense that I would. And proving myself was no longer necessary. I was already a Marine.

Just to be clear: I don't make any claims of being a model Marine, let alone the best ever. Everything I achieved was because of this: I was obsessed with not messing up.

Camp David had all sorts of complex procedures and systems, and it was really easy to muck something, even if you were a great Marine. I succeeded by being paranoid. Ordinarily I'm not a type A personality like my father, but when it came to the Corps, I was all in on that.

But now it was time to move on. And so, on February 9, 2016, I completed my separation paperwork, gassed up my Jeep, and drove from California back to Texas where my family had relocated after my sister finished high school. Happy not to have a boss, a responsibility, or even a plan, I was ready for the rest of my life.

TWO

LOVE AND FATE

I don't know how to describe those first few days and weeks. Then again, there's not much to describe. I came home and stayed in a room upstairs in my parents' house. And slept.

And slept some more. I was making up for five years of missed sleep. There was no PT in the morning, no younger Marines to check on. No little problems that leadership made big problems. Sock on the floor? No one cared.

Yeah, I left socks everywhere.

I didn't have PTSD or anything, but I did have nightmares. I dreamed I screwed up something and would have to go to the brig. I'd wake up nervous and shaking, trying to remember what the hell it was that I had messed up. Then I'd realize I hadn't done anything wrong, and wasn't in the Corps anymore.

Playing video games all night and sleeping until the afternoon didn't sit too well with my parents, especially my dad. I wasn't doing much else—not partying or even seeing friends. One afternoon my father came and sat on the bed. "Hey buddy. You're sleeping a lot."

"Yeah, I'm tired," I told him.

"You might want to find something to do. A job? School?"

"Yeah."

I think it was the next day that my friend Jordan called me up and asked what I was up to.

"Hanging," I said.

"Let me guess," he started. "You live with your parents and you're sleeping until one p.m."

"Yep."

"You have a job?"

"Nope," I confessed.

"Are you going to school?"

"No."

He laughed. "I did the same for three months when I got out. You want to make some money?"

"What do I have to do?"

I didn't know where the conversation was going. I mean, that's the sort of question drug cartels ask naive tourists, right?

"You don't have to do much," he told me. "It's real cool."

He wasn't pimping for drug dealers. It was a legitimate job, though the tasks were considerably more than he let on. Jordan worked for Triple Canopy, a security firm that had contracts with the US and others to provide services overseas. Triple Canopy was one of several companies under the umbrella of a private contracting company known as Constellis. Security was just one of Constellis's specialties, but that was the area that I was qualified for.

My friend had me send my resume to a recruiter. To my surprise, I got a call the next day from Academi, another sub-company of Constellis.

"Hey, your resume here looks awesome," the recruiter told me. "But also, no offense, there's a lot of stuff in here that's pretty hard to believe without evidence."

"Okay. Well, what do you want?"

"I need a letter that confirms that you actually did this stuff and guarded the president."

Getting letters of recommendation from previous employers can be a bit of a hassle, but imagine trying to run down the President of the United States for one. Fortunately, I was able to get ahold of the head of security at Camp David, who just happened to have worked under me when I was there. He sent a letter out pretty quick.

And just as quick, the recruiter called back and said they wanted a letter from the unit's commanding officer.

"How about the XO?" I asked, knowing that the executive officer was more likely to take the time to write, or at least sign, a letter confirming my bona fides.

"That'll do."

And it did. Even though Academi employed high-speed SEALs and Green Berets, this lowly Marine's experience guarding the president and his family fit perfectly with what the company was looking for—someone who could work overseas providing security for State Department personnel and other US assets. While the State Department's Bureau of Diplomatic Security and the US Marines are responsible for the direct security, they're heavily augmented by private contractors, who are usually under the direction of State's RSOs, or Regional Security Officers. Academi was one of those contractors.

"Okay, this is awesome," said the recruiter after I forwarded the letter. "You should come to training in three days."

"Three days? Whoa."

After a bit of discussion, he agreed to make it two weeks so I could get my affairs in order.

After I hung up, I went to tell my mom and dad.

"Hey, I got a job," I told them.

"Great," said my father. "What kind of job?"

"I'm going to do security stuff in Iraq or Afghanistan with this private company."

"What private company?"

"Used to be Blackwater, and now it's called this other thing. I just have to go pass the PT test and the training course."

"Why are you taking that job?" he asked.

"You told me I should get a job."

"Yeah, but not that kind of job. What's the pay?"

"I don't know. I forgot to ask."

The pay turned out to be pretty good. I believe I started at $459.33 a day. Why the odd number? Dunno. There were a bunch of benefits as well. Sweet, especially compared to my salary in the Corps.

Of course, I could get killed at any moment guarding someone a terrorist wanted dead, but I didn't figure that into the equation.

It's kind of funny now, but I remember there was a job I applied for before I heard from my friend: security at the Fort Worth Zoo.

They rejected my application. Apparently guarding the president did not qualify me to keep an eye on giraffes and elephants.

I did six weeks of training in the US. The hardest part might have been the psych evaluation.

Pre-evaluation, they gave me a questionnaire to fill out. There was a wide range of questions, but the ones that jumped out concerned pornography.

The first was *Have you ever watched child pornography?*

Easy *no* to that.

Have you ever watched pornography?

Hell, find me a twenty-five-year-old American male, or female, who hasn't.

But was "yes" a safe answer? Or "no"? Or . . .

The guys being screened with me couldn't decide. Maybe it was really a question about honesty—I mean, you have to be lying if you say no, right?

I saw no point in lying. But I was nervous about it when it came time for my in-person screening.

It didn't help that the female psychologist was an 11 on a scale of 1–10.

She didn't ask any porn questions. I was a little disappointed.

Most of what she asked were hypotheticals, designed to see if I was a sociopathic killer. Apparently I'm not, because the questioning continued routinely, until finally she asked if I was married.

"No," I told her.

"Kids?"

"No."

"Is it easier that way, to just kind of come and go as you please?" she asked.

I shrugged. "I guess."

She smiled and I left. It turned out, none of my friends had been asked about being married or having kids—information she would have had from my application.

"She was looking for a date," suggested a fellow trainee.

"Nah."

"Yeah," he insisted. Others agreed.

Maybe. I'd never been interviewed by a shrink before. Or an 11. Next time I'll be better prepared.

The training itself was mostly straightforward. There was a lot of emphasis on small arms, from pistols to grenade launchers. I was already familiar with all but the Glock pistols they issued, and learning that gun wasn't particularly hard. The instructors were ex-military, most with impressive credentials. Pretty much every trainee was ex-military and had served in combat zones, though in a few cases I suspect they hadn't actually seen combat, and had probably trained for specialties other than infantry. Cooks and mechanics are very important, but their skills are not necessarily applicable to defending a motorcade. Those who didn't have the skills and couldn't adapt quickly were handed tickets home.

As you probably expect, a good portion of the training dealt directly with protecting "assets"—people—and getting them (and ourselves) out of trouble. Assaulting buildings to rescue prisoners. Defensive driving on steroids. How to move in and out of different situations while minimizing danger.

Less expected, I'd guess, was the amount of time the instructors spent on first aid, aka "tactical combat casualty care." That was something that would eventually be very important to me, though it would be years before I truly needed it.

Our midterm exam: protect the "ambassador" as he makes a speech in an urban area.

Of course he's going to be attacked, right?

We were divided up into teams with select duties. I was on the four-man advance squad. We went in, did our thing, then sat back and watched as the "enemy" moved to ambush.

"We should go in." I pointed out that we could circle behind the aggressors and surprise them. Technically, we weren't supposed to do that; our mission had already been accomplished. But in real life, if we happened to be in that position when stuff started hitting the fan . . .

We caught the enemy completely by surprise. Big score for us.

Then came the debrief. The instructor wanted to know whose idea it was to mess up the exercise like that.

I reluctantly accepted the blame.

"Good job," he told me.

First time I've ever been congratulated for cheating on a test.

Our final was a more realistic exercise off base: escorting a subject in a local municipality, where, among other places, he stopped into an ice cream place and then a Dick's Sporting Goods store on a whim. To his credit, he didn't employ the five-finger discount in either place, even though he would have had plenty of protection getting out.

Private security companies—"contractors," or occasionally "mercenaries" to the general public—handle a wide variety of jobs that most people associate with the government. Protecting Americans probably being the most critical. When I was employed, there were gigs all over the world. Some were comparatively safe, like one in Israel (not at war at the time). Others were riskier, and paid more.

My assignment was to Afghanistan, which at that time rated very high, danger-wise. I arrived in Kabul at the end of July 2016. The trip itself was uneventful until the last leg, when the plane flew so low through the mountains I was squirming before we touched down.

Disembarking, I joined maybe a hundred other contractors in a hangar to wait for my transport. I wanted to ask what the deal was but didn't want to look like a stupid boot, so I kept my mouth shut and waited. Eventually a guy came out with a clipboard.

"Where's my shooters at?" he barked.

I looked at a huge guy to my left and thought, He's definitely a shooter.

But he didn't move. In fact, no one moved. The man with the clipboard checked his papers. "Where's Trevor Reed?"

I walked up.

"Why didn't you say anything when I asked for shooters?"

"I didn't know that was me."

"First time or what?"

I put on a flak vest and hustled over to a Chinook helicopter waiting nearby. The crew chief tossed my gear in and told me to strap up.

"I'm the only one on the helicopter?" I asked. Chinooks, a staple of the US military, can carry something like fifty troops.

The chief smiled. "Yeah, bro, this bird is for you."

Shortly after I arrived at the base, we came under attack. I'd just figured out how to get my laptop online and video my parents to tell them I'd arrived when an alarm began blaring.

"Incoming! Incoming! Incoming!"

A moment later, something exploded nearby. The room shook.

"Gotta go," I told my parents as nonchalantly as I could. "I'll call ya back."

I slapped the computer closed and ran out into the hall. Guys had already lined up, kitted out, rifles ready.

"Come on, bro," yelled one. "You comin' or what?"

"Uh, I don't have a rifle," I said. I hadn't been issued gear yet. "All I got's my Glock."

"What's wrong?" said one of the guys. "You don't want to fuck people up with your pistol?"

"Uh—"

"Just kidding you." He laughed. "You can't go without a rifle."

I stayed back. I never did find out the details on the incident, but it obviously wasn't much. Random shellings and IED attacks were an unfortunate reality in Afghanistan even before the final Taliban offensive in 2021.

Our job was pretty simple in outline. We'd have advance teams; teams with the diplomat or VIP, whatever; and we'd have backups or QRFs—Quick Response Forces—just in case things went incredibly south. Our weaponry was what you imagine: M-4s and pistols, heavier stuff like SAWs (squad automatic machine guns). The teams were a considerable size, ratcheted up because of the environment; there could easily be sixty guys on a QRF, which is where I spent most of my assignment.

I went on my first mission the next day, acting as a driver on a trip to the European Union headquarters. We had to drive through a red zone—red was bad, green was not quite as bad—in a Toyota Land Cruiser outfitted with armor plating. Outside of learning to throw my whole body into opening and closing the vehicle's door due to the weight of the armor plating, I felt I was handling the job fairly well until I saw an Afghani in a car ahead put his blinker on to make a turn. Thinking nothing of it, I did the same—and got immediately called out.

"You just killed us!" yelled the guy in the seat behind me.

The fact that he was the team medic made the criticism all the more pointed.

I expected a roasting when we got back to base. But at the debrief, the mission commander laughed and said I was a really good driver.

"I give you a B plus," he said, explaining later that usually he gave out Ds and Fs. "You're a really good driver, really attentive, watch everything. And you didn't fuck anything up. The only thing you did was turn on the blinker. So we made it into a huge deal to mess with you."

Thanks.

The response teams could be called out for anything involving the State Department, and by extension, anything involving an American. And sometimes more.

In August, about a month after I got there, the American University was attacked by Taliban. (The school was not an American school, despite the name; it was a private college that received donations from a lot of Americans and others, modeled after American universities, but with no official ties.) We hustled over to the embassy to wait for orders to go in, but they never came. The Afghanis had decided to send their own forces, and State apparently didn't want to risk any of us getting hurt.

Well, we didn't get hurt. It did take the Afghanis something like eight hours to clear the place and kill three attackers. In the meantime, seven students, one professor, three security guards, and another guard from a different school were killed.

But there was no scandal or headlines back home.

Political PR decisions like that happened all the time. There were a lot of frustrating aspects to the job, things that must have driven the people above me crazy. The embassy would be shelled by mortars. We'd be sent over there to protect it. Translation: We went and sat on our hands, rather than going out and nailing the terrorists. By the time anyone got after them, they had dispersed, handing off their weapons to others to hide. Many times they were probably already in bed.

As far as I was concerned, one of the biggest downsides of the job was the lack of interaction with women. Given where we were and the circumstances, dating anyone was practically impossible. There were no local pickup joints, or at least I didn't know of any. Eventually, I started fooling around on the dating app Tinder, just to have some interaction with women. By changing my geographic location on the app—possible with certain accounts—I could find myself talking to women all over Europe.

There were some super-hot girls online. I'd talk to them, messaging, etc., not intending for it to really go anywhere, more to pass the time.

And then one day I met Alina "Lina" Tsybulnik.

Lina was Russian. She lived in Moscow. She was definitely pretty, with high cheekbones and a very open, friendly facial expression, but there was more to my attraction than that. She was really excited about life. She was like, "Oh man, life is awesome" every interaction we had.

And that made me feel that way, too.

Russians don't really smile very much, but Lina did. Later on, I saw pictures of her with her classmates. Many looked angry, and the rest didn't smile. But Lina was always easy to pick out. Look for the biggest grin in the bunch, and there she was.

A few days after swiping right on Lina, I stopped swiping on anyone else. Our conversations, whether by message or recorded voice, seemed a little different. Real. It wasn't as if she was practicing English, or trying hard to get into some money-based relationship. We were really talking to each other.

I know it's easy to be cynical about that, or think that I was naive or maybe just lonely. But I truly believed then, and deeply believe now, that something sparked between us. Somehow in those internet images and delayed responses, a connection developed. I sensed she was a good, loving person. Events proved I wasn't wrong.

Lina's mother was wary. Her family was very conservative, and I don't blame them for being suspicious. But though Lina listened to their concerns, she kept up our conversation over the course of some weeks and months.

I had a thirty-five-day leave coming to me that year, and I decided to ask her if she wanted to meet me. We were messaging one day, and I told her I'd like to hang out.

"Okay," she answered.

"I'd like to take you on a date," I said.

"Don't talk to me like that."

"What?"

"I'm looking for a relationship," she explained.

"So what are you upset about?"

It took a bit before I understood that she didn't entirely understand what the word "date" meant in that context.

Ohh . . .

For some reason, she'd translated the word "date" into "table." So she thought I was saying, "I want to take you on a table."

Not what I meant. I wanted a relationship, too, though I didn't realize how deep my feelings were, not really. I was willing to just be a friend, have a platonic relationship—no sex, in other words, nothing but friends.

Where, though? With over a month off, and a good amount of money saved, we could go anywhere.

Lina suggested Russia.

"No," I told her.

"Why not?"

"Well, your government doesn't really like Americans. There's a good chance that they would take me hostage if I went there."

"Are you serious? It's not like Africa or South America. They don't just take people hostage."

A pause here for the irony. Though to be fair, the overwhelming majority of Russians have no idea what sort of things their government does. And holding Americans to trade for people they wanted was not yet a thing.

I suggested America. Her mom forbade it: too dangerous.

"Why do you say that?" I asked.

"You have school shootings and everyone has guns."

"Your country has less than half of the population of the United States," I told her, "and you have more murders."

We went back and forth a bit on that, neither one of us really understanding the actual math of fear. Finally, I changed the subject.

"I've always wanted to see Greece," I told her.

And so, we planned to meet in Greece. It was, in the plan, a completely friends kind of thing. We'd do some sightseeing together, but we would have separate rooms and separate itineraries. "I'm going to be very busy seeing archaeological sites," I told her. "If you want to go to the pool and do girl stuff, that's great."

"Great."

"Great."

Our flights arrived in Athens the same day, but mine was much earlier. I went to the hotel, dropped off my bag, and then went back to pick her up.

We'd had a conversation earlier about how, if I didn't like the way she looked in person, I could just leave. You don't do that to a friend—*I* certainly couldn't've—but it was something she felt very deeply. She didn't yet understand how beautiful she really is, both inside and out, how worthy of respect she is. And of course she didn't know who I was, either.

I spotted her in the terminal from a distance, her head swiveling around. And the emotion I felt was, in a word, "fear."

Absolute fear. Because she was *really* pretty. Far prettier in person than on the internet. So hot I was scared.

I wasn't going to walk away from her. She was going to walk away from me.

I made my way over, took a deep breath, and asked, "Lina?"

"Yes."

"I'm Trevor."

We shook hands.

"Want to go to the hotel?" I asked.

"Yes."

I tried not to stare at her in the taxi, but it was nearly impossible. I yelled silently at myself, *Don't stare!*

My brain went crazy.

Does she have second thoughts about being here? Does she think I'm crazy? Should I not have shaken her hand? Was that weird? What if she thinks I'm ugly? An ugly American? What if, what if, what if . . .

Pretending to look outside the windows, I happened to turn and saw her staring at me.

"Do you like me?" she asked.

"What?"

"Do you like me?"

"Uh—"

"Do you like about my look?"

"It's . . . you're very beautiful." Fortunately, she didn't ask about her English.

She smiled, and took my hand. In the hotel, she gave me a kiss. From that point on, I knew we'd be more than friends. With luck, forever.

Well, it was definitely magical, but not quite that simple. Fate was definitely involved, but so was human error.

When we went inside, it turned out that the hotel had messed up the reservations. Instead of a suite with two rooms, as I'd reserved, they had only one room with one bed.

I argued, but aside from getting a refund on the more expensive room, there was nothing really to be done. I tried for about an hour to get rooms at another hotel, but I couldn't find anything. Tired, we went up to the rooftop to get something to eat and hang out. The Acropolis was across the way. Whatever romantic magic Greece has was on full display.

We spent the night talking. Finally, it didn't matter that there was only one room left. And the kiss meant even more.

Lina had scored well on her exams in high school, which led to a government grant to pay for college. At sixteen, she was accepted to the highest-rated law school in Moscow.

The state grant paid for the schooling, but not her living expenses. She got two jobs to support herself, and shared an apartment with three other girls. When she first told me that, I was shocked. I couldn't imagine a sixteen-year-old on her own in Dallas or Houston, let alone Moscow. But she just shrugged. Moscow is safe, she told me. She never worried about things there.

It takes five years to get a law degree in Russia. After that, Lina had to work for three years with a law firm before practicing on her own. Starting as an assistant, she would become an associate and then a senior associate over the course of our time together.

She'd wanted to be a lawyer since she was very young. She had a strong sense of justice, and liked helping people, defending their rights even if the police were against them, something a defense attorney needed very strongly in Russia.

The Russian legal system is superficially similar to Western systems. There is a constitution, a series of courts, prosecutors and defense attorneys. There is a published criminal code, with provisions for jury trials for the most serious offenses. In practice, though, there are vast differences between the Russian legal system and ours, beginning with severe limitations on the rights of anyone accused of a crime. The idea of "innocent until proven guilty" doesn't exist.

Lina later said that she didn't feel any qualms about defending someone presumed guilty. Everyone had a right to a fair trial in Russia, meaning that their rights had to be observed.

She would prove to have a lot more faith in the system than me.

We spent about ten days together in Greece, touring historic sites, wandering shopping districts, just hanging out. We took a side trip for a few days and just about froze in the cool fall weather. Back in Athens, we walked the city, soaking up centuries of art and history. I remember sitting on the Acropolis as the sun went down, not really believing that I was there. I'd thought about going to Greece for so long, thought about being in love for longer, and here we were.

But then on our last full day together, Lina became distant. I could tell she wasn't having a good time anymore. I asked if she was all right; she told me she was.

"Something's bothering you," I said. "I can tell."

"No."

"Just tell me what it is."

"It's fine," she said.

I kept bugging her. Finally, she looked at me. "You're not going to talk to me again."

"Huh?"

"I'll never see you again."

"No."

"If that's the truth, I won't be mad," Lina said. "I won't be upset, but I would just like you to tell me."

"No, I really, really like you. I want you to be my girlfriend."

She was quiet for a moment.

"If you want that," I added.

"Of course I want to do that," she said.

So, we were a couple. She returned to Russia, and I went back to work in Afghanistan. I told my parents and my friends about her. Lina's mom was still leery, as any mother would be I guess. But eventually that would change, and the rest of her family came to like me as well.

As our relationship went on, I began to think of Lina as the woman I would marry. And maybe in another life, I would have. But that wasn't the life I was destined to live.

THREE

LEARNING RUSSIAN

Jose, my team leader in Afghanistan, noticed I was pretty happy when I got back from my vacation, and not just because I'd had the break. I thought the guys at work would give me a hard time, busting on me a bit—probably because they were jealous. But actually, they were all pretty happy for me. I guess it was obvious to everyone around that I'd really found something in Lina.

Jose was a very squared-away guy, a former US Army Ranger who'd seen action in Iraq hunting insurgents. He'd been out of the Army for a few years, then decided to go into contracting because he missed the action. The money wasn't bad, either.

Those are the two reasons most guys go into contracting, though not necessarily in that order. Jose's experiences in Iraq had been intense; his Purple Heart proved it. But following his tour he felt burned out mentally and eventually decided to leave the military. After a few years of trying to decide what to do, he came to regret not having done more there. He went into contracting and had a few other gigs before joining the protection team.

Given his experience, he found our assignment pretty mundane. Like a lot of guys, he eventually grew tired of being second-guessed by State Department officials. The supervisors rotate in and out, staying for only a few months at a time. They mean well, I'm sure, but like a lot of new officers in charge, they think they have to reinvent the wheel. By the time they come to understand why the team works a certain way, they're often on their way back to the States or another assignment.

One incident in particular got under everyone's skin. One of our posts was attacked by a dump truck that contained a large improvised bomb. Jose responded, organizing a defense and helping the wounded, who were all locals. Rather than being able to help them, Jose was ordered to immediately take his team to another location quite a distance away. In his mind, the order was not only improper—the other area wasn't under direct attack—it meant he had to leave people to die. The incident galvanized him, and he'd eventually leave for another job.

No US citizens or personnel were injured in the attack.

Granted, the right thing to do was not always immediately obvious. The World Bank building was attacked one morning—the explosion sent a massive mushroom cloud over the city—but we remained at our post. Good thing: it turned out that the security team at the bank building thought they were being attacked by the security at the building across the street. They shot at each other for hours before realizing neither side was the Taliban. Fortunately, no one was killed.

A lot of my time was routine, and even a little boring. We were always aware of the possibility of an insurgent attack, but weren't actively going out to find trouble. Downtime was nice. I could get some great food at the PX that was part of the military complex. On my time off, there'd be a lot of poker games and occasional cigar smoking.

Pranking other team members was a thing; always check your boots before you put them on.

Oh, and there were some smoking women at the pool in the embassy complex. Can't forget to mention that.

I was the youngest member of the team at twenty-five. Some of the guys were not only married but had kids. I'm sure the separation was rough for them, harder than being there was for me.

Things got exciting when the Taliban decided to kidnap two professors from the university. We were called to respond to provide security and backup at a sensitive location. We geared up and hopped in the truck. The driver, a new guy, revved hard and barreled through the city, just about launching us into outer space when he went over a speed bump en route.

I lifted off the seat, slamming back down on the bench. Between the weight of my body armor, gear, and weapon, my backbone was crushed.

We ended up going over to the embassy without seeing any action, but I was still hurting when we returned to quarters at the end of the day. The next morning, my back was so stiff I had to lay on the floor to get my boots on. A buddy who happened to be a medic saw me and sent me to medical to get checked out.

The physician assistants were sympathetic, and may even have believed me when I told them I'd just slightly strained a muscle. I was due to go on a home leave soon, so they told me to have it x-rayed while I was there. That was actually a favor, since if they had x-rayed it and it turned out I was hurt, I would have been sent home immediately, endangering my job.

Long story short, I ended up with an actual back injury. Nonmedically speaking, I lost one of my discs. Medically speaking, I seriously screwed the heck out of my spine.

I went back to Afghanistan after my leave, managing to work for another two months until I jumped out of a BearCat during a training drill. I don't know how many times I've jumped out of an armored vehicle, but this was one time I won't forget. At first the pain wasn't too bad, and I actually completed the drills. But later, after taking my gear off, pain started shooting up my legs.

Whoof.

I got sent home then.

The university professors were kept in custody by the terrorists for three years.

The injury ended my career as a security contractor. I ended up going through a lot of bs to get approved for surgery. I believe it was literally an entire year before I finally had the operation. I was under for six or eight hours, had a bad reaction to some of the painkillers, and after being manhandled by a physical therapist harder than most of my drill instructors, managed to walk decently again.

But not completely without pain. It was weeks before I could take the stairs semi-comfortably. I hobbled around the neighborhood like an old man at first, my progress measured in feet, not yards.

My relationship with Lina was going strong, and she'd encourage me, dismissing my fears of being paralyzed.

"If you can never walk again," she joked when we talked long distance, "then I will take care of you. I'll lock you away in another room and when people come I'll say you're busy. Then we will have fun by ourselves for the rest of the day."

Her idea of fun was not what you—or I—was thinking: "I will make you watch *Twilight* and other movies I like and you won't be able to escape."

I wanted to continue my education. My heart was in it now; I decided I'd make a career out of foreign service, working with the State

Department if I could. I started with community college—the operation slotted conveniently between semesters—but I found the classes annoyingly easy, and decided to transfer to UNT—the University of North Texas, one of the largest schools in Texas.

I liked North Texas. The students seemed more serious, and the instructors better qualified in general. But ultimately, I needed to go to a different school to complete a program in International Studies, my selected field. As the end of my second year approached, I looked into Texas A&M and its prestigious Bush School of Government and Public Service. They told me I was likely to be accepted as a transfer, but I would need to meet their language requirements. That meant two years of college-level foreign language classes.

I had zero.

But in lieu of that, I could take a proficiency exam. I could study for that on my own, then transfer in. Assuming I passed.

I figured that Russian, Chinese, Farsi, and Arabic were more likely to get me a job. They were spoken in countries that were potential or pseudo adversaries already. If I applied for a job and went in with Spanish, say, it wouldn't set me apart from anyone else. But if I knew Farsi or Chinese or Russian, it would make me a more desirable hire.

Out of those, Russian was the obvious choice. Now, I didn't know if I had the linguistic ability for Russian, but I did know, or at least thought, that Chinese and Farsi were more difficult. So on that score alone, Russian was a good choice.

And I had a girlfriend who spoke Russian and might be convinced to tutor pro bono.

A plan formed: I would go to Russia, study the language intensely, come back, and test out.

And along the way, spend time with Lina. We felt very serious at that point. I had visited her family; she mine.

I'd been nervous about her meeting my family, especially after my dad grilled me about the possibility that she might be after me for my money.

Don't laugh.

I knew she wasn't, and not just because I didn't have any.

When she came in February 2017, she immediately charmed everyone in the family. My father couldn't have been sweeter, and my mom practically adopted her. If they were forced to choose between us, I'm not one hundred percent sure they would have picked me.

There was a language school in the building where Lina worked as a law assistant. We arranged for what amounted to private lessons, working with two different instructors and the head of the school. I had three hours of class five days a week, on top of being immersed in the language every day. After class I would often hang out with the building receptionist and other people in the lobby, practicing as much Russian as I could.

It was surprisingly hard. Physically hard. My head pounded every day. There were times when my thoughts were so jumbled that I couldn't think at all. At one point I told Yulia, who ran the school, that my brain was degrading.

"I'm learning less Russian than I already knew."

"That's a sign of your brain changing to adapt to the language," Yulia said confidently. "You're going to start learning at a rapid pace."

Really?

She explained that I would hit a plateau, then seem to go backward again, forgetting stuff and learning less. "You'll pick back up after that."

I did, actually. All these Russian words started entering my dreams. It was still a workout, mentally and physically, but I did make good progress. My teachers took different tacks. One was a sweet, little ol' grandma, who taught me rudimentary grammar as if I were an elementary school kid, which in some senses I was. The other teacher took a more conversational approach. They'd have me talk to their English students; I learned from them, they from me.

Thinking back—way back—I'm remembering that I had some sort of Russian alphabet book when I was a kid. Why or how I bought it, I don't remember. Maybe it primed me for everything that happened as an adult.

The headaches gradually subsided. The Russian in my dreams became more vivid. And grammatical.

I wasn't an expert speaker by any means. My vocabulary had a long way to go, and my understanding of grammar was . . . pathetic. But I could get by at a basic level, which was huge.

Obviously, there are a lot of cultural differences between the US and Russia. Part of my education in those weeks, informally anyway, involved them.

People are people everywhere, but they do approach things differently. In Moscow, the strangers I met did not smile, as a general rule. It wasn't that they weren't friendly. On the contrary, if you went up to them on the street and asked for directions, they would stop whatever they were doing and give you directions. They would go out of their way to make sure you understood, often to the point of actually leading you there.

In the US, if you ask someone how they are, ninety-nine times out of a hundred they'll say "fine," even if their head is about to fall off their body.

If you ask that in Russia, they will take the question literally, and you will likely get a very detailed medical and psychological report. You'll know all their problems by the time they finish talking. I had to train myself *not* to ask.

A lot of Americans remember Russia during the end of the Soviet era. We have stereotypes: a lot of drinking, long lines at the shops, beaten-down economics. When I was there, what was said to be the biggest McDonald's in the world was in Moscow, right down the street from the Kremlin. Go into a shop and you'd get treated extremely well. There was a lot of capitalism and entrepreneurial spirit, at least for small businesses.

But outside the city center, I'd never seen an industrialized nation so poor. And drinking was still a thing.

According to Lina, I didn't stand out as an American, maybe because of my thick reddish beard. But I was regularly stopped by police in public places and wanded by security personnel looking for weapons. Apparently I looked to them like a terrorist.

It wasn't just me. Middle Easterners were often stopped and questioned in public places like the subway or a shopping mall. There were video surveillance cameras in a lot of public places, though that's not all that different from much of Western Europe or even the US these days. It's the number that seemed crazy. I looked up the statistics while I was there. A website claimed there were one million cameras in Moscow alone. There's probably more now.

That's not so much about fighting crime as a demonstration of state control and the ability to monitor every action a citizen might take. It was a constant reminder that I was in a country run by a dictator with a very organized state security system that keeps a lid on dissension.

There were good and bad places in Moscow, just like any other city. Lina sometimes seemed less cautious than I thought was safe. Even allowing for the fact that she knew the capital far better than I did, there were plenty of times when I thought we shouldn't be walking where she wanted to go. It seemed to me nothing bad had ever happened to her, and so she didn't have the extra bit of caution that people growing up around bad neighborhoods seem born with.

"We really need to get off at another stop," I'd tell her. "The lights there are better, and it's not as sketchy looking."

She'd just shrug.

Big US cities have a lot of homeless. Moscow seemed to have a lot of drunks. They all seemed to have homes, though, even the ones outside liquor stores begging for change.

Not that we didn't drink ourselves. Visiting Lina's family, we'd do shots the whole dinner through. Admittedly, my hosts didn't get as drunk as I would have guessed they would. I didn't even get as drunk as I thought I would.

Some of the vodka was particularly good, especially the stuff her family shared. But there was also a good amount of fake vodka around. It could be hard to detect. You'd have criminals bribe government officials for the proper stamps, then sell phony alcohol in what looked like legitimate bottles. I heard about poisonings every week or so, as the government attempted to crack down.

No Second Amendment rights in Russia, obviously. Guns are far rarer than in the US, and generally outlawed. The official statistics show more homicides there than in the US, which has roughly twice as many people. There are a lot of murders with knives, but bullets still somehow show up in corpses. I also heard stories about drunken policemen shooting and killing suspects indiscriminately.

No way to prove any of that at the time, but it didn't increase my confidence.

One odd thing about Russia: when you order food in a Russian restaurant, a fancy place or even a fast-food joint, the food will come out looking exactly like its picture on a menu. The first time Lina ordered food in the States, she was stunned to find that wasn't usually the case here. I was surprised to see the other side of this; pleasantly surprised.

State-run TV is completely slanted to suit the Russian government. I didn't understand exactly how slanted until I understood Russian better and started watching the news regularly. There's an obvious bias against the US. Broadcasters seemed to go out of their way to blame anything bad that happened to Russia on the West. That was especially true during the build-up to their invasion of Ukraine. Everything was NATO's fault. NATO was the devil, and the devil made Russians do some awful things.

One impression that Americans have about Russians is true: they really aren't the greatest drivers. Lina was in two taxicab accidents during the time we dated. Both times she suffered whiplash. Both times the taxi and the other vehicle were totaled.

The Metro was a lot safer than subways I'd taken in the States, though I quickly learned to stay away from drunks. Pretty women, including Lina, were often hassled and harassed in ways that would be criminal here. It was accepted that men would act like dogs and no one would do anything about it. Even so, there are a large number of women in the workforce. Who, by the way, are generally paid less than the men.

One thing I didn't understand: everyone seemed to be obsessed with luxury brands and the cachet they allegedly bestow. Some of the goods, granted, were counterfeit; I doubt every Gucci bag I saw on the street originated in Italy. Still, people would spend three- and four-months' worth of salary on things like handbags, sacrificing a host of necessities to have some bit of luxury. On the street, men and women wore fancy clothes. If they found out I was an American, they would take pity on me because obviously I was poor: I wasn't wearing a fine pair of pants or new boots.

Someone asked me how much I made. I told them what I'd made as a contractor: $11,000 a month. A fortune in Russia, even in Moscow. They were astounded, and unable to comprehend why I didn't sport the latest and fanciest clothes and jewelry.

Lina's apartment was small, but typical; maybe four hundred

square feet. She didn't have much furniture; she slept on a blow-up mattress on the floor. Granted, she was still a few years from being a full-fledged lawyer; still, her standard of living and that of most Moscow residents was far below what you would expect elsewhere in Europe, let alone in the US.

It didn't seem to bother her. She hadn't become a lawyer to get rich. She truly believed in fighting for people's rights.

And she loved me.

Our relationship, though, started to fray as the end of my stay neared. Lina felt that I was becoming very controlling. I was suggesting things she could do to come to America, like getting her visa, but she didn't follow through. I saw us getting married and living in America. She seemed to want to get married, but didn't do any of the things that it would take to do that. That put a lot of doubt in my mind. I took it as a sign that she didn't want to be together and decided if nothing changed, I'd break it off.

I completed my Russian lessons. I was light-years better than when I'd arrived, hopefully good enough to pass the basic competency exam I needed at college. I had a plane ticket to return.

August 15, five days before I was to return to the US:

Some of Lina's friends planned a party for Lina's and a coworker's birthdays at a park on the edge of Moscow, about forty-five minutes away from the apartment. Lina said she was tired, and thought about not going. I was tired myself, even after taking a short nap.

Her birthday had actually been a week or so before. Going out didn't really appeal to either of us.

But . . .

In the end, we decided to go. We had to buy some food—it's a custom in Russia that the person whose birthday it is buys the refreshments—then got a ride to the park from one of Lina's friends.

The park reminded me of many in the US: picnic tables and grills. There was a flat area of concrete, kind of like an outdoor patio, but without any utilities.

It was dark by the time we got there. We mingled, grilled up some kebabs. I talked to a few of her acquaintances; one had been a policeman, though now he was off the force. I had a few other conversations, still struggling a bit with my Russian. At one point we thought of leaving, but Lina's phone had died, and I had no cell service, so we couldn't call for an Uber or taxi. We decided we'd wait until someone could give us a lift.

As the night went on, I had a few drinks. I'm not really sure how many. I didn't think it was many at the time, but it must have been, because within an hour or so, I was blind drunk.

The next thing I would remember occurred several hours later, in a much different place.

FOUR

ARRESTED

We've pieced together what happened next with the help of Lina and others. While there's a bit of variance in the different accounts, they all agree on one point: as the party came to an end, I was a belligerent drunk.

Lina had never seen me that drunk, let alone that aggressive. As far as I can remember, it had been quite some time since I'd even been drunk. But I was clearly out of my mind, blackout smashed, arguing and surly with everyone, including her.

Two acquaintances offered to take us home in their car. I got in, and we may have gone a short distance before it became clear that I had to throw up. The driver didn't want me to lose it in her car, obviously, and stopped to let me out.

I stumbled around, possibly got sick. Probably got sick. There was foam around my mouth, like I was a dog with rabies. I ranted incoherently, possibly in English, though whatever I said wouldn't have made sense in any language.

I didn't want to get back in. Whether I was hallucinating or simply paranoid, I made it quite clear that I wasn't going through the door voluntarily. Given that I was still very fit, and had considerable martial arts and wrestling training, no one would have had an easy time making me.

Lina tried to calm me down: I wasn't having it. At some points, it didn't seem like I even recognized her. I didn't hit her or her friends, but I was clearly a danger to them and to myself. The bizarre creature that had taken possession of my brain and body wanted to . . . I don't know what. Become one with the primal forces of destruction, maybe.

As my ranting continued, one of Lina's acquaintances decided she should call the police for help getting me in the car.

I should point out that being drunk is not an uncommon experience in Russia. Public intoxication is not considered the taboo it is in the US. It's not encouraged, but it's accepted.

And I wasn't driving or about to drive. But I was, to use the proper medical term, falling-down drunk.

Very.

By the time the police arrived, I was unconscious. The police didn't appear to know exactly what to do. I hadn't committed a crime, but since they had been called, they apparently felt they had to do *something*. Or at least that's what they said. So they decided to transport me back to their station, where apparently they thought I could sleep it off.

Back in the day, it was common for police departments in the US to have drunk tanks, bare bones holding cells where the intoxicated can sleep it off. They were fairly common in Russia as well, until a reform movement closed most of them down. Recently, there has been a move to revive the concept as "detoxification centers," a fancier and maybe more hopeful term for roughly the same thing. But there was no *vytrezvitel* at the police station where I was brought.

It was decided that I would stay there until I sobered up in the morning. Call it catch and release.

The police said they couldn't put me in a holding cell because I hadn't committed a crime. So instead, they moved me to the duty office and left me to sleep on the floor.

Lina called my parents, telling my dad what was going on. She mentioned that the police might be angling for a small amount of money to compensate them for their "emotional distress," aka a bribe to look the other way. Not only did they know I was American by that point, but they were also aware that I had the equivalent of several hundred dollars in my wallet, money that I had taken out to pay the last of my school bill on Monday.

While there were hints, no quid pro quo was laid out. Lina held off without making any overtures herself, then took the police officers' advice to go home and get some rest. She was told to return in the morning with clean clothes and a ride.

By the time I came to in the morning, the situation had calmed down. The police officers were even joking about it. The humor was at my expense, but that was to be expected. I earned it.

With my brain back online, I asked the lieutenant who had let me sleep in her office if I could use the station's wi-fi to call my girlfriend. She said that I could, but added that she had already called Lina and she was on her way. She said I was free to go.

I should have gone out the door when she said that. You don't know how many times I've thought of that exact moment, and wish I had. Rarely can you pinpoint an exact place and time where a 180-degree turn, or in this case a stroll down the block, would change your life forever.

Those sorts of moments are usually tied to fatal or near-fatal accidents and bizarre, unpredictable events. As was this one.

I'd arrived at the station somewhere around one a.m. By now it was early morning, around shift change. I sat in the lobby. A handful of people came in on business, filing complaints and whatnot. I sat near the door watching, climbing toward full sobriety when the station's chief walked in. He took one look at me and immediately began asking questions about what was going on.

The night lieutenant explained that I had come in very drunk, had slept it off, and was now waiting for my girlfriend.

The chief walked into the back. About five minutes later, he came back with two officers.

I was told I couldn't leave.

Lina arrived with my clothes. She took one look at me, saw bruises, then walked to the nearest police officer.

"Why did you beat him up?" she demanded. The officer claimed to know nothing of a beating. Lina pulled out her phone and began taking pictures of my face. I had black eyes and other bruises that hadn't been there when she had left.

The station started to liven up, but things still seemed loose. I could have skipped out at that point, though I imagine it would have been easy for the police to catch up with me.

Lina asked why I couldn't leave. The police said I was being detained for assaulting a police officer.

"Where?" she demanded.

"In the police station."

"When?"

"As we brought him in."

"I was with him when he was brought in," she snapped. She pulled out her ID. "I'm a lawyer and I want to see your security footage," referring to the station's video cameras.

At that point, the police stopped talking to us. Lina called an attorney from her office, then left to get food and water for me, since I hadn't had anything since leaving the party.

The lawyer soon arrived. After talking to the police, he came over to me sweating, his face red. He paced back and forth.

"What's wrong?" I asked.

"The police called the FSB."

"Is that normal?"

"No," he told me. "I think you're going to have a political issue."

The station chief had apparently decided to call the Federal Security Service or FSB, officially Federal'naya sluzhba bezopasnosti Rossiyskoy Federatsii (I'll spare you the Cyrillic, here and elsewhere). Things had suddenly become very serious.

The FSB is sometimes compared to the American Federal Bureau of Investigation. There are some superficial similarities. Both investigate serious crimes. Like the FBI, the FSB investigates and tries to prevent terrorism, though the US and Russian concepts of the job and justice differ significantly. Organized out of the ruins of the notorious KGB at the end of the Cold War, the FSB does a fair amount of spying on Russian citizens. It also includes the Russian border guards, the coast guard, and a modest air force that boasts Mi-24 combat helicopters.

The real difference between the two organizations has to do with their role in the country's business life. The FSB might be best described as a gang of kleptomaniacs. Though it has had its scandals and well-documented abuse, the modern FBI does not attempt to take over successful American businesses for its and its employees' own gain. The FSB does.

Lina's attorney seemed nervous, sweating quite a bit, pacing even more. At that point, I didn't understand exactly what FSB involvement might mean. But I realized that if I was interviewed by them, they would probably ask me about my career in the Marines. I knew I didn't want to talk about what I had done as a Presidential Guard. Even small slips about security might inadvertently hurt the country.

Two FSB agents arrived, looking rather bored. They were middle-aged guys, in their forties, with shiny black shoes and nice dress watches. One had a beard. They wouldn't have stood out in a crowd. No devil horns or pitchforks, just frowns.

After talking to the police, they told me they were going to interview me. I told them I wanted my attorney there—very American of me—but they wouldn't allow that and started to lead me off.

"Good luck," the attorney told me, with a scared look on his face.

Thanks.

The police chief tried to listen at the open door, but they pushed him away and shut the door in his face. I wasn't cuffed, though trying to run out would have been silly. I mentally prepared myself: maybe I get tortured now.

The FSB agents didn't torture me. I kept expecting them to, but for the record, they didn't.

We sat at a large table and they started grilling me. It wasn't the third degree or anything like you see in the movies; it was professional, and mostly perfunctory. They weren't friendly, but they weren't gruff, either. Think two bored functionaries trying to fill in the blanks on some bureaucratic form before going home for the weekend.

My military service was the only thing that might be remotely interesting to them. Since the visa forms I'd filled out to come to Russia told them I'd been a Marine, I thought that must be why they were here. I figured these guys wanted to find some military secret. So I had a choice: (1) Not say anything, which would make them think I was hiding something and get me arrested, then probably tortured; or (2) bs around for as long as the interview took, feeding them the most uninteresting information that I could think of until they decided I had zero value.

I figured I would chose option two, hoping they were maybe a little pissed at being called out to waste their time talking to a drunk.

And let me be clear: aside from my duties at Camp David and the Presidential Guard, I had nothing of any value for anyone.

I started talking in Russian, hoping this would allow me to lie with impunity: if they found out later that I had lied, I could just say that I didn't understand the question. They weren't too worried about that, apparently, and probably weren't very competent in English, because we spoke Russian the whole time.

After some preliminaries, they asked off-handedly if I had served in the military.

"Yes," I told them.

They seemed surprised. Which surprised me as well. But they didn't follow up at first.

"What are you doing in Russia?"

"I'm a student."

"You did an exchange program with your university?"

"No, I studied at a private school."

They asked about the school. I didn't have the address, but that didn't seem to bother them much.

"What did you come here to study?"

I started to say the language. The guy with the beard said something that implied I'd come to get drunk. I laughed and explained that I needed language skills for my university. "I have to study a foreign language."

"Why did you choose Russian?" he asked.

"Because my girlfriend's Russian, and I wanted to be able to talk to her family."

That seemed to make sense. "What job are you going into? Where you want to speak Russian?"

"I want to work for the State Department and do humanitarian stuff with USAID or diplomacy or whatever."

Their eyes may have rolled at the mention of humanitarian aid, but otherwise they took it in stride. We went through details that were in my passport: date of birth, home address, etc. We got to my military service, and they asked what I did.

"I was in the Marines."

"What's your specialty?"

I told them I was a rifleman—true—and they asked what unit I was in. I told them the battalion I'd been assigned to after Camp David.

"Did you deploy to a combat zone?"

"Not really."

"What does that mean?" they asked.

"I just went to Kuwait. But there was no war there then."

"Is that the only place you went?"

"No. I went to Hawaii. I went to United Arab Emirates."

"What kind of operations were you doing there?"

"We didn't do any operations," I told them. "We just did training."

"But in these countries, what did you do?"

"I just had beers in those countries. We didn't do anything."

"But this was a deployment?"

"Well, it was more of a cruise."

"So it wasn't a deployment?"

"It was an actual deployment, but we don't do anything on them. We just float around in the ocean."

"How does it work with the fleet with these deployments?"

"I have no clue. I was a Marine. I was sleeping the whole time. We don't work on the ship. We don't know anything about the ship. We just sleep on there."

Which is not false, right? Marines are not ship's crew; we do our own thing. Which isn't much unless there is fighting ashore.

They asked what I did in Hawaii. So I told them in great detail:

We went hiking in the mountains, we practiced on some firing ranges. I went to eat at a cheeseburger place . . .

My shamefully boring career as a middling rifleman annoyed them a bit. I gave excruciatingly accurate details of the most mundane parts of my life in the Corps. Honestly, there wasn't much that was truly interesting, anyway, as I've already laid out.

"What was your rank?"

"Corporal."

"The whole time you were a corporal?"

"I got out as a sergeant. But I was only a sergeant for four months."

"How much money did you make?"

I told them my salary. They were impressed.

"For America," I told them, "that's pretty low."

"If it's so bad, why do people go into the military? Are they drafted?"

"No. It's volunteer."

That seemed to surprise them. The idea of patriotic duty was strange, I guess. They asked some more about military service in general. Then they asked if foreigners could join the military.

I told them they could.

Is it a difficult process?

No, I said, adding that you got citizenship when you left the service. Their expressions made me think they were going to ask me how to sign up themselves.

"Do you know anyone who works in the government?" they finally asked, meaning back in the States.

"My buddies are police officers."

Not what they were looking for, I'm sure, but that set off another round of questions about police forces in general.

"How much does it pay?"

"The average is probably about $60,000. It varies."

I'm sure they would have filled out applications on the spot if I'd had them.

We talked for about two hours. They would double back on details, probably to see if I was lying. But I wasn't. Maybe I was leaving things out, maybe a lot of things, but everything I told them was truthful. If they'd asked me point-blank if I had a security clearance, that would have been harder to deal with. But they didn't. And in the end, they looked like they had concluded that I was a nothingburger, not worth their time, let alone the government's.

Lina ran up to them as they walked me back downstairs.

"Did you hurt him?!" She started crying.

I told her they hadn't touched me, and that I was fine.

While I was being questioned, Lina had been out getting food for me. Back in the station, she saw the officers who had taken me in the night before. They had been talking to the chief in the back. (We later heard from a witness who had listened at the door that the chief had told them they needed to get a jacket to use as evidence against me. Lina didn't know that at the time.)

My attorney hadn't been of much use, but Lina was already using her legal skills. It was obvious now that I would be arrested. The police fingerprinted me, then said they wanted to take pictures of my tattoos.

"You can't," she told them. The tatts weren't exactly top secret, but they did include what had been my badge number at Camp David. If they figured out what it meant, it would only cause me more problems. "The law says that unless they're gang-related, you cannot do that without his permission," she told them. "He denies you that permission."

More important, Lina realized that at least some of what had happened while I was in the station would have been recorded on video cameras. She would spend the next few days trying to collect those records, knowing that they would be automatically erased in the camera after a certain time so the memory could be reused.

In the US, the police who apprehend you are generally the ones who gather evidence, which is then turned over to the prosecutor. In Russia, the process is different. An investigator working for a separate organization is called in after the arrest is made. (The organization, Sledstvennyi komitet, or the Investigation Committee, is often referred to as the SK or SKR in the West.) The investigator does interviews and gathers evidence. He or she then decides whether there is a case, and what the charges are. Investigators don't work directly for the police or the prosecutor, and play a pretty big role in things as the case goes through the system.

The investigator here was a young woman. I have no idea what experience she had, but she came off as very young, barely Lina's age, if that. The stiff blue uniform she wore didn't make her look any older, not even with its light blue stripe (police officers wear red trim) and baggy pants.

Her questions made it obvious that the chief of police wanted to have me charged with assaulting his officers. Admittedly, I had been blacked out for a while; even so, I was pretty sure that I hadn't hit anyone. Lina had not seen me hit anyone. No one had talked about my hitting anyone. No one had any obvious wounds, and no one had gone to the hospital.

The investigator asked the police officers who had taken me to the station what happened. Their answers were very straightforward, and truthful: I was drunk at this time, this place. They transported me to the station.

Nothing about me assaulting them. Nothing about anything that might or might not have happened in the station.

"But what crime did he commit against you?" the investigator asked.

"I don't know," said one of the cops.

"You don't know?"

"I can't remember."

Great, I thought. *I'm getting off.*

"Did he assault you? Did he beat you? Did he grab you? Or something?" asked the investigator.

"I don't know."

My lawyer interrupted. "You don't remember him committing a crime?"

"No," said the cop.

"Do you have any claims against him?" asked the attorney.

"No."

The investigator asked if I had any claims against the police officers. I said no.

Instead of being released, the police officers took me to what looked like a closet at the back, and had me undress for a search. The investigator and my lawyer filed in behind me to watch.

It was a bit crowded.

When I got dressed, they handcuffed me.

"What's going on?" I asked my attorney.

"They don't know what to charge you with."

"They just said they had nothing against me."

He kind of shrugged. *This is the way Russian justice works.*

It was at that point that I knew beyond any doubt that I would be arrested. And I had a bad feeling that I was going to have trouble making my Tuesday flight.

Lina had had no luck getting help from the US Embassy. Technically, I wasn't under arrest; I was simply being "detained." Which of course made sense, since they didn't really know what to charge me with.

I don't know why the chief had decided to get the FSB involved. Probably he was looking for some sort of internal political advantage. Maybe he'd been told to be on the lookout for an American who might be a useful political pawn. Maybe he legitimately thought I was a spy. Maybe he didn't like Americans.

Whatever it was, it was eventually decided that I should be transported to the Investigation Committee headquarters.

A dozen men armed with AK-74s, the newer cousin of the venerable but ancient AK-47, met us at the huge Moscow building. The place was locked up, either because of the weekend or the hour: it was now roughly two a.m., twenty-four hours after I'd been picked up. We had to wait for someone to arrive with a key, or maybe just to figure out which door we could use. I complained to my escorts that I was hungry and had a headache. After quite a bit of pleading, they decided to let Lina in with food. The officer who undid my handcuffs said something menacing, like, "If you try to escape, we'll kill you." But most of the cops seemed indifferent to me; a few may even have been sympathetic, since it was obvious that I was being set up.

The investigator seemed embarrassed by the whole charade. She showed up at the building after I did.

I didn't know this at the time, but me being brought there was a huge break from the usual procedure. Suspects *can* go to the SK to talk about their case, but they are generally not brought in for questioning.

The investigator tried to get me to sign some paper that I couldn't read. Two translators were brought in, and I was told I could take my pick. One was an extremely good-looking blond, who was whispering something to the other staff members as she entered. The other was a fat, ugly dude who *talk in stiff language no sense grammar*.

Like that.

He told me he was very qualified, and could speak excellent Farsi, which of course I don't. Maybe my beard made me look Iranian.

I chose him anyway. He seemed less of a suck-up. Both translators were working for the government—he said he was a freelancer, as opposed to a staff member like the blond, but his checks still came from them. I had to go with the lesser of two evils.

It proved to be a decent choice, since he told me I was entitled to have my attorney present, and gave me a few other hints I wouldn't have known and surely wouldn't have gotten from the blond.

My attorney looked over the paper and advised me to sign it. It seems to have been a summary of what I had said at the police station about the incident. But I never saw the document again, so I can't be sure.

"Your lawyer says you should apologize," the Farsi-speaking translator told me after I handed the paper back.

"Apologize?"

"To the police."

"What?" I looked over at the attorney, and asked him in Russian if he had said that.

He hadn't. It was the translator's idea, a play to get some sympathy from them.

My lawyer proceeded to ball out the translator. It was a good tirade, proving that he was at least capable of expressing anger, if not for his clients, at least for himself.

Giving rotten legal advice was his job, after all, not the translator's.

My time with the investigator was more tedious than anything, or would have been had I not been hungry, tired, and still a bit hungover. She seemed to have a conscience, and was honest with Lina about what was going on. Granted, we were entitled honesty—and more—under Russian law. But being entitled to things doesn't mean you get them.

Russian justice.

A lot of the people in the system know what a farce it is. Sometimes their humanity shows through. Lina persuaded one of the guards watching me to let her in with some food. He uncuffed me so I could hold and kiss her before I was taken off.

I gave her my watch. It was an Omega, worth a few thousand at the time. I told her to sell it if she needed money.

"I'll be okay," I told her. "Go."

I knew she was going to cry and I didn't want to see that. I also knew I had to pretend not to care about what was happening to me. I had to show her, and the Russian authorities around me, that I was strong. I had no worries. I was confident that this was a bs case. I was getting out in the morning.

I almost believed that.

I was charged with Violence Against a Representative of the Government, in this case police officers—officially, Article 318 Part Two of the Russian Criminal Code. The crime was punishable by ten years in prison, though the usual sentence was a fine and maybe time served waiting for trial. "Part Two" meant that I had used violence, threatening serious bodily injury or death.

I hadn't done any of that, which was already obvious from what the police officers had said at the station. At that point, I did think that the charges would *eventually* be dismissed or, if the case did go to trial, I'd show they were bs and walk.

What I was worried about was an espionage charge. While equally bogus, I suspected that would be far harder to deal with.

Incidentally, taking me to the Investigation Committee building was apparently a bit out of normal procedure. A suspect can go on their own, but they have to go voluntarily, not with a dozen automatic rifles stuck in their face.

Lina left. I froze my face into stone, my eyes a thousand-yard stare, as I was led for transport again.

My next stop was a building about twenty minutes away, where I was to be held for a hearing that would determine whether the charges were substantial enough for an actual trial, and if so, whether I could be released on bail.

At least, that was how it was supposed to work. Not all that unlike in the US, except in the US you're presumed innocent, and the evidence isn't made up.

They patted me down and put me in a cell. I told them I was hungry. By now it was late on the seventeenth, past dinner or whatever meal they planned, which meant tough luck.

The cell had a half dozen or more bunks, but I was the only prisoner. The guards gave me a mattress and a pillow, neither of which was more than a slim pretender of the real thing. But I was so tired I fell right off to sleep. The next morning I joined a group of other prisoners in the back of a transport van making its way to the court building. The van made frequent stops, picking up prisoners from other facilities. Two guards sat in the back with us, behind a barrier. They smoked nonstop, adding a fine haze to the fetid sweat and mold of the prisoner area.

Russian courtrooms put the defendant in a barred cage for the proceedings. It's an obvious sign of what they think of you.

Made of simple, white-painted metal bars, the cage takes up a small portion of the room at the rear. A few paces back and forth were all I could manage. There's usually a bench, but I stood during the proceedings. My translator would stand at the side of the cage, explaining what was being said. Guards hovered nearby. The door to the cage was locked with my handcuffs, which the guards would remove once I was inside.

Except for the cage, the room didn't look too different than a courtroom in a small county courthouse in the States. Plain and relatively small. The judge sat at a desk rather than a fancy dais. The prosecution and defense attorneys sat at a table across from him. There was a jury box to one side, very similar to the US, though very few crimes in Russia require a jury, and there was never one for me. Spectators sat on a few pew-like benches.

The lawyer Lina had hired and the translator hadn't shown up when I first arrived. One of the guards spoke English, and we started talking a bit after he asked why I was there. Eventually the conversation got around to the military, and I blew him away with the possibility of a decent (for Russia) salary. I really could clean up as a recruiter, at least in Russia.

Eventually my lawyer and the translator showed up.

"This is a preliminary hearing to decide if you have to be held in jail or get bail," the attorney explained. "Your family sent us documents to attest to your character."

"Okay."

The investigator I'd met the day before arrived, along with the prosecutor. The judge, Dmitry Arnaut, came in a short time later.

The prosecutor launched into her presentation, talking far too fast for me to understand what she was saying. The translator left a lot of what she said by the wayside, concentrating on the highlights.

"She's saying you should be remanded to custody," he told me. "Is that the right word?"

It was the right word, just not the right outcome.

My lawyer took his turn with the judge. The translator told me he was saying I was a good boy.

I doubt that was a literal translation, but I got the gist. He asked for house arrest, the Russian version of being released on your own recognizance, or bail.

Then the investigator spoke. She didn't have much evidence, mostly because there was none. This annoyed the prosecutor, who snapped at her. They had a few words back and forth, until finally the judge told the investigator to read the charges. She held up a piece of paper and started to read it before suddenly bursting into tears.

The judge leaned over to scold her. She snapped back, saying something along the lines that she did not want to press charges, though those weren't the exact words.

"It's your job!" shouted the judge.

She got up and left, tears streaming from her eyes. Both the prosecutor and judge yelled at her as she fled.

Meanwhile, I stood in my little cage wondering what the hell was going on. The translator stopped talking, as stunned as I was.

When everyone recovered, my lawyer asked to give the judge some documents about my character that had come from the US Embassy. As he walked up to the desk, I saw a picture of me in my dress blues with President Obama.

Damn!

My parents had sent the picture to the embassy, which forwarded it to the lawyer, apparently thinking that it would somehow impress the Russians. I'm sure it did, just not in the way we wanted.

If there was a picture of me with the president, then I must not be a know-nothing, worthless Marine who'd gotten drunk and ought to be released with a small fine and a vicious tongue-lashing. No. I was a very valuable personal friend of the president, someone who could be worth quite a lot as a political bargaining chip.

I know now that I would not have been released and my case would not have gone any differently without that photo. But at that point, I was outraged, sure that it had just convinced the Russians to make a big deal of me.

I do think that the photo impressed the judge, at least momentarily. He looked at it for a full twenty seconds before placing it with the other documents, letters from friends who were police officers saying that I would never assault a cop, etc.

The judge closed my folder and looked at me. His expression as he spoke told me more than the translator did. I wasn't getting house arrest or bail.

"Trevor, I'm sorry," said the lawyer.

"You are going to prison," added the translator. "But don't worry. Everything will be okay."

"Yeah? How's that?"

"Trevor, you are going to have a great time in prison. You have an awesome crime for Russian prisoners. They are going to love you. You're going to be a hero to them."

Right, dumbass. Sure.

That was about all I could think of as I was led back down for transport to prison.

FIVE

WHAT MY PARENTS HEARD

Back home, my parents knew absolutely nothing about what was going on. The first word of trouble they got was from Lina, who called from the station. Moscow is nine hours ahead of central Texas; one a.m. in Moscow would be four p.m. the day before in Dallas. I'll let my dad tell the story (with a little help from my mom and my coauthor, Jim DeFelice):

Lina called us in the afternoon or early night. It was obvious she was upset.

"Dad"—she called Paula and me Mom and Dad—"Trevor's been arrested. We're at the police station."

I could hear him in the background, yelling, drunk. I'd only seen my son drunk once or maybe twice before, but his condition was pretty obvious from the way he was talking.

Lina gave me the whole story of what had happened. She thought the police were angling for a bribe—they'd seen that he had the money to pay for his school in his wallet. It was hinted that half that money could make the problem go away.

She said she'd been noncommittal—it would be very easy to say the wrong thing and implicate herself in some sort of bribery scheme—but she was sure at that point that he'd be released in the morning, when he would sober up.

Paula and I were upset, of course, but at that point we felt it would work out. I spent the rest of the night worried, doing some research on the internet, waiting.

The next call was the scary one. It was hours later. Lina cried hysterically. She said the FSB was involved. Trevor had been detained.

"Call the embassy," she said.

Their phone number was on a website. The only person I could get on the phone was a Marine guard, a corporal. He took my information. A while later, an embassy official called back. The Consular Affairs Officer wanted to know where Trevor was held and his information. We called Lina and got the address of the station.

The embassy called back and confirmed that Trevor was at the police station, but otherwise he had not been able to get any information. He tried to put us at ease, but there was a complication—because of the weekend, he didn't think he'd have any real information until Monday.

We told him we already knew from Lina that Trevor was going to be arraigned on Saturday and asked if the embassy would send someone. He said something to the effect of "we can't go to jail or court every time an American gets arrested in Russia."

The Saturday arraignment was unusual, though at that point I didn't know that. The fact that the embassy wasn't fully informed was disheartening. Paula and I also wondered how many Americans were being arrested in Russia. (Not many, fortunately.)

Lina hired an attorney, and we were told to get some information that would prove Trevor was an upstanding citizen. That wasn't hard—he'd been an Eagle Scout and a Marine. But there I made a mistake: I sent a picture of Trevor with President Obama. Possibly that made the Russians think he was much more valuable as a prisoner than he really was. In my defense, the embassy had already made it clear that the Russians would know about Trevor's military history, so there seemed no reason to downplay his service, which after all had been exemplary.

It soon became obvious that the embassy didn't trust Lina. I'm guessing they thought she was somehow involved. But we trusted her. She was giving us much more information than they were. We also knew her, and knew she wouldn't be involved, as her actions continually proved.

Lina was very brave. Everything she did put her in danger with the government. But she never flinched.

I decided right away that I was going to Russia. It took a few weeks to get everything arranged. Lina recommended two very experienced attorneys from her office, Sergey and Victoria.

When we notified the embassy that I had gotten a visa and would be coming to Moscow, they were a little surprised. Apparently, few Americans went there to help family members in trouble.

Paula, meanwhile, put in her notice at the chiropractor's office where she'd worked. Partly it was so she could take care of what needed to be done at home, for us and for Trevor: contacting congressmen, staying in touch with the State Department, and eventually trying to get public support to bring Trevor back. To be honest, she had a hard time focusing on anything other than her son. She spent part of each day crying.

A friend started a GoFundMe page, which Paula later managed. Trevor saw red when he heard about that. But the donations that came in from people around the country helped us get him food and other supplies in jail, and covered a small portion of my expenses overseas. Later I set up a website as a clearinghouse for the public as well as journalists and politicians to get information and updates on the situation.

At first, Trevor didn't want us to contact the media or elected offi-

cials, probably worried that it would make his case more valuable to the Russians. Eventually he would agree it was a political case and it would require presidential help, but that still lay ahead.

You have to understand, Trevor didn't want us to do anything. He didn't want me to come—he blew up when the embassy arranged for us to meet a few days after I arrived in Moscow. He's still probably a little mad. But how could we have left him there alone? Our son?

I'd traveled to Japan and Korea back when I was a Marine, and had been in Mexico and the Caribbean. But I'd never been to Europe, and my conception of Russia was way out of date, based on the bad old days of the late Cold War when I'd grown up. So my first experiences of the country were surprising. Getting the visa—I went as a tourist, without giving any details—was easy. Passing into the country was simply a matter of walking through a gate. The apartment I stayed in at first was run-down, but I quickly found something better with Lina's help. People were friendly and helpful, even though I knew no Russian.

One phrase I did know: Ya ne govoriu po-russki.

"I don't speak Russian."

I mastered that quickly. Otherwise, I made do with English, bits of poorly pronounced Russian, and pointing as best I could.

SIX

MAKING BAIL

I was sent to a pre-trial detention center in Moscow known as SIZO-5. SIZO is an acronym for Russian words that literally mean "investigative isolator," though generally they're translated as "detention center." The American equivalent would generally be a county jail, but SIZOs are a far more intense beast, intended to wear a prisoner down before trial. (While similar in some ways, the Moscow SIZO-5 is a different facility than the one famed dissident Alexei Navalny was held in at one point during his ordeal, FKU SIZO-5 FSIN, in Krasnodar, southern Russia.)

When you first arrive at a Russian jail, you're checked over medically, then sent to quarantine for a few days until the administration decides what to do with you. I was taken to the medical office, where the nurse had me get undressed. She looked me over quickly, then told me I could put my clothes back on.

"What kind of prison is this?" I asked her.

"A regular one."

"But what kind of prisoners are in here?"

"All kinds of prisoners," she said. "Murderers, terrorists."

"You have terrorists in here?"

"Yes, of course."

"Uh—"

"Oh, don't worry," she told me. "It's Russian *mafya* here."

She was trying to be reassuring.

The guards took me to a small holding cell to await a cell assignment. Looking around, I happened to spot a piece of door hinge in the bathroom trash can. I grabbed it, thinking I might be able to use it somehow as a weapon if things got desperate.

I figured things were about to get desperate real fast. The guards came and led me to a cell, my pulse doubling with each step. The guard opened the door and I found myself staring at six guys, trying to figure out who I would have to fight first.

The biggest prisoner came over as the door closed behind me. He had a thick black beard, a good amount of muscle, and a gruff voice. He was a Chechen. Adlan, I'll call him.

"*Shto za bida?*" he asked.

That's prison slang for "What are you in for?" But the words translate as "What pains you?" or "What's your problem?" so I had no idea what he was saying.

"*Kakaya statiya u tebya?*" Adlan asked.

I gave him another dumbfounded look. The words are literally "What article do you have?" and refer to the criminal charge, a specific article in the Russian penal code. But I had no idea what he meant. Adrenaline surged through my body, confusion mixing with the anticipation of a fight.

"Paper," he said, pointing to my prison admission forms.

A smile spread across his face as he read it.

He turned to the others and started reading out loud. The others began laughing and clapping, then ran over to me, wanting to hug and shake my hand.

Apparently holding official papers that say you nearly killed two policemen is one of the best ways to make friends in a Russian prison.

"Come sit down, brother!" they told me. "Have some tea and bread!"

"I don't have to fight anyone?" I asked Adlan, who turned out to speak enough English to translate for me.

"No. You don't fight anyone. It is against our code."

"Code?"

"The mafya code."

Over the next two or three days, I was given a quick but intensive lesson in prison life and the role of the mafya in Russian prisons. Everyone follows their rules.

As long as you do that, you're okay. You're "in," so to speak.

If you don't, or if you're a cop, a pedophile, or gay, you're out.

You don't want to be out. Being out means no one will associate with you. You'll get the worst jobs. You will probably be taken advantage of. You may get beaten. You may even be raped.

Trustees, who by definition are cooperating with the authorities, are also out, though their duties can put them in a position where they can help the mafya.

The extent of mafya control varies from prison to prison. Those that are largely mafya run are called "black." The government's are "red." Rules tend to be slacker at mafya prisons, with more amenities like clandestine cell phones available. Ultimately the government is in charge, but there are incentives for both sides to maintain the status quo.

The level of the security at the prison doesn't necessarily indicate whether it is red or black, but political prisoners always go to red prisons. There are hard black prisons, and easy ones. Same thing with red.

International monitoring agencies have claimed the highest incidents of torture and other abuse occur at the red prisons. Alexei Navalny, the most famous Russian dissident in recent years, died while in custody at one; he was far from alone.

In the mafya system, regular, low-level prisoners are "men": *muzhiki* ("muzhiki" is plural, *muzhik* is singular). Rank doesn't depend on the crime or number of incarcerations; a muzhik may have been in prison six or seven times, while a *brodyaga*, a member of the hierarchy, may be serving his first sentence.

Mafya rules cover a variety of situations. When you are to be placed in a cell for the first time, you're supposed to ask if "men" live there. If the answer is yes, you can join them. If not, you *have* to demand another cell. Men don't cooperate with the authorities. They don't snitch on other inmates. They don't kill other mafya members; if they fight, they are liable to be tried in a mafya "court," which can punish the wrongdoer. The most common punishment for small infractions, including minor fights, is a slap to the face of the guilty party. (The victim can refuse the reward and say he has no claims.)

As you'd expect, a certain amount of slang is used in prison, which I had to learn besides regular Russian. There are different accents, especially Chechen, which can be very difficult to decipher.

The quarantine cell had bunk beds and cots lined up against the walls, with a table in the middle. Though the size of the cells differed, the arrangement was generally similar elsewhere in the prison and the overall system. All of the prisoners I was in with in quarantine were first timers. They asked me where I was from. When I told them I was American, they were impressed—kind of: *You came all the way here just to mess up our cops? Good job.*

I told them that I hadn't actually assaulted the police officers, and explained the circumstances. They realized that I had been set up, especially after I mentioned that I'd been in the military.

Ironically, Adlan never really liked me once he found out I was a Marine. "He fought against our brothers," he told the others, referring to his Muslim background as a Chechen.

Even the other Chechens just shrugged. I explained that the US wasn't against Islam or Muslims, just terrorists like Al Qaeda. That didn't make much of an impression with him. He remained far less friendly than he'd been, but continued to translate for me, since the others couldn't speak English.

After three days in quarantine, I was sent to Spetz Block, a section generally reserved for prisoners of special interest to the FSB. The mafya has less influence there, but I continued to follow their rules. Given that I quickly came to hate the Russian government and decided I'd never cooperate with them, it wasn't hard. And I already knew my stance was one strongly approved by the mafya.

I was in several cells in Spetz Block. All were more or less the same, except for the size. In my first, there were two sets of bunk beds on the left and right, with a table in the center. I had to turn sideways to pass between the table and the bunks. There were open shelves for food and whatnot on the walls. There was also a TV. We would keep personal belongings in bags under the beds.

The bathroom area—a toilet and sink—was separated from the cell by walls that didn't quite reach the ceiling. Prisoners would shove orange peels into a hole in the wall and burn them to kill the smell.

Some of the cells had long fluorescent tube bulbs for lighting. The windows would open a few inches; beyond the glass were bars and barbed wire.

Hot water pipes served as radiators. There was no AC. It was muggy and hot in summer, though fans would be brought in, the air blasting over the beds.

We had a mini fridge in the first cell I was in; the larger cells had a larger refrigerator. We had a primitive arrangement to cook, using a heating coil, a plastic bowl, and a square Tupperware box. The box was the base. The heating coil was placed inside. The bowl, filled with water, sat on the box. Food would be put in a plastic bag or other container and placed in the bowl. Another bowl would then be placed on the top to trap the steam. It worked the way a double-boiler might, the water rather than the heating coil warming or cooking the food.

Prisoners got showers once a week, though you could pay to have a second shower. The shower room was just an open area with four pipes, no spray heads. The guards would escort the prisoners from a cell to a holding area just outside the room. Four at a time would then go and wash up as best they could.

Each floor had its own guard post. There were storage areas for prisoners near them, but guards and even inmates were known to steal from it, so nothing valuable would ever be kept there.

At least not for long.

Every morning the guards would inspect the cells for contraband. The prisoners would go into the hallway, put their hands against the wall, and wait to be searched, either by a metal detector or pat down.

Random inspections were more thorough. The guards would tear the whole room apart. I saw dogs used for searches in SIZO twice; in the work camp later they were used once a week.

The men I'd been with in quarantine were "regular" or "common" criminals, arrested for theft or robbery or armed robbery or grand theft auto, whatever. My new cellmates, though, were different. There were drug dealers, yes—but these were big-time smugglers, not street guys. If they had been caught with cocaine, it was a ton or two, not a baggie. Others were bankers or business owners or government officials who'd crossed the FSB or someone powerful. They were there for swindling or corruption or espionage or terrorism.

Not that the charges against most of them held any truth, as I would soon learn.

Anyway, my cellmates were all high-value prisoners, generally pretty smart, and often well-off, even by Western standards. A lot of the guys on Spetz Block were highly educated, with doctorates or master's degrees. A lot spoke English. A few, admittedly, were high-level criminals and members of the mafya. There was even a *vor,* a member of mob royalty.

A vor (from "*vory v zakone*" or "thieves in law") is a leader at the highest rung of the criminal mafya, and ordinarily is kept in complete isolation in prison. They go on walks by themselves, have no one in the cells next to them, and cannot walk through the halls when other prisoners are in the hallway. But at SIZO, I saw him twice in a hallway when the guards messed up. He walked up and shook our hands; the guards were afraid to tell us not to.

The reaction I got from my cellmates in Spetz Block was a lot different than the one I'd gotten in quarantine, at least at first. Basically, they were scared of me. They thought I was a thug, and it took at least three days until they warmed up to me. But once they were convinced I wasn't going to beat on them if they didn't beat on me, we got along fine.

You can divide the Russian prison system in half: the jails you go to before you are convicted, and the prisons (the gulag or work camps) you go to after your trial.

In the Russian system, long stays in the pre-conviction prisons are common. It can take more than a year for a case to get to trial; appeals after conviction can go on for months if not more. All of that time is spent in SIZO, unless you're lucky enough to get some form of house arrest or bail.

I knew several inmates who'd been in SIZO for four years or more; two had been in for six. Stays at the pre-conviction prisons are credited against your sentence, with a "bonus" depending on the severity of the possible punishment. In my case, I was credited a day and a half for every day in SIZO.

Generally, prisoners say that SIZO is the worst part of their sentence. Prisoners are locked up twenty-three hours a day and have limited access to packages and visitors and such. The severity and conditions vary—mine was said to be one of the worst, even though the structure was relatively new—but none of these places are hotels. Physically, they are far worse than American prisons. Dilapidated concrete, faulty drains, mold on every surface. The amount of heating in the winter varies from scant to purely imaginary. Prisoners bake in the summer. Rats and all sorts of vermin are plentiful. Disease, especially tuberculosis, is rampant.

Prisoners have a lot of different ways of coping. It's possible, even routine, to bribe the guards. I was told it was even possible to bribe the warden to put in a good word for you with the parole board while you were serving your sentence.

During my first transport from court back to SIZO—I ended up going back and forth a lot before my trial was adjudicated—I met a prisoner I'll call Cuban who had killed someone. When I asked why, he and everyone around him just laughed. I found out later that he'd killed in self-defense, but there must have been some funny or ironic story attached that I never was told. On the same ride, another prisoner rolled up his sleeve and showed me a series of scars that ran down the length of his arm. They were perfect cuts, a ladder-like hash up his arm. I thought maybe he had a mental illness. He might have, but these cuts weren't the result of it. He'd done it to get sent to hospital prisons.

Like twenty times, if my count was right.

The hospital wasn't an actual hospital. It was a prison that provided inmates with some token care. Usually it would have better food and living conditions, relatively speaking. Going to a hospital prison when you were serving in a work camp after conviction meant you didn't have to work, so that was another bonus. From SIZO, though, hospitals were especially difficult to get into, since going to one automatically gave a prisoner an excuse to receive house arrest, something the Russians were loath to grant. It was doubly hard because the case investigator was in charge of deciding if you could go or not, not the prison staff. It happened a few times that the authorities let prisoners die rather than taking them.

Prisoners might be in for any sort of crime. I met a Chechen in for kidnapping. Maybe that was legit; kidnapping was a thing. Another Chechen had bought part of a motor for some sort of job, and ended up being arrested for arms trafficking. The piece had come from a helicopter; neither it nor the job had anything to do with terrorism. But . . . *Russian justice.*

You never knew how accurate a person's charge might be. The prisoners themselves could be very honest: ask an armed robber if he did what he was accused of, and he'd often admit it. But as I quickly found out, a load of the guys I was in with were innocent. Some may have done something bad, but not what they had been charged with.

Russian investigators might know that you committed some crime, but couldn't prove it. So they'd make up something to charge you with. Or perhaps you had the bad luck to be near a real criminal when the police came to arrest him. If you were scooped up with the crooks, it was very easy to end up with charges no matter your protest or alibi.

The taxi "terrorists" were a case in point. Taxi drivers seemed to be a particular target for the legal system. A driver I met during a transport explained what had happened to him: An actual terrorist had hailed a cab. When it came time to pay for the ride, he'd use a card linked to an account that had been used for terrorist or criminal activities. Unfortunately, the investigator used that as evidence that the driver was involved in terrorism as well—he'd benefited from the crime.

The guy broke down while telling me the story. The fare had been about six dollars. He was labeled an international terrorist and kept away from his family because he'd done his job giving someone a ride.

Disclosure: there were *actual* terrorists in jail. I got along fairly well with the few I met. They didn't like the Russian government, and neither did I.

Some of the prisoners were in jail because of baseless charges by spouses, business partners, or rivals. Adlan's British-tinted English was the result of being in business with a Brit a decade or so before. Years later, another partner had been embezzling money from the company. After being confronted, he went and told the police that Adlan had kidnapped him.

As I mentioned, kidnapping is big business in Chechnya, so the charges weren't necessarily far-fetched. I never was entirely sure in this case.

Partners weren't the only ones who would create a story to get your money or your business. FSB agents did this quite a lot, muscling into legitimate companies the way the American mafia used to do in the 1950s and early '60s. Just on a much bigger scale, and with the "law" on their side.

A lot of prisoners pled guilty to make sure they got a relatively short sentence. It was extremely rare to be declared not guilty at trial, so they believed it was far better to plead and keep things quick and clean. Russian jail sentences for typical crimes seemed generally shorter than those in most US states, and rarely did convicted criminals get anything close to the maximum permitted sentence.

In my case, for example, the maximum sentence for beating a police officer was on the books as ten years, but no one ever got that.

In fact, from the moment I got to SIZO-5, I was told I would likely get out with a small fine and time served.

Murder someone? The criminal code said you could get fifteen years, but no one ever did. According to the inmates I talked to, the likely sentence was less than six years; higher was considered harsh and required particularly grotesque circumstances.

On the other hand, I met a guy who had stolen a laptop. He was looking at a likely sentence of five years. And he had returned the laptop before being arrested.

His story had a "happy" ending—he ended up getting out after six months without going to a labor camp. Russian justice was unpredictable.

The notion that you were innocent before trial was pretty foreign. The fact that a good percentage of people charged with a crime in the US end up being judged not guilty blew a lot of minds. Russians valued fairness as much as Americans; they just didn't expect to see it in the legal system.

"The fact that you live in such a place," one man told me when we compared court systems, "is incredible."

Tell Russians about the death penalty, though, and their opinions quickly change. It was barbaric, even if the trial that led to it was fair.

I'm on the short side for an American, but I'm roughly average for Russians. I was pretty jacked when I went to jail—I'd been working out seriously for more than half my life. So to a lot of prisoners, I seemed physically intimidating. And I'm sure I could have trashed everyone in my first cell.

Maybe not Adlan.

But fighting wasn't necessary. The guys who had money and connections on the outside were, of course, highly valued by other prisoners . . . and the guards. But there was a kind of strangely democratic feel to the prison, or at least the cells I was in. *We're all screwed here, so let's make the best of it. Maybe I help you today; maybe you help me tomorrow.*

I wouldn't trust it to last under pressure, but people tended to be very helpful to and even protective of their cellmates.

At the pre-trial prison, cigarettes, tea, and a few other staples and luxuries were provided by the mafya. Drugs and other contraband, including cell phones, came from them as well. In exchange, each cell paid dues to the criminal hierarchy. The guards were part of the system, presumably taking in good money to look the other way.

Every morning the guards would bring bread and oatmeal. I called it oatmeal, but it was really more like a bowl of water with some amount of grains floating in it, not necessarily oats. One day it'd be oats, then wheat, or buckwheat, or some grain no one could identify. The bread was tough and dry, but edible, a large loaf baked by prisoners. We were offered a knife to cut it with, but in quarantine, no one would sign—it represented a submission to authority, against mafya rules. In Spetz Block, someone would sign, and we got the knife. It had a rounded edge, but it was sharp—absolutely a weapon if someone chose to use it as one. The guards always managed to collect it.

Many of the prisoners in my wing were well off; that was why the FSB had arrested them in the first place, hoping to put the screws to them and get whatever it was they wanted. Prisoners with money would spend it on things like outside food, which was permitted; this would (usually) be shared with cellmates. Certain things, drugs especially, were impossible to get. But bribery made much possible. Cell phones were common throughout the rest of the prison but the rules forbidding them were strictly observed in my block. Even so, someone managed to get one or more in, undoubtedly with help from the staff. There was hell to pay when they were found, though.

Bribes ranged from trivial—cigarettes for a guard who shrugged at some minor offense—to hundreds of thousands of dollars and the equivalent to prosecutors and judges.

I heard a story about someone who'd been charged with all sorts of made-up crimes. (I'm not saying he didn't commit crimes, just that the ones they charged him with were bogus.) The usual sentence for his charges totaled twenty years. He passed enough money around to get the sentence down to, like, nine years. He then filed an appeal and bribed the judge to get the sentence down to, like, six years. Between house arrest and SIZO he had enough time accumulated to take it down to three. Another bribe got him to a certain prison, where for a little more money he got a letter from the warden saying that he met the requirements for parole and should be freed.

It was generally thought better to spend less money for a prosecutor than a judge, since you were far more likely to get a reduced sentence than an acquittal. And the difference in price could be pretty large, amounting to tens of thousands of dollars, either in rubles or something like a Mercedes G-Wagon. I imagine not *every* judge or prosecutor would take a bribe. But there were many stories circulating, and I'm sure most would, unless the FSB was involved in the case.

Bribes also helped people to keep some portion of their wealth despite going to jail. There, the main players were usually the investigators. They'd say, "We know you have two BMW 5s, a G-Wagon, and two houses. If you give me one of the BMWs, then I won't know that you own this other house or this G-Wagon."

Easy decision, I'd say.

If you were *really* successful, the bribes were bigger. An FSB official or go-between might say something along the lines of: "You own ten factories. What I want you to do is this—give my FSB chief 51 percent ownership of your company, and then you only go to prison for three years."

Russian justice made many people rich, and just as many poor.

●

Even if I had been Russian and an "ordinary" visitor, Lina would have had a difficult time arranging visits since we weren't married. She maneuvered around various roadblocks by claiming to be my fiancée or by playing the lawyer card. She knew the law better than most of the people who worked at the prison, and she wasn't shy about pushing for her rights, or mine.

She managed to get into SIZO soon after I was arrested. We sat across from each other in a visitor's room, separated by a sheet of plexiglass. She held her hand up to the glass. I reached across and put mine there as well. It was the closest we could come to a hug or a kiss.

My main thing was to just make her understand that I was all right. I wanted her to know I wasn't scared. I gave her a bunch of things to tell my parents.

I'd found out from my cellmates that she could send letters; Lina had already worked that out. We arranged that I would write to my parents through her.

"They need to call the embassy," I told her.

"They already have," Lina said. "But your embassy isn't doing anything. They are crap."

"They have a lot to take care of." That was the first and last time I ever defended the embassy. Lina's description of their efforts proved far more accurate than mine, at least until my trial was over.

She asked about my cellmates.

"They're all rich guys. Bankers and businessmen." An exaggeration at that point, though it would later be largely true.

I don't know that she believed that. Nor did she believe me when I told her I'd be okay.

Finally, it was time for her to go.

"Hey, don't worry," I told her. "Everything's okay."

She forced a smile. It didn't fool me, though I wanted it to.

The embassy had not contacted me directly to that point. I was told later that the Russians gave them a difficult time, turning down a request to visit me. One theory for the delay was that the Russians wanted time for my bruises to heal.

I don't remember when an embassy official finally visited. It may have been August 21, the Wednesday after my arrest. The meeting did not go particularly well. To be honest, I got the impression that checking on Americans accused of crimes was not a priority. The representative they sent seemed to know very little about the Russian legal system, or the inner workings and machinations of Russia in general.

We were seated in a cubicle, separated by plexiglass, not unlike the arrangements common in many American jails and prisons. We were supposed to talk on a phone, which was undoubtedly being recorded for later translation. I had a hard time persuading the embassy guy not to use the phone, even though it wasn't difficult to hear what each of us was saying without it.

While I'm sure my phone there was tapped, I don't think all of the cubicles were wired for eavesdropping, since I was nearly always taken to the same cubicle at the far end of the room. At least once, I was abruptly pulled out of the room while talking to someone, probably because whatever recording arrangement they had in place failed.

Anyway, the embassy official told me they were going to do whatever they could for me blah-blah-blah. What he said didn't raise my expectations that I would be out soon.

I let him have it about the photo. His blank look only got blanker.

"You should be prepared to be here for a long time," he told me when I finished. "And you look great."

"Are you serious?"

"Genuinely, yes. When we meet people in these places they are usually crying."

"I was a US Marine."

"Yes. It's obvious that that does something for you guys."

The delay in seeing me, the ineptness at the prison—those were not confidence builders. But the worst bungle was that picture. I knew my parents had sent it, but the embassy should have had the sense to understand how it would be received. It seemed like everyone, with the exception of Lina, was doing everything they could to make things worse for me.

Not on purpose, but just the same . . .

It was a pattern that would repeat and repeat. When the FSB wasn't screwing me on purpose, everyone else did it accidentally.

That's not charitable, I know. It's not fair. My family was doing everything they could to help. The embassy not so much, but I really was a non-important person who had the bad judgment to get black-out drunk, so maybe their inaction was understandable.

Hard to forgive, but understandable.

I got a graduate-level seminar in Russian justice those first few weeks, between the arrest, the hearing, and jail. I still had a lot to learn, but I already realized that hiring an expensive lawyer would be a waste of money.

So my father's decision to pay the two lawyers from Lina's office an exorbitant sum (for Russia) to represent me angered me no end. And that anger was impossible to suppress the first time he visited soon after he arrived in Moscow on September 11.

Let me say, number one, that I respected those attorneys and their efforts. Sergey and Victoria were very experienced; Sergey had been a judge, in fact. They worked as a kind of tag team, playing to each one's strengths, be it precise legal citations or persuasive arguments. They did a lot of work on my behalf.

That work had exactly zero effect on the judicial outcome, but it did help me convince people back in the States that the trial was a monkey show and I was a political pawn. Very possibly I would still be in Russia had that not happened.

Number two, I love my dad greatly. Immensely. Deeply. We have a close relationship. I will do anything—*anything*—for him. And if it wasn't for my father hounding the embassy, I'm pretty convinced that they wouldn't have done anything for me.

But he has a habit of doing things against my advice. Like paying too much for the lawyers. Or coming to Moscow in the first place. I raged at him for both of those things, and gave him a hard time about it for the three years of my incarceration. Sometimes still.

My father thinks I don't know how much that was. I may not. But I do know that at least $40,000 went straight from my bank account back home to the lawyers. I also know that at least another $10,000 in donations from a GoFundMe account went for appeals. As lawyer fees go in Russia, those amounts are absolutely insane. The going rate for a criminal case, according to my cellmates, was between $5,000 and $10,000.

My father disagrees, of course.

Here's one thing I definitely know: hiring a good lawyer in Russia does very little to affect the outcome of the case, unless he's the one bribing the prosecutor for an easy sentence. That wasn't going to happen here. No lawyer, not even one related to Putin, was going to get me off.

Back to my father's visit, which was September 13, a couple of days after he arrived. The guards typically don't tell you who your visitor is when they meet you at your cell. They escorted me down, took me to the room: and there's Dad.

"What are you doing here!" I screeched.

The Russians didn't need listening devices to hear me. Putin probably heard me over at the Kremlin.

My first thought was that they would arrest my father as well. I told him that. About half my words were spelled with four letters.

His face grew red, but he remained relatively calm. And insistent. No way in hell was he leaving.

And great if they arrested him, too. Then they'd *really* be in trouble.

Right.

"The best thing that could happen for your case is for them to arrest me, too," he claimed. "That'll get the media's attention and maybe our government will do something."

I didn't have much faith in that. Nor did I think the publicity of a father and son detention would embarrass the Russians. My language and attitude deteriorated as my father talked about how I needed a strong defense, which the lawyers were promising. And how this would translate into my being freed.

The nicest thing I called him was "dumbass."

This is clearly not the fucking United States! This is an enemy nation with a dictator that hates America. Why would you think that they have the same values as us and that their system works the same way?

I tore into him about everything, including the embassy. *Are they retarded? Are they trying to screw me on purpose?*

There was worse. I'm ashamed of how I treated him. I treated him pretty poorly on most of his other visits as well.

He took my tirades better than I deserved. Usually, he was insanely calm.

My mom's theory is that my dad was the only safe person I could vent to. That is true. But there was more to my anger than that, or to any pop psychology theories that spring to mind. I already understood that I was going to have an extremely difficult time surviving prison. My only hope of doing that was to harden myself so completely that the Russians could not harm me psychologically.

I could not allow myself to be vulnerable.

Nor could I let them think I had *any* vulnerability, because they would absolutely use it against me. If they thought I loved something or someone, that person would be used in some way to get what they wanted from me.

My father had just presented himself to them as a tool to be used. A torture device. Defying them might very possibly mean hurting him.

But so be it.

In my fury, I thought he was forcing me to harm him.

The Russian authorities never directly used my dad. They severely limited his visits. Maybe they thought that would give them some leverage, but the opposite was true. In fact, there came a point where I told the lawyers and the embassy that I would not accept any communication or visits from him at all, until he agreed to follow precisely any directions I gave him.

Eventually, my father agreed. I'm sure it took superhuman effort. He's a good man, but he's not humble when he thinks he's right. And he still thinks he was right. Mostly.

How much the Russians knew or cared about any of that, I have no idea.

My father was *very* optimistic, at least when he talked to me. Early on, probably to cheer me up, he told me he'd heard a new *Top Gun* was being released very soon, and promised we'd see it together in a few weeks back in the States.

I doubt even Tom Cruise could have been as optimistic.

I was very skeptical of Sergey and Victoria the first time I met them. My experience with my first lawyer had pretty much turned me off to all Russian lawyers. Even though they had come from Lina's company, I was hesitant to even sign the agreement letting them represent me.

My skepticism was so obvious that Victoria, in broken English, gave me a figurative slap across the face: "You're going to have to trust us at some point. We are attorneys. Your attorneys."

They were good advocates, definitely on my side. They had me taken from the prison to a doctor's office to evaluate my bruises. The injuries were close to healed by that point, but the fact the lawyers could arrange that made me feel more confident of their abilities.

The examination was a joke. The thing that really impressed me was how lackadaisical the guards were when they escorted us there. I could easily have run off. I wouldn't have gotten very far since I hadn't formulated a plan, though.

My lawyers prepared a list of items they wanted from the investigator—the equivalent of discovery in the American judicial system. There were also some requests for the court. The stack of requests was several inches high.

We want all of the cameras from the vehicle where this supposedly occurred. We want all of the cameras from inside of the police station, all the recordings. We want a list of all of the police officers who are involved and who were on duty at that time . . .

It was an impressive list, impressive enough to shake some of my doubt that my conviction was preordained. And while I wasn't optimistic when a bail hearing was set for the end of the month in front of a new judge, my father got excited, thinking that the odds of bail had greatly improved.

Maybe they weren't ten million to one. Maybe just 999,999 to 1. Even the embassy didn't think I would get bail.

Few prisoners in Russia are let out on bail before trial once they have been put into the detention center. You may get bail if you bribe the prosecutor to go along, or if the judge sees beyond any doubt that you're innocent. You won't get out of a conviction, but you'll at least have a year or more out of prison before the case comes up and you go to the gulag.

The prosecutor wasn't going to go along, but the judge might see the obvious.

And if that happened, I knew exactly what I was doing: finding a way to leave the country and never come back.

We had serious evidence showing that the police were lying. Slam-dunk evidence in a fair system.

The original charges had claimed I was violent in the police station. Apparently when they realized that footage from the many video cameras in the station would show that wasn't true, the charges were amended to claim that I was violent in the car, causing it to careen all over the road. (They also failed to produce any video footage; we'll get to the reasons later.)

Lina had followed, so she could testify that this hadn't happened. Better, there were video cameras along the route. She obtained videos showing that the police had driven normally, calmly, along the route to their station. There was also video evidence showing that I had been passed out when carried into the police station.

My attorneys had presented some of the video evidence to the investigator. He responded by throwing it in the trash.

Now at the bail hearing, my lawyers told the judge about the video of the car, which they still had copies of. The investigator denied that he had ignored it. My lawyers said there was video showing I'd been carried in. The prosecutor hemmed and hawed.

The judge didn't look particularly happy. The obvious conclusion was that the prosecution really had no case. But knowing Russia, and warned by my fellow prisoners, I figured that would all be disregarded. So I was stunned when the judge sternly announced bail was granted and set at one million rubles.

Don't be too impressed, or dismayed. That was $15,000 at the time.

I think the deciding factor for the judge was the investigator's continued defiance of our request for video from inside the car where the alleged incident (hadn't) occurred.

The attorneys were jubilant. One of them let out a shriek and jumped up and down in disbelief.

I had to go back to prison until the money was posted, but my father had an account with the embassy and would gladly wire the money. Paperwork signed, I'd walk out.

I'd been in for roughly six weeks. Six more hours, and I'd be free.

SEVEN

MORE LESSONS

It was Friday afternoon when the judge made his decision. And that turned out to make all the difference.

The evidence, or I should say the lack of it, was overwhelming. It was obvious that the case against me was bogus. My lawyers arranged for me to stay at a house in the city, and when the judge asked why I wouldn't run, I told him that I was innocent, and confident that a trial would prove that.

I was surprised I got bail. Stunned. In fact, I thought maybe I was wrong about the case being political. Maybe the station chief had just not liked me. I went back to SIZO-5 to wait while my father got the money. My cellmates were as surprised as I was, and congratulated me.

The first hint of a problem came when my dad tried to get someone at the embassy to arrange to get the money, which the court required in cash. But the consular affairs officer told him they would have difficulty gathering up that much cash, especially given that most of the staff were at a going-away party for Ambassador Jon Huntsman.

Whatever. Two more days, no sweat.

My father got the cash Monday morning. He went directly to the court and gave them the money, well within the allotted time.

But I wasn't let out.

A few days later, I was taken from my cell to the second floor of the prison. Seven judges, including the top judge of the Moscow Region, Olga Egorova, heard the case by video. The government translator was so inept that one of the judges had to stop the proceedings and tell me exactly what was going on: the prosecutor had filed an appeal to stop the release.

Following the hearing, my case was sent to another lower-court judge, who reversed the first judge's ruling on a technicality. Further appeals would follow.

They did change my indictment after the video evidence was included in the case by the judge that granted bail. The new indictment would claim that the violence happened on a stretch of road where cameras could not see.

Of course, it was still bs, as events at the trial would show.

It was clear that I was denied bail because the government wanted me in prison. My value as a political pawn was higher there. They could control my interactions, and put pressure on me if necessary.

Or at least they thought that. All they really did was make me angrier.

Side note: the Russians did refund the money. So there's that.

I was moved from my cell a number of times. I'm not sure why. Maybe they wanted to avoid me having too much contact with other prisoners. Maybe they wanted to put people in who might be able to get information from me. Maybe it was just a staffing thing, or a reminder of who was in charge.

Moving was a minor hassle. It involved rolling up my mattress, taking it and the rest of my stuff to wherever my new home was. But it gave me the opportunity to meet a lot of other prisoners, and hear their stories.

Given the amount of corruption in Russia, it must be hard for any businessman or entrepreneur to get far without paying someone off. I met so many people who clearly were being screwed that it's impossible not to see the country as a cauldron of crime and financial lust perpetuated by a kleptomaniac government. You needed money not to be screwed, but if you had too much of it, someone more powerful would come and take it.

If you had no money or power, you were screwed even worse.

One of my cellmates was a fellow named Aleksei, who was apparently pretty famous in Russia. He was a bank manager whose boss or bosses had stolen an incredible sum and fled overseas. I think it was the equivalent of $2 billion. He had been arrested because the authorities had no one else to charge, and with a crime that large, someone had to go to jail.

Another cellmate, Sasha, was also a banker charged with corruption. He was regularly pressured to testify against people in exchange for a lighter sentence, even though he had no connection to the people or knowledge of their cases. Their interviews would go like this:

Do you know about so-and-so and his crime?

No.

Well, if you do know, you'll get a lighter sentence. So, do you know?

No.

He always held out, at least while I knew him.

I realize that happens in bad cop movies in the US, but that's why they're bad cop movies. In SIZO, it seemed like every inmate I met was pressured to invent something to make his sentence easier.

Not to get off entirely, though. The FSB or whoever was controlling things would only go so far. The idea of "justice" had to be upheld.

I'd guess most people go along. Sasha was an exception.

Poor guy. Every couple of months, the government lodged new charges against him. When he first arrived, he was charged with a minor crime. When he wouldn't cooperate, they added embezzling.

Still not helping? We are now charging you with bribery . . . part of a criminal enterprise . . .

I don't know where it ended. The stress it put these guys under was visible. They had families outside. Some I'm sure had stashed money overseas, but most were as broke as I was. Worse, since they were Russian.

It didn't matter if the case made no sense on its face. An investigation into corruption in the city of Sochi resulted in charges implicating the vice mayor. "Anatoly" was brought in and charged with the crime.

All good, except that he had not been vice mayor when the crime occurred, and in fact was an official in a different city, without access to whatever was going on.

The poor guy thought that if he just explained that, he would be released. Apparently, he naively thought all he had to do was say who he was, and the charges against him would be dropped.

They weren't. Instead, the investigators insisted he must be an accomplice.

"I served in a different city!" he protested.

"Well, you told [the actual criminal] to steal the money."

And on and on.

Then there was "Andre," who worked security for the Russian version of the State Department in South America somewhere. He had been arrested for smuggling cocaine. According to the police, he was involved in a conspiracy with two other men, one of whom had been in Russia the whole time.

Andre had his own alibis, but no matter. The men were accused of bringing a massive amount of cocaine into the embassy and then transporting it via airplane to Russia. The mechanism to do so involved a complicated and highly unlikely bureaucratic chain of falsified documents and a lot of officials looking the other way. Not that it would have been impossible, just very far-fetched, even for Russia.

The thing was, though, the Argentinian police had found the cocaine at the airport or on its way there *without* connecting it to Andre. When they began to investigate, the Russian authorities told them that Andre and the other embassy worker were responsible.

Believing them, the Argentinians investigated, only to realize that neither man was involved. Argentina eventually just dropped the case.

The Russians did not. Another country was investigating a separate but similar situation in another South American country. It wasn't going to take much digging to realize that the FSB was running a pretty extensive drug smuggling operation.

Something had to be done to take the heat off. So Andre and the others were arrested. He wasn't sure exactly why he had been targeted. Possibly it was because he had angered someone. He also had the authority to be near an aircraft to transport the drugs, though he didn't appear to have been near the one in question.

His "accomplice" was an even further reach: he cleaned toilets. The only possible reason he could have been picked was the fact that he had a nephew back in Russia who lived in the same city where the drugs were to be delivered. You guessed it: the man's nephew was the third person charged in the conspiracy.

There was a story, plotted and tied in a bow. Mind you, no drugs were ever delivered, since the Argentinians had seized them.

Jury trials are rare in Russia. You can only have a jury if the crime is very serious. Drug smuggling qualifies. But the problem in a high-profile case—something like Andre's, for example—is the huge pressure on the judge. Cases are only brought if the powers-that-be want the person convicted. So if things go badly for the prosecution and it looks like the jury will declare the accused innocent, the judge will find a reason to declare a mistrial or transfer the case. It's back to square one.

Andre had quite an odyssey in the court system. At his first jury trial, the prospective jurors included six current and former members of law enforcement. His attorneys whittled away the most obviously prejudiced jurors, but the panel was still weighted against him.

An FSB agent testified about events he witnessed in South America . . . only to be shown documents by the defense that indicated he was not even in the country at the time.

The jury saw a yacht that Andre had allegedly bought with the proceeds.

Oops. It turned out that the photo came from the internet. Andre didn't own a yacht. Or a South American villa, another piece of false evidence that somehow made it to court before being easily refuted.

The case went so poorly for the prosecution that the judge soon found a reason to transfer it.

Do-over time.

Andre, who smoked more than a steam locomotive, then had a stroke. His lawyers tried to get him out on bail to recuperate at home. Somehow the records relating to his stroke disappeared from his file.

Andre had lived in Germany at some point, and had a house there. He managed to leverage that into a request from the German embassy to check on his condition. After that, he started receiving somewhat better care and attention from the authorities. He stayed in jail, though.

Maybe you're thinking: My friend was a pretty smart guy who had enough wits to use the system, and apparently enough money to hire lawyers. So maybe he was not guilty of this, but was complicit in something else.

That's what Russia does to you. There is so much corruption that it's impossible not to suspect everyone of something, if not everything. But I honestly think Andre wasn't involved in the cocaine plot, or any crime at all.

I learned a lot from Andre. Most important, he taught me how to write legal complaints.

As twisted as the Russian legal system is, no one involved wants to admit how utterly corrupt it is. In an odd way, this can be used against it. Formally notifying the authorities that a rule or a law has been broken can generate a flurry of action. It can even get things changed, at least a little.

Not always, but often enough that it's worth pursuing, especially if your goal is to harass the authorities as much as possible.

"Listen, you are writing this complaint to the head of the prison," Andre would explain, instructing me on how to protest some violation or other. "But he doesn't care. Writing to him is a waste. What you need to do is write to his boss. He also won't care. But at the same time, you write to all of these other people here and here and here. They will then ask the boss what is going on. That, in turn, will put pressure on the head of the prison."

Stuff rolls downhill, in other words.

Andre had an encyclopedic knowledge of Russian law, at least as it related to prisons. He also had a library of Russian law books in his cell. He explained quite a lot about how the system worked, where a protest might help, where an appeal was useless. He urged me to write letters to the European Court of Human Rights, explaining that opening a case there would anger the Russians, since it was bad publicity and would generate work for some bureaucrat or other. It would also make them more careful about violating my rights—life was annoying enough in Russia without having to put up with hassles caused by a random American.

Also, there was the possibility of winning a case and getting money from the people and government who violated my rights. So why not?

I wrote to the European Court, protesting my treatment. I soon got a visit from some official or other at the prison who demanded to know why I had asked the court to open a case.

"You guys are violating my rights," I told him.

He threw the court papers at me and left.

They kept violating my rights. I kept complaining. The biggest sticking point, aside from the arrest, the denial of bail, etc., was the fact that they would not give me medicine.

I'm not talking about exotic, costly medications only available in the West. I mean aspirin and similar painkillers. Among other body parts, my back, which I'd injured in Afghanistan, was a constant problem.

I began keeping track of the denials, then formed that into a complaint.

I did finally get the meds, either because of my complaint, actions by my lawyers, or pressure from the embassy. Most likely all three.

Letters and protests only took you so far, as Andre readily admitted. The system was thoroughly corrupt, and the more I talked to people, the less hope I had that I would get out, let alone find a tiny bit of justice.

I heard about a guy—let's call him Boris—who was under arrest and charged with the same crime I was: assault on police officers with the intent to cause serious bodily injury.

Boris was even less guilty than I was. He'd been arrested while filming a protest in Moscow, taking footage of the police beating people. The police ran over to him, telling him to stop, which he did.

But one of the cops running over tripped on a curb and broke his collarbone. Because of that, Boris was arrested and charged. In court, the prosecutor claimed Boris violently resisted arrest and threw the officer down.

A lot of people were taking pictures. His attorneys found a video that showed the entire sequence and presented it to the court. Clearly, Boris had done none of the things he was charged with.

The court refused to accept the video as evidence. He was convicted and sentenced to three years in prison.

It's a different situation today, but at the time there was still some free press in Russia. His lawyers leaked the video to the media and it was shown all over Russia. With that background, the case was sent to an appeals court. Under enormous public pressure, the appeals court decided it had no option but to reverse the guilty verdict.

Well, not exactly. They *upheld* the guilty verdict but reclassified the charge to a lower level. They then sentenced him according to the lesser crime, carefully setting the amount of time to what he had already served. That meant he was released.

That's what passed for a victory in the Russian legal system.

The parallel to my case was hard to miss.

The embassy's support was very hit or miss. Sometimes it was just not competent. My attorneys needed a statement indicating the Russians had delayed allowing embassy personnel to see me after I was arrested, and that when they had finally gotten in, I had some bruises and other injuries. When my father finally got the letter to give to the attorneys, it was so poorly written that it made it seem the opposite of what was intended. That touched off a testy back-and-forth, until finally my dad appealed to higher authorities at the State Department. He got a new letter after two months of struggle.

Things went better from that point on, in his opinion. Not so much mine.

The main thing you have in prison, any prison, is time. It can be valuable, but it can also be a curse.

I had plenty of time to learn Russian, which I pretty much had to do to communicate. I also had time to learn their laws, and protest when they didn't follow them, which was often. I also spent time doing mental math. It required a lot of concentration, pushing out other thoughts. I worked word problems, playing with financial situations, like *You have this much money available in a bank account. If you put it in a CD at 3 percent over ten years, how much will that be?*

I debated my future employment. Would it be more beneficial to become a firefighter or a police officer immediately when I got back to the States, or go to college first? Which universities would I want to look at?

I planned an escape. It was more of a mental challenge than an actual plan, but I approached it scientifically. I looked for a wall that I might climb, judging whether I would be seen or not. I asked prisoners for information that was relevant to escaping. I contemplated what part of Russia would be easiest to get out of.

Could I get near the border with Ukraine? The Ukrainians won't extradite me.

The curse of time was thinking about things that made me weak. Prime among them was thinking about my family. I saw how that made others despair.

There was no way to completely shut those thoughts out, even as I filled my head with other things. What I eventually decided to do was set aside a specific time to think of them: at night, just before going to sleep.

Thinking of my family was dessert. I favored happy thoughts, events in the past, things we would do in the future. Only good things. I limited myself to an hour—maybe two hours if I was feeling real bad or couldn't sleep.

I found two types of Russians in prison, both in SIZO-5 and later in the work camp, when it came to attitudes toward America: ones who were super pro-Russian and didn't like America, and others who were really interested in America, to the point of wanting to move there.

Sometimes I'd argue a little with the first type, though there was no way to persuade them that maybe America wasn't as evil as their news media's propaganda insisted. The lies about America and NATO were so ingrained in the reporting that it was no surprise that people began repeating them. You hear something outrageous for days and weeks and years, and you can't help but think it's true, or close to true.

I think that explains why so many people, even lawyers, were so naive about the Russian legal system. If you had no actual interaction with it, it was easy to think that there was nothing behind whispers about how badly justice was perverted. The things you heard about so-and-so were so horrendous, they had to be true. Why would anyone make that up?

But then, when you came in contact with the legal system, what you saw could only make you cynical.

Very cynical. If you were there for something you knew you didn't do, you thought everything the government said was a lie. And not just *your* government, and not just governments. The world itself was false.

How do you survive that? How do you find anything that is real? Can you even believe in yourself?

For many, skepticism led to cynicism. Beyond that, despair.

I never lost hope. As much as I raged, I knew I could survive. I absolutely knew I would. There could be no other thought in my head.

It wasn't a mathematical equation. It was belief. Whether it was genetic or came from how I was raised, my experience in the Marine Corps, my ups and downs in life, my love for my parents and Lina . . . No, it was all of those things, and more. It was a conviction in my soul, in every cell of my body, that I would get through this. I would do it by hardening myself every day. I would not allow myself to be weak. I would not give the Russians a weapon to use against me.

And at some point, somehow, some way, I would get them back for all of this. I would have revenge.

EIGHT

PARENTAL SUPPORT

After a lot of arguing back and forth with my parents, and at one point not answering letters, I agreed to let the embassy discuss my situation with them and for them to contact elected officials to seek help. I was just a pawn in a much larger chess game—a war, really. I could fight, and I would fight, and I wouldn't surrender.

But I couldn't fight entirely alone.

The wheels of Russian justice ground on. Spring approached, as did my trial, set to begin in early March.

My dad's point of view:

By the time I came home in January 2020, Trevor had agreed that it was a political case. With his approval, Paula and I started reaching out for help.

The first politician we reached out to in January 2020 was our senator, Ted Cruz. After a few emails and phone calls, his staff told us that they had spoken to the State Department. They also informed us that the Moscow embassy website stated that former American military personnel may be at risk of questionable detention in Russia.

We concluded they were a dead end.

We reached out to Paul Whelan's attorney in Washington to try and get some guidance. He gave our number to the Whelan family, who contacted us and were a great help.

In February 2020, I returned to Moscow. Paula stayed busy making fliers and yard signs to put up around our area. She handed out cards and fliers at businesses. She put up yellow ribbons in our yard and made calls and sent emails to politicians.

What she really wanted to do, though, was come to Moscow for the trial.

I tried very hard to talk her out of it. But mothers' instincts are strong, and Paula's will is even stronger than mine, certainly when it comes to her kids. Trevor's sister Taylor insisted on coming as well, so the whole family was in Moscow City Court the day his trial began March 11.

I didn't tell Trevor beforehand because I knew how he would react. He'd given me hell when I first showed up in Moscow—he's still mad, I think, though he claims to have forgiven me. I saw no point in making him worry about things more than he already had to worry about.

Our meetings were contentious, the few we were allowed to have. Trevor was focusing very hard on simply getting through each day. Worrying about us—Paula, Taylor, myself—made it exponentially harder for him to do that.

We were standing in the hallway as the guards brought him up. He came into the hall and there we were.

Anger quickly replaced the look of shock on his face. He said nothing, walking past quickly.

Cameras started flashing and clicking as he turned the corner. Besides the local press, news services from around the world had decided to attend. First the shock of seeing his mother and sister, then that. His heart must have started beating out of his chest.

Even though we'd done everything we could to get media attention, I was still surprised by how many news organizations were covering the trial. Between our press releases, my freshly opened Twitter account, and personal appeals, we'd spread the word to so many people. I'd convinced a New York Times *reporter to attend the pre-trial hearing, and he wrote an article, helping increase Trevor's profile. Now that we had media attention, we realized we'd have to convince their readers and viewers that Trevor was innocent.*

I knew by now that Trevor wasn't going to get anything close to a fair trial in Russia. I also knew only the US government could get Trevor back home. But they would only do that if there was political pressure. And that pressure would only be generated if people knew Trevor was innocent.

The two police officers whom Trevor had allegedly injured were scheduled as witnesses on the first day. The first officer was inconsistent and outright lied, claiming that Trevor had physically injured him, which was directly contradicted by videotape evidence.

A bomb threat emptied the courthouse as the second police officer was called to the stand. Court was adjourned. There would be a series of bomb threats during much of the trial, apparently called in by supporters of Alexei Navalny, who was being tried around the same time, though in a different building. As far as we know, no bomb was ever found, and none ever went off.

Paula and Taylor visited Trevor the next day, with permission from the judge. Trevor scolded them, but he couldn't stay mad at his mother or his sister very long.

Being angry with me was another story.

Two days later, the prison system and courts shut down for COVID.

We'd known that the virus was spreading across the world since the end of 2019. The first case in Russia was publicly declared around the beginning of February. The World Health Organization declared a worldwide pandemic March 11, prompting countries to begin closing or severely restricting their borders.

Taylor managed to find a flight and returned to the US. Paula didn't want to go. She claimed she didn't feel well, that she was sick. I strongly suspect that she was faking, telling me that so she wouldn't have to leave her son.

"Maybe," she confessed later.

You can't blame her. Not only did she have a fierce mother's love for our son, but she felt a little out of the loop watching from back home. Even though she'd been handling dozens of important things, the distance made her feel as if she wasn't really doing everything she could. Eventually, though, she realized it was important for her to get back while she could. In many ways she was more important than I was.

The small size of the apartment and my snoring probably helped her make that decision.

Flights quickly became few and far between, and she might have gotten her wish to stay had we not heard that the embassy was arranging a last flight back to the States.

I took her to the airport, and waited until she boarded. I hadn't left the terminal building when my cell phone rang. It was Paula, on the plane.

"We're coming back to the terminal," she told me. The flight had been canceled just as it started to taxi.

We never learned exactly what happened. According to the Russians, New York had declined permission for the plane to land. According to the authorities in New York, that wasn't true; they claimed the Russians had decided to cancel the flight.

A few days later, the embassy arranged another flight. I managed to persuade Paula to take it. Good thing: it's said to have been the very last plane out of Russia before total quarantine.

When we arrived at the terminal, we found embassy staff there, helping Americans with boarding documents. Among them was their boss, Ambassador John Sullivan, who was there handing out masks as a precaution against COVID.

That was the first of what would eventually be several meetings I had with the ambassador. I liked him a lot. He was in his late fifties or early sixties at the time, and very personable. He'd started his career as a lawyer in the Department of Justice, worked for George H. W. Bush, and had represented international trade interests as a private counsel before coming back into public service as a deputy general counsel in the Defense Department. Before his appointment to Russia at the end of 2019, Sullivan had been Deputy Secretary of State.

Up until our meeting, I didn't think the embassy had been very helpful. Maybe it was because I believed what I read on State Department websites that among their priorities is to assist Americans detained in foreign countries. I came to realize that's not always possible because of hostile attitudes in some of those countries, as well as a shortage of embassy staff.

From what I've seen, when you get arrested overseas, the US government really doesn't do much. If you're not a spy—or someone accused of spying—they generally aren't going to say anything about your case at all. You may not even be designated as "wrongfully detained" by the State Department when by rights you should be.

To me, there are four ways that you can get our government's attention when you're wrongly accused in a foreign country: you can be very famous, or ultra rich, or extremely well-connected to someone in the government, or able to create enough pressure through the media or political influence.

While some of our local congresspeople had been sympathetic, it was really up to the president to pressure Russia on the case. And President Trump had not chosen to do so.

●

After meeting with the ambassador and his staff, I went back to my apartment, where I would spend months researching information and doing whatever I could to help Trevor's attorneys. I'd tweet throughout the day, trying to build up publicity for the case and make contacts with reporters.

Like cities around the world, Moscow was in lockdown. Aside from a small area around the building, I needed permission from the mayor to go anywhere in the city. When I needed to shop for food or go to court, I had to go online and make a request to go out. Once approved, you needed to carry the permit with you at all times.

One poor guy was arrested for taking his dog to a park. They made an example out of him, fining and jailing him.

My Russian remained worse than primitive, but by now I was an expert at using translation apps and figuring things out.

Trevor, meanwhile, remained in prison, his case temporarily on hold.

NINE

FAKE JUSTICE

Getting past the initial shock of my mom and my sister being in Moscow was not easy. I couldn't really stay mad at either of them, though. There was so much to focus on, even when COVID shut the world down.

The actual start of the trial was a relief in some ways; for me, limbo was worse than hell. With the trial there was more to do, and a resolution at least in sight, even if the resolution was sure to suck. I'd lost my appetite and had trouble sleeping as the trial neared; now at least I could eat and doze off semi-reliably.

More than six months had passed since I was first arrested. My lawyers had filed appeals and arguments after my bail was denied; we worked through a series of hearings, mostly remote. They also labored to get my complaints on the record. At one point, Sergey got into a shouting match with a judge over whether I was entitled to have the complaints listed.

He won—for most, though not all.

The fact that we fought bothered the hell out of the Russians. The fact that I resisted at all bothered them beyond belief.

My lawyers had discussed a number of strategies in the weeks leading up to the trial. The problem was, all of their strategies added up to the same thing: plead guilty for a lighter sentence.

I was *not* guilty. I had *not* assaulted those police officers. There was video evidence showing I had not.

No. I could not, would not, lie about that.

We would meet to discuss the case and strategy in a concrete-walled room, sitting on stools bolted to the floor, a table between us. It was uncomfortable to sit there for too long, which I assume was the idea. My keepers didn't want me or my lawyers to be comfortable. The Russian investigators did whatever they could to harass me, though generally in a way that made it difficult to prove they were more than just incompetent.

Petty stuff, mostly. I'd have to wait for my attorneys, sometimes for hours, not because they were late, but because . . . because whatever excuse the prison officials could come up with, no matter how far-fetched. I'd sit on the stool and wait. Eventually, my back would start to ache. I'd look at the windows and fantasize about pushing through their narrow openings, dropping to the ground and escaping, if only for a few hours.

A Metro stop sat nearby. I could jump, run, take the train, fly away.

Those windows: At some point, the people who ran the prison decided that being able to see through the windows and breathe the air—even if the view was horrid and the air metallic—made things too comfortable for a prisoner and his attorneys. So they cemented over them.

My attorneys kept coming, and kept making their pitch for me to accept a guilty plea.

We understand that you're not guilty, and we understand that in America, if you're not guilty, you would plead not guilty. But in Russia, if you plead not guilty, it's like punching the judge in the face. He'll take it as an insult. You're basically saying they're lying.

To which I'd answer, "They *are* lying."

Yes, but they might give you a harsher sentence because you do that.

I was pretty sure I was getting a harsh sentence no matter what.

The lawyers tried and tried to get me to plead guilty. I refused. Then, finally, after I'm not sure how many hours in how many concrete-walled rooms, they came up with a possible compromise. Not a compromise exactly, just a tactic that might lessen the insult to the judge, or at least delay it long enough for us to present our case.

Ordinarily in Russia, you made your plea—guilty or not guilty—at the start of the criminal proceedings. But there was also a provision under Russian court procedure that let a suspect delay his plea until the end of the trial.

In other words, I could wait to punch the judge in the face after all of the evidence was heard.

I agreed.

I knew it wouldn't make any difference in the judgment. I also didn't think it would make much difference in my sentencing, to be honest. It might be that after hearing all the evidence, seeing how much of it was pure bs, the judge would go easy. But I doubted that. If anything, he was likely to feel I'd just kicked him in the judicial balls, and would have a lot less time to forget it, or at least recover from the blow. But it was a way to satisfy my attorneys, and it might possibly make it easier for them to argue the case, since the judge would not be as pissed off—at least until the end.

My strategy wasn't to win. I had no illusions that I would find justice in Russia.

What I needed to do was to convince the people back home that

I was innocent. I had begun to believe in my parents' campaign to get me out of prison.

I'd started out not wanting them to do anything. I don't know if there was a specific moment when my mind changed, and I can't say that I really had any faith that I would be released, or even that the US government could apply meaningful pressure on the Russians. But as the trial started, it was important to me that my countrymen knew I was being framed.

It's one thing to be innocent, and another for people to know you are innocent.

I liked Victoria more than Sergey. Sergey was very focused on the legal aspects of the case, and no doubt an expert. But Victoria seemed to care more about things that mattered to me, like getting my medicine. She seemed to understand why I didn't want to plead guilty. I think she was more emotionally invested in my cause than her partner.

Yulia, who headed the school where I studied Russian, became an important part of my team, acting as translator after my lawyers argued that I should be allowed to select and hire my own. There were a few times when the courts tried to force me to use a different translator. I'd just pretend I couldn't understand what the translator was saying, and eventually the judges would relent. Most often, I didn't have to pretend; the government translators tended to be subpar.

I don't know that the Russians really cared who translated for me, but I did. Yulia was a familiar and soothing presence.

She was also a teacher, first and last. She'd have me say something in Russian, then correct it, working with me until I had the pronunciation correct.

Lina, meanwhile, worked behind the scenes, gathering evidence and helping prepare the case. She, too, was an important conduit to the outside world, though her visits were not as open as the lawyers'.

She was also helping my father. She often took him shopping, and all in all made it possible for him to live in Moscow. Besides bothering the embassy, which was immeasurably valuable, he was contacting news media, and helping my mom attempt to get support in Congress back home.

On February 3, 2020, the Constitutional Court of the Russian Federation ruled that the Moscow City Court had inappropriately revoked my bail and proper procedures were not followed. The high court sent the case back down to the Second Court of Cassation, a high appellate court.

In other words: no bail. More process to suffer through.

My relationship with the embassy was still shaky. I didn't think they were doing a lot, and they still tended to treat Lina as if she were a Russian spy. But they were at least working with my dad.

Occasionally they were very helpful. Anton, a consular affairs officer, intervened before a hearing when a guard scolded my father for asking me a question. Anton got up from his seat in the audience, walked around the cage, and stuck his hand inside to shake mine as he introduced himself. The guard made the mistake of taking a step toward him and loudly giving him a warning. Anton retorted in loud Russian that he was an officer of the United States embassy and had the right to speak to his citizen.

Surprised, the guard mumbled something and took a step back. Anton then had a brief discussion with me, nodding to my dad when he returned to his seat, as if to underline the small victory.

Typically, though, my father didn't get to talk to me before hearings. He would ask Yulia to ask me a question, which I would answer in English. There was no rule against him speaking with the interpreter, and of course she could talk to me as the proceedings went on.

The first day of the trial, March 11, was more important from a PR point of view than a legal one: we were definitely getting the story out, judging by the large number of international news crews packing the courtroom, the hallway, and the area outside.

"There are a lot of news media here," said Judge Arnaut, looking around before the start of the proceedings. Arnaut was the judge who had originally sent me to jail to await the trial; he would preside over the rest of the proceeding. "I have dozens of requests for journalists to be present. I want to ask everyone if they're okay with that. Trevor, are you okay with that?"

"Yes, I support it."

He asked my attorneys, who agreed. He asked the cops, who were to testify first. They said fine.

"No," said the prosecutor. "I don't support this."

"Well, I'm okay with it," said the judge. "Let's get underway."

I don't know if the news media affected the judge's attitude. It was my impression, though, that he wanted to do everything by the book. It was undoubtedly an important case for him, in a personal sense at least. He was an older guy, and in my mind I conjured a backstory: a man who entered the legal profession with high ideals, only to see those ideals turned inside out. And then finally a case with real meaning came before him. He was attentive and serious, if occasionally amused by the ridiculousness of the prosecution's case and antics.

Maybe it was all an act, but I like to think it wasn't.

The prosecutor presented the official indictment. No surprise: it had been altered to avoid some of the more blatant lies my attorneys had already pointed out. The videos that had been ordered in at the bail hearing would now be "explained" by testimony claiming I had attacked the officers at a minuscule spot along the route not explicitly covered by the cameras. It was ludicrous, but right in line with the rest of the case.

We had our own evidence. Evidence that showed that the police testimony was false. Expert testimony proving their claim about their clothes being torn was false. Medical records demonstrating that the police were uninjured. Witness testimonies.

The prosecutor objected. The judge overruled him, allowing our evidence to be used.

In America, a trial generally runs on consecutive days until a conclusion. Even if there are interruptions for motions or unusual events, things still progress in a relatively compact amount of time. Russian trials aren't necessarily like that. There can be pretty wide gaps in the timing. They might proceed on every Monday, for example, for months.

COVID complicated everything. The virus had been spreading in Russia for weeks, but the government had claimed only a very small number of people had it. Their propaganda tried to portray the virus as a Western illness, one more example (for them) that Russia was superior.

And then all of a sudden: *Hey, guess what? We have a hundred thousand cases. A lot of people are croaking. And more to come!*

A cynic might point out that the admission was necessary because of moves the government had to make to keep the economy afloat. Or maybe it was just reality slapping Putin and his government in the head. Whatever the reason, restrictions began slamming into place. Travel was cut off. Schools, museums, government offices were closed. Court sessions, including mine, were postponed. On March 25, Putin told everyone in the country it would have a week's paid vacation the following week, but they'd have to stay in their home or risk arrest. Russia had joined most of the world in a massive shutdown.

SIZO-5 went into lockdown mode. No more visits from family or even attorneys. The employees had to stay in the prison as well.

A nurse came by the cells every morning, taking our temperature, looking for early signs of infection. That might have worked better had they not changed the base temperature on the thermometer by three degrees. The adjustment meant that no one at SIZO was ever officially sick.

Whatever box that checked off positively in the Russian bureaucracy, it didn't work well in the real world. Within a short period of time, COVID was rampant in the prison.

Officially, I didn't get COVID at that time. Unofficially, though, I had COVID-like symptoms and felt weak right around the time my trial was going to start. Whether I had a fever or not, I don't know. But I did pass out at one point.

Not exactly a rock-solid medical diagnosis. But probably as good as any of the ones the medical personnel were making at the prison. I informed my defense team the next day during a video court hearing. The embassy submitted diplomatic notes requesting a doctor examine me and asked for copies of my medical records, but the Russians never responded.

Speaking of nurses . . .

One was always flirting with me. She was blond, and very pretty. If I hadn't been in prison, it would have been hard to resist.

She called me handsome; she said loudly that she wanted to get married. She also gave me acetaminophen, which was probably the biggest giveaway.

Lina asked if I was getting my medicine. I told her I was, but only from the blond captain.

"Why does only this one give you medicine?" she asked.

"I don't know."

"What does she look like?"

"She's tall, blond, and sexy."

"You should flirt with her."

"What?"

"This way you can get your medicine," Lina explained.

"You won't be mad?"

"Trevor, sweetie. How do you think I got this meeting with you? I flirt with your investigator."

As far as the actual trial was concerned, the months of April, May, and June were basically washed out. The Russians had wanted to continue the trial by video, but my lawyers had managed to squash that, arguing that I was entitled to attend court in person. The Russians acquiesced, and we waited for roughly two months until prisoners were allowed to be transported from SIZO-5.

It was during this period that the Russians held a secret trial for Paul Whelan.

Paul had been arrested in Russia on December 28, 2018. He was charged with spying, after allegedly receiving a USB flash drive from a friend who was an FSB officer. Contrary to evidence presented at the trial, the Russians claimed that he had bought secret information from the FSB agent, and was in fact a US spy.

On June 15, Paul's sentence was announced: sixteen years for espionage. Ambassador Sullivan held a press conference following the sentence; my father was among those who attended.

On July 2, my trial resumed. We picked up where we had left off, with more lies from the prosecutor. The prosecution contended that I had been pummeling the police, injuring them and tearing up their uniforms. Over the next few weeks, the court heard the phone call Lina's acquaintances had made and some laughable "expert" testimony on how drunk I was. The jacket that the prosecution alleged had been ripped by me—a jacket probably older than the cops and several sizes too small—was shown by one of my experts to have been purposely ripped, not mangled in a fight.

Pretty much all of the evidence the prosecutor presented was refuted by my attorneys and witnesses—and often contradicted by the prosecution's own witnesses.

There had been seventy cameras in the police station. Not one of them was working that night . . . or so the investigator claimed, without any technical explanation of why that was. Or even proof that they weren't operating.

The lieutenant who had allowed me to sleep my drunkenness off testified that she hadn't seen me hit anyone, or commit any crime.

"What are you talking about?" demanded the prosecutor, trying to get her to retract the statement.

"As far as I remember, this man was drunk and his girlfriend and her friends brought him here because they couldn't control him," said the lieutenant.

"But he assaulted police officers during this time!" insisted the prosecutor.

"If he assaulted police officers, I don't know about that."

Furiously mad, the prosecutor waved some papers at her. "This is your testimony."

She shrugged. The investigator had apparently written up the statement himself and had her sign it, presumably without her reading it. Among other things, they had the wrong date for the arrest.

And on and on.

Russian court procedure allows a defendant to question a witness after the prosecution and the defense lawyers have had their turns. I used the privilege with the lieutenant to underline the fact that the FSB was behind all of this.

"Why did the FSB interrogate me about my military service?" I asked.

"I don't know about the FSB."

"Do you have any idea why the FSB raided my girlfriend's apartment? And her grandparents'? In another city! To search for evidence if I had supposedly assaulted police?"

The judge interrupted, saying he wouldn't allow the question.

But I'd made my point for the media, showing the FSB had been involved. Someone had broken into Lina's apartment before the trial. Another agent came a night or two later and tried to get in again.

She didn't have any evidence, of course, but the security agency's interest made it clear this was not a case about a drunk going nuts in a police station.

The FSB wasn't the only agency involved in the case. After the police changed their story from me fighting police in the police station to it happening in the police car, my attorneys requested footage from inside the police car. The investigator denied this for three months until he said that it had expired or been erased.

But my attorneys accidentally stumbled upon a document that showed the video from the police car had been retrieved by the Russian agency responsible for police internal affairs: in theory, they were watchdogs who keep the police honest.

Some theory.

My attorneys requested the footage. The agency responded that the handling of video surveillance equipment was confidential and a matter of national security, so they could not provide any information about the who, when, why, or where of the video.

I have to say, the fact that the trial lasted so long was almost entirely due to my lawyers. They raised every objection imaginable, made every interruption possible. Instead of giving a few words in rebuttal, they gave paragraphs.

Part of their strategy was to get things on the record so they could appeal. And they were playing to the world outside of Russia, showing how overwhelming the evidence in my favor was.

There were times even I was tempted to tell them, "Enough already."

The policemen's attitudes toward the testimony seemed pretty interesting. Cross-examined about their changing stories and shown to be lying, they shrugged and said they might have been mistaken . . . or had imagined the whole thing.

Their comments caused some giggling in the courtroom; even the judge grinned.

When the officers were asked about locations and photos in the official report, they admitted having no knowledge about those spots.

"That's strange," said my attorney. "You signed the report."

Each man said they hadn't. When the judge showed them their signatures, they said they weren't in their handwriting.

They gave off the impression of men who'd been told to lie, were willing to do so, but whose hearts just weren't in it. Maybe they realized the whole thing was a charade and wanted it to be over. Maybe they just wanted to be paid, as is customary with charges like mine, for alleged pain and suffering. Ordinarily they would have been asked to give a victim statement at the end of the trial; that never happened, even though I had supposedly caused them great distress.

My back caused me more and more pain as the trial went on. Finally on July 16, the fifth day of the proceedings, I requested a doctor. The judge ordered an examination.

I was really in pain. Often waiting for court I would be put into a cell the size of an old telephone booth. With barely enough room to stand, I'd sit and curl up with my arms around my legs. I'd have to stay either standing or sitting like that for hours until it was time for my case. Getting simple painkillers like Tylenol remained a huge project.

I wanted some relief. But I also knew that the trial was being covered by the world media. I hoped they would report about this, noting the terrible treatment I was getting in prison.

They did.

July 16 was also the day I testified. Aside from the questions about my military service, which I would not answer, I told the court everything that I knew had happened. I testified truthfully, and as fully as I was allowed.

Lina testified to what had, and hadn't, happened. We had experts refute what little evidence the prosecutor presented, and back up ours.

With everything now on the record and both sides aired, the judge turned to me and asked how I wanted to plead. Guilty or not guilty?

"Not guilty, based on the evidence we've seen."

Not f'ing guilty. No f'ing way.

Closing statements were made July 29. The prosecutor ignored pretty much everything that had been presented in court by our side, brushed past the facts, and after a few minutes of pro forma bs, told the judge and the world that I should be sentenced to nine years and eight months for my crime. It was the longest sentence ever levied in modern Russian history for the crime.

I think we were supposed to view that as lenient, given that it wasn't the maximum.

The maximum being ten years. Which no one ever got.

The usual sentence, even in a case where there was real evidence that a police officer had been injured, amounted to three years or less. If I had been a rich Russian, I would have paid off the policemen for their "injuries" and "mental anguish" and walked. If I had been a regular Russian, the case probably wouldn't have been made at all.

My father timed the prosecutor's speech. It came in under twenty minutes. My attorneys spoke for nearly seven hours.

And then it was my turn. I rose, and gave my own short plea for justice. I went over all the evidence presented against me, the discrepancies with that evidence, and the actions the prosecution took to conceal it once it was proven to be false. Then I summed up:

> *Your honor, I understand in this country that pleading guilty may lead to you having a shorter sentence, but I think it would be unethical and immoral to plead guilty to a crime that I truly believe I did not commit.*
>
> *And if I'm going to be given a prison sentence, I would rather stay in prison an honest man than walk free tomorrow a liar and a coward.*

According to my dad, everyone in the courtroom—including him—was crying when I finished.

Everyone except the judge, who adjourned the session, declaring a verdict would be rendered the next day.

I warned my father on my way out of the courtroom that he had to be prepared for a really long sentence.

Lina, nearby, shook her head. "No."

"Don't listen to Lina," I told my dad. "The amount they asked for me to be sentenced to right now, they don't ask that much for murderers. So tomorrow's sentence is going to be very big. I would say probably close to ten years. Just prepare Mom that that's what's going to happen."

"Are you guilty?" asked one of the reporters as I started to leave.

"No."

I wanted to say a lot more, but I cut myself off. I knew I'd be found guilty, but there was no sense pissing the judge off before the sentencing. And really, what else could I have said that I hadn't already?

The guards tugged at me to leave. I went back to SIZO-5 to await my fate.

TEN

F*** YOU, PUTIN

Just in case you think the FSB cared so little about me that they skipped the trial:

There was one person who attended every court session: a pasty-faced young guy in an ill-fitting suit who always sat to the side, same spot near the front, listening. Lina went up to him one day and asked who he was. He gave her some bs about being a law student. The thing was, she knew too much about the school for his bluff to fool her. He clearly had been planted to keep an eye on the proceedings, just in case things took a direction the FSB didn't want, like me getting bail.

On July 30, 2020, I was marched back to the court to learn my fate. Camera crews and reporters crammed the hall and room. Lina and some friends, along with my father, were already sitting in the small audience.

I was wearing the same shirt and pants I wore to every hearing. The guards held me back while they moved the crowd, mostly media and friends of Lina, away from the cage door. Inside the cage, I turned my back to the door as they closed it, then pushed my wrists close to it so the guard could unlock the handcuffs and put them on the door.

The judge walked in, wearing a COVID mask. To this point, he had been animated, even enthusiastic, about what he was doing. I had the impression that he enjoyed playing a real judge, not that he was fair or just in any way. As I see it, to work in the Russian government, you must be amoral.

He started to talk. Ordinarily his voice was strong, easily carrying through the courtroom. Today, he was mumbling. I strained to hear him. I noticed the papers in his hands shaking. He was trembling.

Not a good sign.

He rejected all of the evidence we had presented. He agreed that I had violently grabbed the police, even though we'd proven I hadn't.

Guilty.

No surprise there.

The judge continued, quickly reading the sentence: Nine years in a labor camp.

And one hundred thousand rubles (in the area of $1,350 at the time) to each police officer for physical and moral damages.

Lina jumped up, screaming. "Nine years! Are you kidding me! Is this what Russia is?"

I yelled at her to calm her down. Two bailiffs came and grabbed her, hustling her from the courtroom.

My dad started to get up to stop them, but the embassy representative grabbed his shoulder. There was nothing my father could have done but get himself put into jail, compounding our collective trouble.

The judge exited in a flash. Still in the cage, I looked out to the hallway, where the guards were now speaking calmly to Lina, imploring her to calm down. They were human now, no longer acting like tough guys for the courtroom. They'd hustled her out of there to show the Russian news channels that they wouldn't accept any dissent.

My father came over and told me he loved me.

"Do you have anything you want to say?" yelled one of the reporters.

"Anyone who's been in this courtroom and has eyes or ears knows I'm not guilty."

I mentioned some of the evidence that had been tossed.

"I've spent my life serving my country," I said. "I hope that, or I would like to ask that, Congress, the president, and the State Department help me." I also asked that they help Lina, since I was afraid the government would now go after her.

My attorneys came over. Tears welled in Victoria's eyes. Sergey stood stone-faced, deflated.

"I'm sorry," he told me.

"It's not your fault. You did everything you could."

"We have grounds to appeal. We will meet you Monday."

As the guards led me out, I heard Lina tell a reporter for Radio Free Europe that I'd been framed.

"Trevor is not guilty! I was there! They made this up. This is a disgrace to Russia!" she said. "I'm embarrassed to be a Russian," she continued, working into a rant. "I didn't think my country was like this."

It was accurate and eloquent, but it was also the sort of statement a Russian citizen, let alone a Russian lawyer, should never make. I tried to hush her. Then, maybe sensing the injustice they'd just witnessed, the guards let me give her a kiss.

As I was prodded down the hall, I saw my father go to her and then tell the reporter her statements couldn't be used.

Outside, my father gave a news conference, then was taken over to the embassy, where he worked with the ambassador on a statement protesting the charade of my arrest, trial, and sentence.

The Russians had always denied that I was arrested to be a pawn in their plot to exchange me for someone legitimately arrested in the US. But for some reason, the suggestions that I might be a candidate for a prisoner exchange started circulating on Russian media almost as soon as I was led away from the court.

What a coincidence.

Just to show you how unusual my sentence was, after it was announced some of the prisoners took to calling me "Yuri," a reference to the first man in space, Yuri Gagarin. I was the first man to receive such a ridiculous prison sentence.

After the sentence was announced, I was taken down to the holding cells to wait for transfer. There is a custom among prisoners to scrape their sentence and crime on the soft wall board. That gives other prisoners waiting for trial some sense of what to expect.

I thought to myself, if I write my sentence, some poor guy is going to commit suicide. It's nowhere near a typical sentence. The highest sentence I had ever seen for assault on police was six years—but it was the fourth time the guy had been jailed and he had stabbed the police officer multiple times.

So, no, I couldn't write my sentence down. But I had to write something.

I carved my name, rank, and last unit in the Marines on the wall.

And:

Fuck You Putin

Fuck the FSB

Then I carved a gigantic *USA* into the wall.

I carved some other stuff, cursing the FSB. I stood back—not very far, because the cell was tiny—and admired my artwork. There were plenty of other messages on the one wall, many cursing the dictator and FSB.

The other prisoners in the transport going back to jail couldn't believe how long my sentence was. Even the guard who took me back up to my cell at SIZO-5 was sympathetic.

My cellmates had seen the news on TV. They hugged me when I came back and tried to be supportive. They asked if I was going to appeal. It was a good idea to do that, they told me. Prison sentences were always shaved down during appeals.

I knew that wasn't going to happen for me. But I would appeal.

My lawyers thought they failed. Our next meeting began with a long hug from Victoria and apologies from both, saying they were sorry.

"You didn't fail," I told them. "All your trials are fake."

"It's our job and you're paying us as lawyers," said Sergey. "We are going to appeal."

They were convinced that they could find something that would get me released or mandate a new trial. I doubted that would happen. I had a different goal: delaying my transfer to a labor camp as long as possible.

I wanted to stay out of the gulag for several reasons. I would most likely be outside of Moscow, which would make it difficult for anyone to visit me, even Lina. The news media had been great—but maybe that would stop if I was far away. There was also a very practical calculation: every day in SIZO-5 counted as a day and a half off my sentence. In theory, I could work off the nine years in six if I stayed here that long.

That wasn't going to happen, but every bit helped.

That was what my attorneys wanted to hear. They went back to their office and started formalizing appeals. The court's review of each would eat up a lot of time. We demanded translations of relevant court documents, another stalling tactic. Eventually, the court grew so frustrated with the translations that it authorized me to hire my own translator—Yulia again.

I still had doubts about how much support I would get from the US government. The embassy hadn't proven to be a paragon of efficiency. Even the news release they prepared about my arrest had to get some judicious editing from my dad.

But if Russia wanted to use me as a pawn, I needed them.

One morning, three guards came to my cell and snapped out orders. "Trevor, get dressed immediately and wear your best clothes."

"What?"

"You have a meeting." They used a word in Russian that can mean "embassy." The fact that three guards had been sent to get me was a little weird, but ordering me to dress up was unprecedented.

"The embassy is here?" I asked.

"No." They repeated the Russian word, this time with a modifier that made it clear it was the ambassador himself.

Oh.

"And be sure to mention that we've been treating you all okay."

Right.

John Sullivan was not what I expected. To my mind at least, an ambassador was a tall, very stiff, very proper gentleman who wore a tuxedo all the time, knew where to put his pinkie when he drank tea, and delivered dire pronouncements on the state of the world as bon mots. The ambassador I met in the SIZO-5 meeting room was a really relaxed, laid-back fellow. The kind of guy you might throw back a few with on St. Patrick's Day. He had a really friendly, happy demeanor. Confidence practically dripped from every pore. He was wearing a suit, but with a bright green tie that definitely clashed. Maybe for effect.

He introduced himself and an assistant, as well as a translator.

"So that was kind of shitty," he said, referring to the trial and sentence.

From that moment, I knew he was going to do everything he could to help. How successful he would be would depend on the Russians as well as his boss, President Trump. But Sullivan was going to give it an effort that in my opinion had been missing until now.

We talked for a while. I assured him that Lina was not a spy, and that she needed help. He didn't seem to think she was a spy at all, and seemed concerned when I told him about what had happened to her in court.

"So what does it look like now for your court cases?" he asked.

I told him about the appeal. "Once that's over, I go to prison camp."

"How long do you think the appeal is going to take?"

"Preferably it takes years, because I get a day and a half for every day that I'm in here."

"Okay. If you don't mind, I'm going to just start coming to your court sessions," he said. "Maybe that will put some pressure on them. Or will that make things worse?"

"Oh, no sir, I don't mind. If you can come, please do. I think at this point probably pressure's the only thing that's going to work."

We talked a little more, some of it serious, some of it about football, though I'm not that big a fan. He promised to visit every month while I was in SIZO-5, and he kept that promise.

My medicine started coming regularly after Sullivan's visit. I think the administration and the guards decided that, since I obviously knew the ambassador, messing with me too much might eventually get them in trouble.

I told Lina she should end our relationship.

"You're young, and I'm going to be here for a long time," I said. "You should find someone and have a family and a life."

She burst into tears.

"You really think I would leave you!?" she cried. "I love you. If I was in this situation, would you leave me?"

"Well, no," I admitted.

"I don't care how long you are in prison," she said. "I will wait for you forever."

She paused, then added, "Like Odysseus's wife when he went to prison."

"Actually," I told her, "he was at war and then lost at sea for a long time."

"Whatever."

We both started laughing.

Lina visited me at SIZO often, and wrote a letter to me every day. She was a constant presence, always optimistic, a messenger of outrageous hope.

Long after I was released, she admitted that she had known our romantic relationship had ended before I was even convicted. But if she truly felt that way when I was in SIZO-5 or the gulag, she kept up a strong face. She would tell me that I would only be in prison a short while, compared to the number of years we would be alive. I think maybe she wanted to stay optimistic for my sake. She thought I had little to hope for. But I was already hardening myself for the long run. I was going to win this by outlasting the Russians. Or I was going to win by making their lives miserable. Or I was going to win by never giving in.

I had no doubt I was going to win. It was just a question of how that victory was defined.

I'd lost a lot of weight in SIZO-5 waiting for the trial. That continued. The prison food had always been skimpy; now it got even thinner.

The prison authorities were apparently skimming the food or the food budget, which left less for the guards to skim, which meant even less for us. (We heard that one of the deputy heads of the prison was arrested for skimming the food and selling it at the farmers market in Moscow, though he went right back to the same job afterward.) When meat came with our meals, it was mostly just fat. Unless it was chicken; then it was basically bones.

My rich cellmates were moved into different cells, and their replacements couldn't afford as much food. My clothes got looser and looser. My cellmates had shown me how to use duct tape to take in my dress pants at the waist, preventing them from falling down when I went to court. But I had definitely shrunk.

I did what I could to keep up my strength. I was able to exercise by doing pull-ups on a bar in the open walking area at the top of the building. There were bars instead of rafters overhead, with some sort of covering preventing prisoners from seeing the sky.

Because it was open, it was very cold in the winter. I'd do some push-ups, and some calisthenics. Like other prisoners, I'd walk in circles, around and around to get more exercise. Sometimes we would get to go to an area that had free weights in it. Even so, I lost a lot of muscle mass just from stress, and not having enough food.

Things between myself and my father had calmed down. He was doing what I asked. And I was more in control of my anger, more aware that it should be focused on the real enemy, Russia.

With the verdict delivered, he was allowed more visits. He would bring me food at the jail about once a week, usually on Fridays. The process was elaborate—after buying things at a food store, whether nearby or at a mall in the city, he'd show up at the prison and wait in a crammed vestibule to be called. He'd have to submit a list of the food in Russian, and enter his name on a long list. Not knowing Russian, he came up with a hack to know when it was his turn: he'd watch who signed the ledger before him, wait until that person was called, then know his turn would be next. He would give the food over, and eventually it would be delivered to me.

It could take hours just to be called. At some point, he befriended the son of another prisoner. The son spoke some English, and they would wait together in the younger man's car early in the morning, hoping to be among the first in line to get in.

Visiting was equally draining; probably more so, since he'd typically have to wait for hours until the guards brought me down. We'd always be given the same little booth at the far end of the small room where interviews were held. Our conversations must still have had some interest to someone.

So much interest that they occasionally went to great lengths to make sure they could hear. During one of my father's visits, a guard arrived inexplicably soon after we began talking. I think their eavesdropping equipment might have malfunctioned, but I got no explanation as the guard brusquely escorted me away to a back room. I began shouting and making a ruckus, banging on anything I could find, demanding to be allowed to see my dad. Finally, they grew tired of my commotion and I was led back in.

"What was that hammering racket?" my father asked.

"Me, banging on the bars."

He was surprised. "It sounded like construction."

ELEVEN

HOMEFRONT

My dad left Russia to go home just before New Year's. I was all for it. I'd always wanted to know that he and the rest of my family were safe. I could never feel that while he was in Moscow.

The trial verdict had hit him hard, harder than I can say. So I'll let him talk about it:

Trevor's speech before the verdict was one of the bravest things I've ever heard. It was like something from a movie.

But we weren't in a movie. We were in a fight for his life.

I was prepared, and I wasn't prepared. It's like you're in a knife fight, and you know there's a high probability of getting stabbed. It still hurts when you get cut.

I cried in the hall when I said goodbye to Trevor, and later when I relayed to Paula on the phone what had happened. Outside the courthouse, I told the media that Trevor had been railroaded. The embassy

President Obama, me, and my dad, Joey, in the Oval Office, 2014.

Lina and I in Greece, October 2016.

SIZO-5 pre-trial detention center, Moscow.

An exercise room in SIZO-5.

My sister, Taylor; Anton, from the US embassy; and my parents, Paula and Joey, at Moscow City Court, March 11, 2020.

Moscow City Court, July 30, 2020.

Ambassador Sullivan and my dad planning a press release, US Embassy, Moscow, July 30, 2020.

My mom in front of the US Capitol with Congressmen Mike Conaway and Michael McCaul for the introduction of House Resolution 1115, calling for my release, September 16, 2020.

IK-12 labor camp in Molochnitsa, Republic of Mordovia, Russia.

A solitary confinement cell in a Russian forced labor camp.

My mom and sister Taylor outside the Fort Worth VA Hospital, waiting for President Biden's visit, March 8, 2022.

My parents meet President Joe Biden in the Oval Office, March 30, 2022.

Boarding a Russian jet with FSB Alpha Group at Vnukovo International Airport, Moscow, April 27, 2022.

The prisoner exchange on the tarmac in Turkey with me (*second from left*) and Konstantin Yaroshenko (*middle*), April 27, 2022.

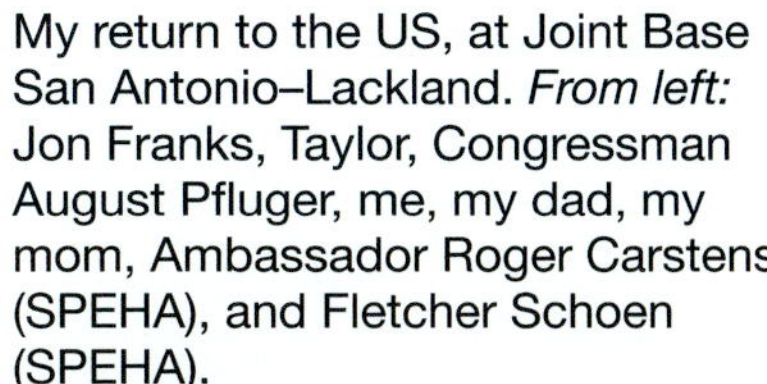

My return to the US, at Joint Base San Antonio–Lackland. *From left:* Jon Franks, Taylor, Congressman August Pfluger, me, my dad, my mom, Ambassador Roger Carstens (SPEHA), and Fletcher Schoen (SPEHA).

Right: My sister and I after I returned from Russia. I was a shadow of myself at roughly 120 pounds, but soon began to regain weight and muscle.

Left: Behind the scenes at the Jake Tapper interview in Florida. *From left:* Jake Tapper, my mom, me, Jon Franks, Taylor, and my dad, May 2022.

My friends really came through for me, helping me get back in shape for Ukraine. *From left:* Kyle Nance, me, John Michael Sidwell, and Cody Cockrell.

From left: Teddy, Super Dave, me, and Yan in Ukraine, 2023. They called me "Gulag," for obvious reasons.

Russian shelling obliterated much of the Ukrainian landscape, including this forest near Bakhmut where we were fighting.

Below: Getting ready to mount an M113 personnel carrier with the rest of Rogue Team for the final assault in July 2023.

Engaging an enemy SPG-9 team with an MK46 machine gun on the Siverskyi-Donets Canal during the 2023 Ukrainian counteroffensive. An incoming shell explodes in the distance to the right of my position.

staff took me over to meet with the ambassador, and we worked together on a statement.

Ambassador Sullivan was all in. The verdict was a kind of closure, but not an end. More like the end of Act I in a long-running drama. The next act would be appeals from Trevor's lawyers. But our real hope was with our government, and the possibility of trading Trevor for someone the Russians wanted. Which was the point of his persecution all along.

We'd been working hard to raise awareness about the case back in the States, hoping to put some pressure on the administration. Jonathan Franks had joined us that spring, before the verdict. Paul Whelan's brother David had recommended we talk to Jon when we were brainstorming ways to get more support. With a family background and connections in media and politics, Jon had become a public relations specialist. He'd already helped some Americans detained in foreign countries. (More famously perhaps, he'd worked with celebrity Montel Williams, the television host and actor. Williams was very supportive behind the scenes.)

Jon volunteered to help us pro bono, and he hit the ground running from that moment on. His first question to me was: "Do you have a Twitter account?"

I set one up that day.

We relied on him for connections, resources, and the occasional shoulder to cry on. He was a good person to bounce ideas off. Jon took no money—and honestly, there was no way to put a price on what he did for us. Media strategies, hints on who to talk to in the government, contacts. He became part of the family. I love the man to this day.

Among other things, I credit him with persuading Senator John Cornyn from Texas to talk with us in July. I compiled a draft congressional resolution based on one for Paul Whelan; in August, Senator Cornyn introduced Senate Resolution 667 calling for Trevor's release.

Representative Mike Conaway, our local congressman, agreed to help push a resolution with the same aim in the House. Michael McCaul, ranking member of the House Foreign Affairs Committee, volunteered to help Conaway with what became House Resolution 1115. (August Pfluger would replace Conaway at the next election. He adopted Trevor's cause.)

The resolutions called on the Russian government to immediately release Trevor and all other political prisoners. They also urged the administration to bring up his case every time there was an official meeting with the Russians.

That September, Paula joined the two congressmen at a press conference in Washington introducing the House bill.

I sent Trevor a picture.

"Wow," he told me. "That's Mom!"

HR 1115 would pass the following December with overwhelming bipartisan support. Cornyn's measure was caught up in the Senate Foreign Relations Committee's internal disputes about when to hold meetings, effectively killing it along with other matters.

Though we had Republican officials in our corner, they had little sway over President Trump, who had praised Putin on several occasions.

Not that every politician was equally enthusiastic. We'd contacted Ted Cruz early on, but he and his staff remained curiously reluctant to get involved. One of his people told The New Yorker *magazine later that "his opposition to the Nord Stream 2 pipeline linking Russia to Germany could have complicated negotiations" for Trevor's release.*

Take that for whatever you will.

Having the backing of Congress was great, but as we knew, the only part of the government that could truly help was the presidency. Trevor didn't seem to be a priority for the administration.

So we tried to work harder.

●

Summer turned to fall. Another Moscow winter approached.

I'd been in Russia for nearly a year. It had been a time of constant depression, relieved only by my talks with Paula, the rest of my family, and a good number of the friends and fellow firemen I'd managed to connect with over the years.

My visits with Trevor were often disheartening. He'd scold me. Criticize me. It wasn't exactly the sort of thing you want to hear from your son, especially when you're trying to help him.

A lot of our meetings ended in tears, though I could hold them until I got back to my apartment. Paula would buck me up.

"You're the only one he can vent to," she'd say. "He can't show emotion in his cell. He can't yell at the judge, or the prosecutor. You're the only one he can vent his emotions on."

She was right about that. It made it a little easier to take—but only a little.

I worked with the attorneys on some of the appeals, and began helping Trevor file complaints to the authorities. He would handwrite his complaint, which would then be passed to me. With help from Lina and some others, I'd send them to the authorities. A lot of times they were ignored, but it was part of Trevor's strategy to cause as much of a disturbance with them as possible.

My visa was due to expire as the year neared its end. I was afraid that I could be arrested if I stayed without the proper extension. The American elections, with Joe Biden and a new administration coming into office, put a hold on what we could do with the government. Until the new administration sorted itself out, our efforts were unlikely to get our son released.

Meanwhile, Trevor's appeals were running out, with the result clearly preordained: he was going to be sent to the Russian gulag system, a labor camp somewhere, until the government decided how they were going to use him.

Assuming he survived.

His mood seemed better now that the verdict had been rendered. He was still hardening himself, psychologically preparing to face whatever the Russians had in store. But he was kinder to me, realizing not only how much we'd tried to do for him, but also understanding that we were doing it out of love.

Not that he necessarily understood that love on a conscious level. He will when he has kids. That's the only way you can really understand what a parent feels for children, the only way anyone can understand what I felt and still feel for him and his sister. It's not simply that you would give your life for them; it's way beyond that, something you can't put into words.

He told me I should go home. I finally agreed. Paula and I could do a lot more for him in the States than we could do in Russia. He had his lawyers and he had Lina. They could help him, to an extent, to stay alive.

The help he really needed would come from the government. And to get that, I needed to be back in the States with my wife.

TWELVE

CARRYING ON

The big holidays were always a difficult time for my parents. They tried different ways of coping. The first year, my dad told me they were going to leave the Christmas tree up until I got home. I tried talking him out of it, but as usual, that didn't work. (It was still up when I returned.) Another time, for Thanksgiving, they kept up an annual tradition by taking a group picture on the lawn with my mom's side of the family. I was there . . . as a big, blow-up poster.

American holidays weren't exactly a thing in Russia. Even Christmas was different. The day is observed according to the Russian Orthodox calendar, which is January 7. It was never a big deal for me.

Well, once. A friend asked if I wanted to attend service with him at the Orthodox chapel. Full disclosure: I wasn't really very curious about the church, and wouldn't call myself very religious in the first place. But he seemed like he needed a friend to share whatever was important to him at the service. So I went.

It was a beautiful service. I didn't understand a lot of what was going on, but the ritual of the mass was impressive. And the mass meant a lot to him.

Yulia came to visit me one dark day that year after my father had gone. As soon as I got into my little cubicle, she leaned forward to talk.

"I have to tell you something. You're going to be an adult about this, right?"

"Yes."

"Your grammy died."

My great-grandmother, Dorothy Jolley, was ninety-nine, so her passing wasn't that unexpected. Still, it hit me hard. I'd lived with her briefly when I was going to school, and would stop by often other times. She had survived breast cancer and open-heart surgery. She had a pacemaker, and a pretty clear mind, given her age.

I'd often visited with her before going to Russia, and she clearly missed those visits, constantly asking my parents about me. My parents told her I was in Russia, but not that I was in jail. I'm sure she wondered why I hadn't come back. That's probably the last thing she thought about me: my great-grandson doesn't love me enough to visit.

Whatever reservations I might have had about taking revenge on the Russians died along with her.

When I get out of here, my goal isn't going to be to just go back and adjust to real life. When I get out of here, I am going to make you pay.

The more time passed, the firmer my resolve became.

In February 2021, Senator Cornyn reintroduced a resolution calling for my release. The bill was discussed by the Foreign Relations Committee in June and approved by the Senate in July with bipartisan support.

The House of Representatives considered its own bill, introduced by our new congressman, August Pfluger, in March. Thanks to a very supportive bipartisan Foreign Affairs Committee, the resolution moved to the House for a vote in June; in the meantime, Pfluger called my parents weekly to check in. Jon Franks helped Pfluger get fifty-seven bipartisan cosponsors, insuring an overwhelming passage. Bizarrely, the vote was held up for a day by Representative Marjorie Taylor Greene. She never explained why.

During one of the periodic searches of our cell, the guards discovered a phone one of the prisoners had managed to sneak in. The discovery caused a wave of searches throughout the entire prison block. They continued for all the time I was there. Our cells and belongings would be turned inside out. Rearranging stuff after the search was a pain, and the petty harassment was one more annoyance, but the searches meant we had to be especially careful about contraband.

As a general rule, I was extremely skeptical about Russian media. But just before my trial, I got a request from a journalist at a small publication. She had done some very brief stories as my case progressed, so I went ahead and granted the interview.

She ended up interviewing me several times, always in a special room of the prison. The interviews were surprisingly thorough. I was very candid. I complained about not getting medicine, but I also tried to be fair, saying that I wasn't being physically tortured or whatever.

I expected that the story, when I finally saw it, would be pretty much like every story the Russian media did about my case: *Bad American. Decadent former Marine who is brute. Etc.*

Instead, the stories she wrote turned out to be very fair. The reporter was forthright about my complaints. It turned out that she was somehow related to or close to a high-ranking government official in the prison system, maybe even the boss himself. I'm sure there were limits, but she accurately described the lousy conditions and deprivations that were routine in Russia at the time. Maybe her stories were intended to influence reform. I never had the opportunity to ask, and I certainly didn't see any evidence of change.

I doubt she could get away with being so truthful now.

One of my cellmates, Vadim, had a psychiatric evaluation done. He ended up giving me an idea that boomeranged.

During my trial, a medical expert had testified that I was so drunk I had to be unconscious. He'd also said that, if I hadn't been unconscious, I'd have been so crazy-out-of-my-mind loaded that I would not be able to understand the consequences of my actions.

That last part should have invalidated the assault charge, lessening it to a simpler case with far less jail time. But in court, the judge dismissed that by saying that perhaps I was an alcoholic, and if so, then my tolerance for alcohol would be much stronger than an average person of my gender, age, and weight.

Yeah, that doesn't make sense. But there was a lot about the case that doesn't make sense.

Vadim needed to be evaluated because he had been accused of being a drug addict, a status that could affect his sentencing. He was sent to the Serbsky Center, a large psychiatric facility in Moscow. Formerly known as the Serbsky Institute, it has a long history of use as a facility to punish critics of the government. Psychiatric facilities in Russia are commonly used to punish critics of the government, even today.

Now, Vadim was definitely a drug addict, but at the same time one of the smartest people I've ever known. He had been a history teacher and was highly intelligent. When he came back, I asked him how it had gone, figuring that it would have sucked.

"No, it's awesome," he insisted. "They have really great food every day. There's no regime at all. It's a big, open facility. The barracks are giant open rooms, and then you can just go from the hallway into other barracks and just do whatever you want."

"What?"

"And you can get more aid packages," he told me.

That was a sore point at SIZO-5; Lina was being limited to how much she could send us.

"How's the security there?" I asked.

"You could probably escape. There's not very much security there because it's a medical facility, not a prison. There's security on the prison side of it, but there are a lot of places on the prison side where there's really big windows. You could go through the window and climb down to the regular medical part. You can escape from there pretty easily."

I worried that one visit would not be enough to scout an escape route, map it, and then execute it. But Vadim assured me that I could get multiple referrals. So the next time I saw my attorneys, I told them I wanted a psychiatric exam to see if I was an alcoholic.

Sergey and Victoria started to laugh. Yulia got very serious and asked if I was worried about my sanity.

I explained that I wanted to delay my case, and had heard treatment there was better than at the prison. I also thought I might be able to escape from there, though naturally I didn't mention that.

My lawyers explained that the process was a lot more complicated than Vadim said, and was unlikely to result in a lesser sentence. But they agreed to try anyway.

The judge thought I was a bit nuts just asking. "Do you understand what your attorneys are requesting? Do you really feel that you need that? Do you think you're crazy?"

"Well, your Honor, I don't think that I'm crazy, but apparently the Russian government thinks I might be an alcoholic, and so I'm curious to find out myself."

The initial evaluation at the hospital in early March was pretty simple: they asked what had happened when I blacked out.

Uh . . .

There were other questions, of course, but nothing very deep or probing. Yulia came to translate, even though by now my Russian was fairly good. Having her there was kind of a security blanket.

The interview lasted a very short time, a screening rather than a full evaluation of my mental state. That would have to wait for another court order. I was sent back for transport. But for some reason, probably to intimidate me, my paperwork had me going to a different prison: Butyrka, and its infamous Cats House section.

Butyrka looks like a castle in the middle of Moscow's Tverskoy District. It is very old. The present building dates to 1879, but there were jails at the site at least two centuries earlier. A long list of distinguished prisoners were kept and tortured there under the tsars and the Soviets.

There are different levels to the Cats House: one for prisoners awaiting transport, one for kids, one for drug addicts, and one for crazy people. My orders sent me to the last.

I asked one of the prisoners during transport what it was like.

"You'll love it," he said.

I didn't.

I wasn't nuts, but the man in the holding cell I was taken to was. He went full-blown orc that night, demanding that he be given his medicine. Apparently he had already been given the prescribed dose, and the night nurse refused to authorize another pill.

It quickly became clear that he would tear the prison walls down if he didn't get more medication. He power walked through the cell, gathering steam and anger with every step. He foamed at the mouth, snarled like a wolverine, and banged on the door every few minutes.

It wasn't his rants or superhuman energy level that scared me; it was the dead look in his eyes that accompanied them. He was the most disturbed individual I've ever seen—and I was a Marine.

The nurse finally gave in. I don't know what the medicine was, but it did calm him down.

Immeasurable hours later, I was graduated from holding to an actual cell. This one had more crazies, though they were not as obviously psychotic.

Not that they were great people. "Everyone in here's a murderer except you and me," one of them told me.

He was a counterfeiter.

There was blood all over the walls, probably left from where prisoners had killed each other, or maybe themselves. A hole in the floor served as the toilet. People walked around like zombies, stoned out on massive doses of haloperidol (a first-generation antipsychotic medicine that has lost favor in the West because of its potential for severe side effects).

I'm not sure now how many days I was there. Every hour seemed like a week. A doctor named Olga realized I wasn't crazy and told me she would work to get me back to SIZO-5. She may have, but it must have been a heavy lift.

The staff tried to give me what I can only guess was an antipsychotic; fortunately, Olga intervened. She also got me ibuprofen for my back. I have to confess I was initially unsure whether to take the aspirin substitute or not, since I had no way of knowing what it truly was.

It was ibuprofen.

I don't know how much longer they would have kept me there if it hadn't been for Lina and my dad. They would speak every day, checking on each other and trying to keep track of me. When they didn't hear from me and couldn't make any contact, they spoke to Yulia. She thought I was being returned to SIZO-5, but wasn't sure. The weekend passed. On the seventh day without hearing from me or getting any letters, Lina called both SIZO-5 and Serbsky; no one could answer her questions. Their emails to me showed they had been delivered, yet I hadn't answered. They realized that meant I had never seen them, which in turn meant I was in trouble.

Lina went into high gear, contacting local news media. On March 11, my father notified the embassy that he hadn't received the weekly phone call I was allowed and always made. The embassy contacted SIZO-5 and was told I wasn't there.

Lina and my father were then informed that I had been sent to Butyrka (SIZO-2) by mistake. The error was being corrected.

I question how it could take them over a week to discover a mistake. How was it that things just happened to clear up the day the embassy started tracking me down?

I suspect—obviously it's something I can't prove definitively—that the judge had been involved in this "mistake." My lawyers theorized that it had been done to scare me, possibly in an effort to convince me that I didn't want an actual evaluation.

I made an issue of it at my next appeal, demanding to know why I had not been sent back to SIZO-5 immediately. The authorities insisted it was a mistake.

The judge asked if I still wanted an evaluation, which ordinarily took twenty days. I told him I hadn't been sure earlier, but the "mistake" had convinced me: I absolutely wanted one.

I gave him an evil smile when I said that.

"Fine," he told me angrily. He'd already set a date.

There are a lot of crazy people in mental institutions. Some are truly crazy. Some are borderline crazy. Some are sane. A few, you just can't tell.

The craziest prisoner I remember was probably sane, or at least sane enough to meet the legal definition. He told me he had killed his wife. They'd sent him to see if he had mitigating circumstances; in other words, if he could plead criminal insanity. After his evaluation, the doctors told him they could do one of two things: They could report that he was sane, which meant that he would be sentenced to six or seven years in a labor camp. Or they could declare him criminally insane, which most likely would mean a year in a mental institution before being released.

He asked me what I thought he should do.

I shrugged. From what I had already seen, though, a year in the looney bin was worth twenty in a labor camp.

"You know what was awesome?" he said while we were discussing his dilemma. "I asked what would happen if I was in the hospital for a year, got out, and then killed someone else. They said I'd just come back here."

Awesome, dude.

I believe in the end he decided to take a year in the mental ward.

The tests they had me do at Serbsky were pretty bogus. There were questionnaires and weird stuff, like one session where they asked me to draw "darkness."

I drew a shaded-in area with little white dots.

The psychologist asked what it was and I said it's night and those are stars. She frowned and asked me to draw "separation."

I knew she would want me to draw, like, a family holding hands with the kid separate and then say I had childhood trauma or something. Instead, I drew a basket of eggs with one egg left out.

"What's that?" she asked.

I explained the one egg was separated from the others.

She was getting frustrated. "Draw 'fear.'"

I drew a bat. Not well, I guess, because she had to ask what it was. When I told her, she asked if I was afraid of bats.

"No," I said. "But Batman is."

I don't think I did too well on that exam; I've never considered myself artistic.

The weirdest and scariest test involved a strange machine with a helmet that was strapped to my head, like something out of an old sci-fi movie. Supposedly it was checking for epilepsy. I don't seem to have it.

They only kept me for eight days, rather than the full twenty. My survey of escape possibilities was cut short. Things hadn't looked too promising, though with enough time I'm sure I could have figured something out.

For the record, my evaluation discovered that I was immature and had a problem with authority. Certainly an accurate assessment.

I got COVID at the end of April 2021.

I only found out because my cellmate Andre was sick. So sick that the rest of us thought he was going to die. The prison authorities refused to test him, let alone actually treat him. I decided to tell the embassy that I thought I had COVID, guessing that the Russians would order everyone in the cell tested at the same time.

I guessed right. The thing was, I hadn't thought I would test positive.

Andre and I happened to be at court when the others in the cell were tested. They were taken away to a hospital prison. The Russians apparently didn't want to admit I had COVID, so instead of going to the hospital, they moved me into a special cell. It was "special" all right: tiny, windowless, and inhabited by thousands of mosquitoes and other bugs.

The guard who brought me there gave me the impression that I'd only be waiting a short while until I was assigned to a better cell in an isolated wing. Several hours passed before the door opened. But instead of being reassigned, I was given a roommate: Andre, my cellmate.

They kept us there overnight. The next day we made a ruckus, yelling and shouting, trying to get ourselves transferred to a better cell. That produced exactly zero response, so Andre came up with a new plan: we'd burn the prison down, starting with a fire in one of our mattresses.

"Bro, I don't think it's a good idea to start a fire in a cell that's the size of a small closet," I told him. "Especially when we're the only ones in it, and the guards don't come around for hours."

"We won't burn it down. We'll just threaten."

There was no one nearby to threaten. By the time anyone came close enough to smell smoke, we'd have choked to death. I talked Andre out of it.

Instead, he took a tin cup he'd been given and started banging on the bars at the front of the cell. He shouted to anyone who could hear him to join in. Eventually, we had quite a ruckus going, loud enough to finally draw some attention.

"A car is coming for you," sputtered the guard who came to see what was going on.

We were transported from SIZO-5 to another prison, Matryoshka Tishena (SIZO-1), which was being used as a hospital. There we received the Russian miracle cure for COVID.

Lemon-flavored vitamins.

They were yellow and the size of BBs. I have no idea what effect, if any, they had on the disease. It would take several more months for the West to come up with drugs that actually had an effect on COVID. (If you want to believe the Russians had found some miracle cure before the rest of the world, I have a bridge you might be interested in.)

On the other hand, the food was a lot better than at SIZO-5. There was also a shower.

I took a hot shower every day. In SIZO-5, you were lucky to be taken to the showers once a week, and you didn't exactly luxuriate in there. This was like being in a spa.

Though one with very sick patients. For me, COVID was little more than a very bad head cold. But a woman in a cell not far from ours began gasping for air one weekend night. A nurse came. It was obvious the woman needed immediate help.

The nurse told them they would have to wait until Monday for a doctor.

The prisoner died that night. It took another day for the authorities to remove her body.

That June, an NBC reporter asked Putin about me prior to the 2021 summit with President Biden in Switzerland. The head of Russia called me a drunk and a troublemaker who couldn't hold his vodka.

Actually, he said I got "shit-faced." I'm told that bit was bleeped out when it aired on US television.

NBC interviewed my parents about it. They were very diplomatic, noting that they had never said anything negative about Putin . . . but adding that words like that didn't seem like those a world leader would use.

Personally, though, I thought Putin's remarks were kind of funny. My guess would be that half of the Russian population has a problem with liquor. Putin must have thought I fit right in.

Despite his slur on my character, he told the reporter he would be open to a prisoner exchange.

That same week, a well-connected inmate told me that someone from the FSB had come by to gather up my files. I wasn't exactly sure what that might mean. Maybe it was one good sign, maybe not. In any event, nothing came of it, and any hope I might have attached to it quickly evaporated.

Which was a good thing. Hope was a luxury I couldn't afford in prison.

By now, my appeals were running out. My attorneys said it might be possible to take some matters further, but we would need more money to spend on experts to testify.

I told them no. We'd already spent a lot of money on the case. I didn't want to go any deeper into debt tilting at windmills, and I certainly didn't want my parents spending any more money. I knew that the lawyers might get a phenomenal expert on fabric or DNA to prove that the jacket hadn't been worn by the officer, say, but the end would always be the same: *appeal denied.*

And honestly, I wanted to move on. I was steadily rotting here.

My prison had not been assigned. The usual practice in Russia is to send a prisoner to their home area. In my case, I had put Lina's hometown as my permanent residence. It would be somewhat convenient for her to visit me there.

With my appeals now done, it was only a matter of time before I would be moved. I started hearing rumors that it would happen. I decided to call my mom and dad, telling them I might be transferred soon.

The next day, I was on my way. No one told me which prison I was going to; they only told me I was going.

THIRTEEN

THE GULAG

Any importance I may have had to the administration of SIZO-5 evaporated on the train to the gulag. I was isolated on the transport, rambling through the country en route to my own version of hell.

I was delivered to IK-18 in Mordovia a day later. Along the way I befriended a prisoner who volunteered to send a message to my parents that I was okay. His promise—he was able to keep it, though I had no way of knowing at the time—was my only communication with the outside world for several days.

There were dozens of police at the Mordovia station, outfitted in unmarked uniforms and ski masks, armed with AK-74s and accompanied by attack dogs. I was cuffed as I exited the train, and led without explanation or even a greeting to a convoy of multiple vehicles.

The only other prisoner with me was an older woman. She must have thought I was Hannibal Lecter.

When we arrived at IK-18, the guards looked at the massive security detail and asked, "Special department?"

My escorts nodded.

Someone asked me what my criminal article was. I told him, assault on police officers.

He was dumbfounded. "That's it?"

They held me for a few days, then sent me to my assigned work camp, IK-12. It was an isolated outpost, a good distance from any sizeable city, and an entire universe away from Moscow, about seven and a half hours by car.

The modern Russian prison system evolved from a horrid network of forced labor camps developed under Stalin in the 1930s. The gulag's roots go even further back to the tsars, who would send dissidents as well as criminals to distant parts of Russia—Siberia in particular—to punish them and keep them from rousing the peasants. It's said more than one and a half million prisoners died before the Soviet Union began reforming the system at Stalin's death in 1953.

Those reforms did away with many abuses, but the core mission of the forced labor camps and their wretched conditions remain pretty much intact. Prisoners are required to work for the state; if they don't, they are severely punished. They are modern slaves, with little if any recourse to justice outside the camp.

The camps continue to be a favorite way of dealing with political prisoners. Aleksandr Solzhenitsyn, one of the most famous dissidents of the Cold War era, published *The Gulag Archipelago* in 1973 detailing the abuse he'd suffered. The book remains a classic, and the description of prison conditions doesn't feel that out of date despite being over fifty years old. Most recently, the most famous Russian dissident of our time, Alexei Navalny, died after being sent to a prison for his criticism of the government. The full details of his death have not, as of this writing, been made public.

No prison in the Russian system is "easy," certainly not by Western standards. You are a slave. You have few real rights, and none if the government or its leader decides you don't deserve them. But there are definitely ones where life is not as hard as others.

By reputation, IK-12 and all prisons in Mordovia are on the harder side. Not as bad as, say, Vladimir Central Prison, but bad. The mafya has comparatively little sway in Mordovia, and the mafya leader in our prison camp was corrupt, working with the prison staff to keep control over the prisoners.

I had only a vague idea of what the prison would be like when I arrived. What I did know was this: I was not going to cooperate with the authorities in any way. I was not going to work. I was going to resist with every breath.

At intake at IK-12, there were only two prisoners, myself and an older guy who'd been "convicted" of fraud or embezzlement. A guard walked up to us and he was like, "Hey, am I going to have any problems with you?"

"Nope, no problems here," said the other inmate. "We're going to do everything you ask."

He laughed nervously. Then the guard looked at me.

"Yeah, you're going to have a big problem," I told him.

The guard looked like he was going to fall over.

"What did you say?"

"You're going to have a big problem. I'm not going to work in your forced labor camp. I'm not going to follow any of your rules or regulations, and I'm not going to do any shit that you want me to."

"Well, that means that you're going to get the black mamba."

I like snakes—I currently have one as a pet—but they weren't offering to put me in the reptile house. The "black mamba" is a stick used for beating inmates, or raping them.

"Black mamba or no black mamba," I told him. "I'm not going to do anything that you want me to."

He left, then came back with other guards, who began telling me that I *would* work, throwing the occasional expletive in for emphasis. I repeated what I told the first one, adding my own curse words. Finally the warden came over. He and I would eventually come to know and loathe each other in an almost familial way, but this was our first meeting and he was simply puzzled.

"Am I going to have a problem with you?" he asked. "It seems like you're trying to start trouble."

"No," I told him. "I'm not trying to start any trouble, but I'm in here illegally, and so I'm not going to do any of your shit. I don't see why I should work for you if you put me in here illegally."

"We didn't put you in here. The criminal justice system did," he said. "If you don't work, you're going to be breaking our laws."

"I didn't break your laws and you put me in prison anyway, so I don't really care about breaking your laws now."

"We're going to punish you."

"I get it, but that's not going to change anything."

"We'll see."

I should point out that my problem wasn't with the work itself; it was the idea of doing anything that would help the government that was oppressing me and other Americans. The jobs themselves were just jobs. There were three main areas: a lumber mill, a sewing shop, and charcoal processing.

The lumber mill processed wood and made a variety of things needed around camp. It was not very safe apparently, because I often saw guys missing fingers. The sewing mill was the largest work area. It was basically a third-world sweatshop. Besides sewing uniforms—they did ours—the men there attached bogus tags to knockoff clothing to make them appear to be the product of expensive brands. I never examined these counterfeits, but apparently they brought in pretty good revenue for the prison.

I never really figured out what the story was at the charcoal plant. There were big mounds of the stuff. Guys would work shoveling it all day into the back of horse-drawn carts. Everyone who worked there looked like they had really dark skin, because the fine dust wouldn't come off.

There were other jobs inside the prison: cleaning, administrative work, and the like. Those jobs would be handled by trustees, off-limits to a muzhik or "man." Taking a position like that would immediately brand an inmate as a collaborator with the authorities.

This was a red camp, meaning that the prison administration and guards generally enforced government rules and could make life miserable at a whim. But the mafya code ruled inmates' lives and day-to-day realities. Cigarettes, candy, good-fitting clothes were given to you as you were in good standing. You could buy extra food and a cell phone, or use one of the common ones, as long as the administration didn't find and confiscate them.

The most popular contraband in prisons is cigarettes. Cigarettes themselves are not contraband, as long as they're bought in the prison store. But there was a steady supply of illegally imported cigarettes from Belarus, which of course were. They're smoked by many prisoners, and also function as a currency.

I was processed and given prison clothes, the usual ill-fitting sack of a shirt and baggy pants. Then I was sent to quarantine.

The authorities send arriving prisoners to quarantine to see how they'll adjust to prison life. That might sound benign in a Western context, but what's going on in the gulag is an attempt to break the incoming prisoner's will. The guards and authorities pressured prisoners to become trustees, working for the administration. They would also try to trick prisoners into working for them, thereby forfeiting any hope of being accepted by the mafya, or at least promotion to a higher rank.

For example, one day a guard gave me a towel and told me to clean up something.

"Clean it yourself," I told him.

That didn't endear me to him, but impressing the enemy wasn't one of my priorities. Taking the rag and doing anything with it—aside from shoving it down his throat or elsewhere—would have been considered working for the administration, a betrayal of the code.

There are some jobs in the work camps that are acceptable to the mafya. At my camp, these were the sewing mill and charcoal processing. The work benefited the prisoners directly. But I'd decided that I wasn't going to do anything the Russians wanted, no matter who benefited.

Refusing to work during the few weeks of quarantine was simple. I was harassed a bit, but not very harshly. I could have been placed in a special punishment cell they had in the headquarters building. It was an extrajudicial cell they used to coerce prisoners into working. It didn't exist officially, but it was certainly there. I'd have slept on the floor there for a month, using a little washtub as my toilet. But apparently the administration was afraid to mess with me just yet, perhaps because of the FSB interest in my case, perhaps because I was an American. They also probably thought I would come around without too much effort on their part. Most prisoners did.

After quarantine, I was assigned to a barracks at the far end of the camp, a good distance from the administrative building.

My stance and the fact that I was an American provoked some curiosity. Who was this foreign guy who could speak Russian and had no fear telling the guards to stick it?

There were a handful of inmates inside when I arrived. I introduced myself, extending my hand. The others took it warily, hoping I wasn't gay—under the mafya rules, shaking hands with a gay person made you gay, and therefore shunned.

Same if I was a pedophile, or an informant. Shaking hands was a dangerous act in the work camps, though turning away was itself an insult.

I started talking with the other prisoners. Things eased up. The fact that I could speak Russian so well, especially with what was now a Moscow accent, surprised them.

An inmate I'll call Malloy came up and told me he'd show me around.

Malloy was a few years younger than me, about my height, and in very good shape, and not just for a prisoner. He had the physique and well-packed bulk of someone who worked out regularly. He was a mafya member, and my first guide to barracks life. He took me around the first floor, an open dormitory-style room, with cots and a large table. He introduced me to a man I'll call Yul, the senior mafya member in the building. Yul was physically larger at five ten, with even more muscled bulk than Malloy. He was Chechen. He had dark black hair, a square chin, no beard. Being clean-shaven was unusual for a Chechen, who were generally Muslim and therefore wore beards.

Yul asked a few questions: What was my "article" or the crime I had been charged with? What prison had I been in?

Easy stuff.

He told me later he had been charged with terrorism due to some weird events that had gone down in Turkey and Dubai while he was working there. I think he was right about the charge of terrorism being bogus, though some Chechens did belong to groups that opposed the government. What he actually did to get in trouble—smuggling?—remained a mystery. Anyway, it was irrelevant to me.

We spoke in a little room I came to call the whiskey locker, though

I don't remember any whiskey being there. It was about the size of a closet, and apparently out of range of any monitoring devices.

I think it was Malloy who asked me where I was going to work.

"I'm not," I told him.

"What?"

"Fuck these guys."

"Respect," said Malloy. "But that kind of sucks."

It sucked because I would eventually be put in SHIZO. And SHIZO really sucked.

They explained a little bit about solitary, or SHIZO (an abbreviation for Russian words that mean "punishment isolator"). Conditions were horrible, the place damp and cold. The cells were mostly tiny, and you stayed in them pretty much the whole time. There was a method of smuggling messages back and forth, but otherwise the prisoners were on their own while they were there.

So be it.

I wasn't just going to refuse to work. I was going to actively resist. Resistance was more important to me than breathing. Even, ultimately, than life.

My idea was this: If my life is going to suck in here, I'm going to make their lives also suck. I'm going to find ways to give the administration and government a hard time. I'm going to file complaints. I'm going to refuse to cooperate, and I'm going to gum up their organization any way I can.

Part of it was, I really didn't have much else to do anyway. But I had come to believe that if I made a big enough fuss and embarrassed Russia—if I was able to somehow cause them problems, even small ones, they might rethink taking Americans hostage in the future.

You know what? We took this jerk hostage and he caused us nothing but heartache. Let's not do that again.

Obviously, that didn't work. But that was my thinking.

The prison was too far for my old lawyers, so my parents arranged to have a local lawyer help me formulate complaints and get them to the right authorities. Aside from that, he was of limited help, to be honest. But he did confirm my lousy health when the media became interested, which probably did help the campaign to get me out. At least a little.

When you arrive at the work camp, you are given a uniform that might come close to fitting—if you're lucky. That is soon replaced by a much better tailored uniform with gray reflective stripes. (There are also blue prison uniforms used as work clothes. Some prisoners wear these because clothes get torn up at their workstations. They put their regular uniform on when not working. In solitary, uniforms have "SHIZO" painted on the back.) All uniforms are tailored at prison sewing mills.

If you have an additional rank beyond a muzhik, your uniform is all black: no reflective stripes. In my case, I was "awarded" the all-black uniform as an *otkaznik*, or refuser, because I refused to work, did not march with the other prisoners, and broke all forms of the administration's rules. When I was there, our prison held roughly one hundred prisoners; about eight, including me, were otkazniks. (Among other senses, the word is the same that was applied, under much different circumstances, to Soviet Jews who wanted to immigrate to Israel and elsewhere in the late 1960s.)

There are also tattoos that signify mafya rank, or in some cases the fact that an inmate has been caught cooperating with the administration or otherwise betraying mafya rules. It was not a tattoo or designation you wanted.

My status accorded me a certain amount of respect from fellow prisoners. It did not put me into any sort of command position. I doubt it especially endeared me to the prison staff.

My first test came the morning after I'd settled into my barracks. I was supposed to line up for work. I said I wouldn't. Not knowing what else to do with me, they confined me to the barracks.

Kind of like getting home detention in grammar school.

I was at the barracks for maybe three days because the prison administration didn't know what to do with me. I was a bit anxious, wondering how I'd be treated and wanting to get the waiting over with. But more than that, I was angry, mad about everything that had been done to me by the Russian government and its henchmen. And that outweighed any other emotion.

The disciplinary system at the prison was like the legal system in Russia: the outcome was predetermined. A convict charged with an infraction was taken before a "commission," tried for his offense, and then sentenced to a certain amount of time in solitary. But while it was essentially a kangaroo court, meaning that you were always going to be found guilty, the administration nonetheless observed rules that made it *seem* fair.

If you didn't know it was all a setup, that is.

I was taken to the administration building. The warden, Alexander Nikolaevich, sat at the head of a long table, flanked by his minions. The proceeding itself was videotaped, so there was a record.

I had refused to work, which was a very serious violation. But I wasn't charged with that. Instead, I was charged with being in a sleeping area—my bed—at a time when I should not have been sleeping.

As silly as that sounds—and is—there was a certain amount of logic to it, at least to Alexander Nikolaevich. This was a lesser charge, even though the punishment meant I would go to solitary confinement when found guilty. There was less paperwork for him, and more flexibility—he hoped to use my stint in solitary to convince me to cooperate.

Finding me guilty of refusing to work would put me into a special category, with very serious consequences, not just for me but for them in terms of how I had to be classified, treated, and ultimately accounted for.

Eventually I learned to use the rules of the commissions against them. Prisoners were allowed to ask questions as well as answer them. Since the proceedings were taped, I would ask questions that showed they had violated Russian law regarding how prisoners should be treated. Physical force, for example. Not only would this anger and occasionally embarrass them, it would send them scurrying to turn off the camera.

At my first commission, though, I didn't know how any of that worked. In short order, I was sentenced to three days in solitary, and was walked over to the building.

The guards walked. I waddled.

There was a good reason for walking funny. The mafya members knew that I would end up in solitary. Before the commission, they had taken me into the whiskey locker out of sight and handed me a wad of cigarettes rolled in black tape. I was told to smuggle them into solitary.

I looked at the wad dubiously, knowing that the guards would examine the small number of items I was allowed to bring in.

And strip-search me.

Yes, that's where I thought I was supposed to put it.

The inmate who gave me the cigarettes realized what I was thinking and laughed. "No, you hide it between your legs, behind your balls."

I'm paraphrasing.

The roll was taped at the back of the scrotum, making it difficult to see. It also made it hard to walk comfortably.

Incidentally, there were cigarette rolls that *were* placed you-know-where, but those were only used by inmates who smoked themselves and needed to bring in many cigarettes.

So I waddled over. The guards kept trying to convince me that it was far better to work than to go into solitary. Every one of them had a different take on how bad the conditions were.

One told me there were rats. "Big ones."

"More protein," I told him.

"You eat rats in Texas?"

"Of course not. They're too little."

Solitary confinement was housed in the oldest barracks at the camp, a single-story building that had once been the prison's headquarters during Stalin's era. The cells were of varying size, from tiny to large enough for six people, though "large" there is only meant comparatively. Generally, I was kept alone in a cell so small my shoulders nearly touched the sides. The singles went about eight feet deep, with a window, a steel sink, and a squat toilet on the floor. There was also a narrow metal bench, a small table, and a rack that was unlocked and folded down from the wall at bedtime. The floor was mostly concrete. To call the place dirty would be to insult dirt. The place wasn't just grimy; it seemed made of grime. Cameras were placed to watch each cell, though I was able to work out ways of hiding what I was doing as time went on.

You slept on a one-inch foam mattress atop wooden planks. When they woke you at six in the morning, they took the pad away and locked the bed against the wall, making sure you couldn't use it during the day. You could rest on the floor, or sometimes against the table, but neither was comfortable.

A hot water pipe in front of the window served as the heating unit.

The cell was brutally cold in the winter, maybe just above freezing. Prisoners were only allowed to wear their prison uniform and one other layer, generally a T-shirt. Wearing a parka or a sweater was considered a uniform infraction.

I would spend whole days hugging the hot water pipe. I'd wrap my arms and legs around it, hold on and shiver. After an hour, my back would be cold. I would turn so the hot water pipe was against my back. After a few hours, I'd get up and walk in circles, or maybe just back and forth for variety. I'd do that until it was ten and my bed would be unlocked and the mattress pad returned.

As soon as I was locked in that first day, I undid the cigarette pack and hid it under a metal lip on the sink. As I stepped back, I heard a voice. It was unworldly, as if coming from above.

An angel in heaven. Though it had a bit of a devil's rasp to it.

Am I hallucinating already?

There was a cough, mumbling.

"Come up here," said the voice.

I started looking around. I was alone in the cell. Not hallucinating. Not yet.

"Climb up on the bars," said the voice. "And yell through the ventilation duct."

The cell had two doors stacked together, the way a screen door might front the exterior door to an American suburban house. The one at the hall was a blast door; the one behind it had bars with bracing that you could climb on. I hoisted myself up, and found myself a few inches from the duct.

"Hello?" I said.

"Are you really an American?" asked the voice.

"Yeah."

"What are you doing in here?"

"It's kind of a long story."

"Are you short on time?"

I laughed. And that is how I met two of the bravest Russians I have ever known, Grisha and Samir.

Grisha had been in solitary for more than four years; Samir about the same. They ran the place, as far as the mafya was concerned. Samir was a Kabardinian, part of the Circassian ethnic group that historically has lived in the Caucasus. He had been put away on terrorism charges and for being part of an armed rebel group. Grisha had been charged with dealing heroin; while he was an addict, the charge itself was bogus.

They seemed to know everything there was to know about solitary, the camp, and the Russian prison system in general. They helped me tremendously. As time went on, I was able to help them, too, at least in a minor way. I made sure to include things they wanted in my complaints and demands. Once in a while, that meant concessions for them.

I loved those guys. They were tough. The men at the barracks were fun to hang out with, but most of them were weak. Grisha and Samir were not.

The morning after I arrived, the guards came to inspect my cell. Guards had inspected the cell the night before, but this was far more thorough. Four men arrived at the cell door, armed with a large wooden mallet. Thor's hammer is smaller.

Wallop!

One of the guards swung the hammer against the table.

Wallop!

He hit the bench seat.

Wallop!

He hit the sink. The cigarettes dropped to the floor.

"What the hell is this?" demanded the guard.

"I don't know," I said. "Cigarettes?"

"You don't know?"

We went around a bit. I told him I'd only come in the day before and didn't know there were cigarettes there. He foamed a bit, but finally just walked away.

Grisha told me later how to hide them better. I won't give all their secrets away, but the solution involved the toilet and thread.

That was hardly the prisoners' cleverest hiding place or strategy. I learned to look carefully around each cell when I arrived. There were often dozens of places where a cigarette or some other contraband might be cached.

Metal spoons were smuggled into cells and became chisels, creating hiding crevices. In one case, the prisoners had managed to get a file into the cellblock, and used it to cut a piece of metal rebar from the cell. It must have taken quite a while, but when the bar was liberated, it became an excavating and grinding tool par excellence.

There was incredible ingenuity in solitary. Inmates were given needles and thread to sew their names on their uniforms. In solitary. I never actually sewed anything on my uniform, but the thread was very useful, especially to send messages; I'll describe a few methods in a bit.

Never in my many stays in solitary could I say that time passed quickly. But I remember thinking as the last day of my first sentence ended that I wished I had more time to learn from Grisha. A firehose of information flowed through the ventilator. Every word of it inspired me to resist even harder.

The warden came to visit as my three-day sentence ended. He was flanked by six of his largest guards.

"Well, did you change your mind?" asked Alexander Nikolaevich.

"Change?"

"Will you work?"

"No," I told him. "You think you broke me in three days? Get the fuck out."

To be honest, I was a little pissed that he thought he could break a Marine so easily. I mean, really.

The warden glanced at one of the guys with him. "Give him eight more days."

Alexander Nikolaevich walked away. His thugs came into the cell to search it. In the process, they decided to search me, instructing me to hold my arms out, spread my legs.

The fattest, Mikhailovic something-or-other, walked over and kneed me in the groin.

I bent with the pain, then straightened and grabbed him by the uniform. I might have done more but the other guard held me back.

Mikhailovic something-or-other smiled. "Sorry. It was an accident."

Right.

With nothing much to do, you're tempted to sleep. But sleeping on the concrete floor, or even on wooden planks in the cells that had them, was dangerous. The slime was thick with bacteria and viruses, and the cold and wet encouraged their growth. Tuberculosis was rampant in Russian prisons, and it would devastate your body in that environment.

The same was true of colds and the flu. I started taking extra towels with me, not only to protect me a bit from the cold concrete, but also to act as a makeshift, very makeshift, blanket.

Another health hazard was kidney stones. The water was very hard with minerals and smelled of sulfur. The other prisoners cautioned me against drinking too much, especially from the sink. The guards were supposed to bring water three times a day, but that rarely happened—maybe once a week. To stay hydrated, there was no real alternative than the faucet with its mineral mash.

My stays in solitary followed a very predictable pattern. I would refuse to work. I would be taken to a commission. I would be given a sentence—the charges and length of sentence could vary slightly, but would generally be between five and fifteen days. I would serve the sentence. I would be brought back to the barracks, refuse to work, spend a day off—that's how I thought about it—go to the commission, return to solitary.

Sometimes I wouldn't get that day off in the middle. They'd find some infraction in solitary, take me to the commission, and bring me back.

There were only so many things you can do in prison, but the Russians were very resourceful at pinning an infraction on a prisoner. It was a one-sided game as far as the prizes went, but I quickly learned how to score difficulty points.

On my second or third stay, I was charged with tampering with their surveillance camera. I hadn't, though admittedly it may have looked like I wanted to. I had climbed up to the duct to try to pass a message through it, and the way I shielded what I was doing must have made it look like I was tampering with the gear.

It still worked, though. But intent—*their* intent—trumped reality. I was convicted of tampering and sent back.

It was one thing to be punished for not working. In the calculus of resistance it was, in a bizarre way, only fair.

But being punished for something I didn't do—well, that was the whole reason I was here to begin with.

You want to put me in here for messing with the camera? I'm not going to sit in here for a crime that I didn't commit.

I'll just own it.

As soon as I got back to my cell, I climbed up to the camera and started whacking at it. Then I took toothpaste and smeared it all over the lens.

Under the Russian mafya's rules, if a prisoner is resisting the administration, other prisoners have a duty to support him. So as soon as Grisha heard me announce what I was doing—another mafya rule: you have to tell the others you're "rioting," or going against the rules—the rest of the men in solitary either broke their cameras or covered them up, too.

"Cell one is offline," yelled one of the prisoners.

"Cell two is offline."

And on and on. Within a few minutes, the entire barracks was blacked out.

Alexander Nikolaevich came down with four guys and marched to my cell.

"What the hell are you doing?" demanded the warden.

"What do you mean?" I asked.

"You covered up the camera!"

"Well, you put me in here for covering up the camera, which I didn't do, so I figured I might as well not sit in here for nothing."

We traded expletives. He had the guards remove the stuff from the lens so they could see.

As soon as they left, I went and did it again. Cleaning the lens wasn't really a big deal, but the guards had to come all the way from the administration building to do it. And not just one guy. Three or four would come together, because they weren't allowed to be in cells by themselves.

I waited a bit, and did it again. And again. I tried to get my timing down so they had to walk the whole distance to and from administration before coming back.

The guards couldn't just blow it off. The camera feeds were being seen by a central prison authority in Mordovia. Losing all the video from solitary prompted uncomfortable questions to the local warden, and the situation had to be rectified ASAP.

We covered the cameras for two days, *Groundhog Day*–style, until finally we got a concession: Grisha and Samir were moved to a larger cell with two other roommates, and kept there rather than being moved around at the jailers' whim.

Guards at the prison wore cameras on their chests, not unlike the devices most police departments in the States use. In this case, though, the guards would regularly turn them on and off. The idea was to document bad behavior by prisoners, good behavior by the guards, and "miss" anything else. One guard in particular liked to egg prisoners on, hoping to get some infraction or another recorded.

Two of the twenty or so guards at the prison were decent, one probably because he was being bribed. The rest were bastards to the nth degree, going out of their way to treat inmates like dirt. The system itself breeds contempt and sadistic behavior.

One other thing was extremely hard for me: disobeying the rules.

I had followed rules all of my life, from school to the Marines. I'd been a Boy Scout, and not just any scout—an Eagle Scout. I'd grown up with the sons and daughters of cops; some of my best friends were policemen now. Following the law was totally what I did.

But not now. I had to resist, and not following the rules was the only way to do that. It was often a struggle with my conscience.

It was also, I will admit, occasionally exhilarating. Being "bad" was a whole new thing for me, and I embraced it.

In September, Ambassador Sullivan visited me, driving eight hours. I'd asked to be supplied with books, which were supposed to be allowed under Russian law. The State Department had arranged to get fifty from the States, delivering them to Moscow via a special flight.

He told me he was worried about my health; it was clearly declining. He said if I continued to refuse to work it would undoubtedly get worse.

I told him ethically I could not work for an enemy of the United States that was taking Americans hostage.

Sullivan remarked that the medical care in Russian prisons was really terrible; if something happened, I could die. I told him that I hoped that I wouldn't but that if I died, the Russians would never take another American hostage again.

Tears slipped down his face. "It will be hard to tell your mom about this conversation," he admitted. "But I understand."

I told the ambassador I wouldn't do anything to embarrass our country and not to worry about me.

"I'm supposed to be here to reassure you," he answered, "not the other way around."

I was glad of the visit, not least of all because the ambassador made it possible for Lina to see me. She had come the whole way from Moscow on her own, and had to wait at the gate outside until it was almost the end of the day.

When Lina showed her documents, the clerk asked if she knew I was a spy.

She laughed. "He's not a spy."

The prison authorities finally let her in after making her wait for hours; they gave her, like, ten minutes to visit with me.

Our meeting was tearful. I told her again that she shouldn't wait for me. She told me again that she loved me and always would.

In the barracks, there were cell phones. It was easy to communicate with the outside world. You could buy one using Telegram, the social media and messaging app. The mafya would arrange to have a package of phones and SIM cards slingshotted over the prison fence, where a waiting prisoner would grab them and hustle them to a hiding spot. The guards rarely if ever reacted quickly enough to catch anyone.

Phones were hidden in special places around the barracks. Occasionally, they would be found and confiscated, so it was also important to hide the SIM cards separately. These small electronic chips contained the number for the phone, and more important, data that could reveal the people in the outside world who helped prisoners or were part of the mafya network. That data was far more important to protect than the phone, so the chips were hidden very carefully. While I know some phones were found while I was in prison, the cards were not, at least not that I knew. Mafya members, and myself, were able to talk to pretty much anyone they wanted in the barracks.

Being in solitary confinement made it a lot more difficult to get messages to the outside world, or even the rest of the prison. But it wasn't impossible. The inmates had worked out a number of ingenious ways of getting messages to other cells, or out to the main barracks.

Some things could be smuggled in and out by prisoners arriving in solitary, as I did with the cigarettes, or by prisoners who were leaving. There were also certain inmates who worked in the barracks who cooperated with the mafya and had ways of moving small amounts of contraband. The trick was to get the messages to a cell where there would be contact and they could be passed on.

One way was to use toilet paper. You would wet it and wad it into a little ball. Then you'd wrap it with plastic wrap, tie a thread around it, and shoot it through the ventilation shaft with a primitive blowgun fashioned from writing paper or a page from a magazine.

Another way was to hide a message in the leftover food after you ate. I'd make a scroll maybe a third the length of a cigarette, rolling it tight. On the outside, I would write who it's addressed to—in my case, often to Malloy, one of the mafya bosses at the barracks. I'd take a scrap of plastic wrap, twist the paper in it, and then burn the ends of the plastic, so it was like a little weatherproof packet. Then I'd hide it on the plate. If I was lucky, there'd be a fish head or something else pretty gross and inedible, but more than once I tucked it into a piece of bread I wished I could have eaten, but didn't so I could get the message out.

The prisoner who delivered the food to the cell would return for the plate thirty minutes after bringing it. You were supposed to give him a code to let him know that there was a message to be retrieved. But the first time I did it, I couldn't remember what I was supposed to say.

"Hey man, do you have any cheeseburgers on the menu?" I asked. Then I looked down at the plate, hoping somehow he'd get the message.

He looked at me like I'd lost my mind.

"Cheeseburger," I repeated.

"No, you dumbass," he said. "Russia doesn't have cheeseburgers."

He took my plate and slammed the door closed.

Damn.

A couple of days later, I tried it again, still not knowing the code. I went through the same routine, asking for a cheeseburger, hoping he'd get the message.

"You're an idiot" was all he said.

And I felt like one. But a couple of days later, when I was released back to the barracks temporarily, I found that the messages had gone through.

"I've been doing this job for nine months," the guy who passed them for me told me later, shrugging. "I'm not stupid." He'd been acting for the guards, in case he was overheard.

Once the message reached the barracks, the contact would snap a picture of it on a cell phone, then pass it on to whoever it was going to. In my case, that generally meant Lina or my parents.

Not long after I arrived, the communications system was compromised. Grisha told me through the ventilation shaft that we'd have to use a different method, one that was a bit more complicated than what we'd used until now.

Call it message fishing.

You started with a full sheet of paper, rolling it diagonally so that it was like a stick. Then you'd lather soap in your hands and coat the paper with it. After thirty minutes or so, the paper would be pretty hard.

That was your arrow.

You'd tie some thread to the arrow, then go to your window and climb up on the sill to reach the part that opened. There were still bars, but the opening at the top was big enough to let air in—or to launch something through.

Holding the arrow in one hand, generally between your thumb and forefinger, you'd smack it on the back with your flipflop, punching it out of the cell. If you were good, and lucky maybe, you could get the arrow to go thirty meters, landing in the grass or dirt outside the building.

At that point, you alerted the inmate in the cell next to you. He would launch his own arrow, hooking its string around your line. Then he would pull your string up. With the thread now connecting the two cells, you tied your message onto the string, and he pulled it over.

There's a bit of a trick to holding everything taut, but given that we were in solitary, there was plenty of time to perfect it. Eventually the note was passed to an inmate who was getting out of solitary. He then would give it to the mafya boss, who would forward it.

I don't know whether the guards figured out what was going on or just wanted to isolate me further, but eventually I was put in a cell with no one nearby. So then I learned another method: parasailing.

Not me. The message.

I'd create a little parasail or kite from a piece of cellophane or plastic and send it out the window, a line playing out behind it. The wind would take it across the side of the building, usually pretty far. An inmate would then send his own line out. Once he had the two lines tangled together, the message could be attached and reeled into the other cell, even if it was a good distance away.

The system worked so well that, even though the administration was blocking me from sending out official complaints and not letting me use the phone calls I was entitled to, I could get messages out pretty much whenever I needed to. When I went back to the barracks—temporarily, that is—I was able to formulate my complaints and send them via a clandestine cell phone, or occasionally give them to my local lawyer.

Time passed slowly, but it definitely passed. Nothing was happening. I was afraid that my case was slipping out of media view. Frustrated with the prison administration's actions—one of my biggest complaints was that they wouldn't let me read any of the books the embassy had delivered for me—I decided to up the ante with them:

I'd go on a hunger strike.

FOURTEEN

HUNGER AS A WEAPON

Starving yourself doesn't sound like a way to fight the system. But it was a powerful tool. Or at least I hoped it would be.

Some background: Alexander Nikolaevich, the warden at IK-12, was a recent replacement. The earlier warden had been a hard-ass, and the prisoners had decided to "riot." They did this by destroying all of the cameras in solitary confinement, sealing their cell doors shut, and slitting their wrists and arms. They also fought with the guards who came to beat them into submission.

News of this got out after they were sent to the hospital. The warden's bosses didn't like the negative publicity, and he was fired.

I figured if news of my hunger strike got out, Alexander Nikolaevich would either get in trouble, or worry that he would. Since I was a prisoner the government was interested in, there'd be a high probability of pressure.

The news that I was striking might—*might*—also push President Biden's administration to move a little faster.

Another important factor—hunger strikes were permitted under mafya rules.

I looked at it as an experiment. If it pressured the Russians, I might be able to use the tactic again, maybe for higher stakes.

As I planned it out, I considered what the prison's response would be. First, they would lie, or try to hide it. So I'd have to make sure the word got out.

I talked to the guards before my next stay in solitary, asking them how long I would be imprisoned—it was an open secret among the staff, and not a closely guarded one. Then I timed out my stay, calculating when I would be back in the barracks before being sent again. A week before I figured I would start my strike, I wrote out a complaint with about fifteen violations. I took a photo of it, then sent the picture to my parents with a clandestine cell phone, explaining that I was going to go on a hunger strike. I told them I wanted them to tell the news media what was going on.

"They're going to say that I'm not doing it," I told my dad. "They're going to lie. So just know I really am doing it."

My father pushed back. "Are you sure you want to do this?"

He had some bogus arguments.

"Okay," I told him. "Well, I just want you to know that how long I'm going to go on a hunger strike depends completely on you, because if you tell the news media and I hear the reports, I'll stop. But if I don't hear anything, I won't eat until I die."

We argued some more. Finally, I convinced him to do as I asked. "And please retype the complaint. I don't want anyone to see how crappy my handwriting is."

I sent complaints to the Prosecutor General of Moscow, the Ministry of Foreign Affairs, the Head of Human Rights, and several other places. My complaint stated that the warden of IK-12 was violating the Russian constitution and its laws. (I don't remember all the violations at this point; one was their refusal to give me books.) I asked for an investigation, and that the violations end immediately.

That was my standard demand. So was my threat to alert the US news media and Congress. To top this complaint off, I added that I would go on a hunger strike.

I made a special copy for the head of IK-12, and presented it during their sham commission sentencing me to solitary.

"What's this?" asked one of Alexander Nikolaevich's sidekicks.

"Oh, I'm going to have a hunger strike."

They turned their camera off.

In solitary that evening, I ate as much as I could. The next morning at six, a guard came around with breakfast.

"No, thanks," I said.

"Huh?"

"Not eating."

"Why?" asked the guard.

"I'm doing a hunger strike."

"Did you tell anyone?" he asked.

"I told the warden and all of the officers on the commission yesterday."

The guard took the food away and went directly to the phone.

The administration ignored me that day, not even bothering to weigh me—generally a precaution during a hunger strike.

It took three or four days before things got serious. The warden himself marched to my cell.

"They told me you're not eating!" Alexander Nikolaevich yelled.

"Yeah. I told you."

"Why?"

"I gave you a list."

"I don't have the paper."

"Did you throw it in the trash?"

He stared at me. "This is a really big deal."

"I know."

"This is going to cause some serious problems for me."

"That's why I'm doing this."

"You should eat!"

"I'm not going to."

"If you don't eat, we'll have to send you to the hospital and they'll force-feed you there."

"Even better."

Alexander Nikolaevich turned around and left.

I'm guessing someone in Moscow called and asked what was going on. The guards redoubled their efforts to get me to eat, bragging about the quality of the food. Which, you know, was pretty comical.

We got you the best gruel. It's going to be yummy.

Not a quote, but you get the idea.

I have to confess that, while I didn't eat any *prison* food during those few days, the guys managed to smuggle in some bits of horse pepperoni for me during the strike. It was pretty good. So was the candy they added as dessert.

A day or two later, Grisha or Samir gave me news through the solitary "intercom."

"The prosecutor general is visiting the prison today," they told me. "He's supposed to come to solitary confinement."

The guards soon came and took me to a building on the other side of the camp. They kept me there for a while before returning me to solitary. I was puzzled.

"When's the prosecutor general coming?" I asked Grisha.

"He already came."

The administration had decided to hide me. But that didn't make their problem go away. The next day I was escorted to the warden's office. The FSB operative assigned to monitor our prison was there.

"You really screwed us," he said. "There are prosecutors here, and they're going to search the prison."

"Good."

Two men in prosecutor uniforms interviewed me about the hunger strike. I told them I had fifteen conditions, all on the declaration I had given to Alexander Nikolaevich days before. That surprised them; the warden had apparently told them he didn't know about the violations or the strike.

Tsk-tsk.

I shrugged. "It's on the tape," I told them, referring to my earlier statements to the administration during the commission.

The prosecutors offered to meet a couple of demands, including getting me books and allowing me to talk to my attorney in English and to have phone calls.

But they drew the line at doing anything about reversing the trial and its verdict. Which was only fair, I guess, since they hadn't been involved.

"Can you stop doing your hunger strike?" one of the prosecutors asked.

"No."

"Why?"

"You didn't meet all of my requirements."

"This is a big problem for us, Trevor. They wrote an article about you here in Mordovia being on a hunger strike."

I did a silent victory dance. My test had proven I had power over the administration. Limited power, but some. I was still newsworthy, and the authorities could be persuaded—forced?—to make some concessions. Limited ones, granted.

"My media or yours?" I asked.

"Both," said one of the prosecutors. "Can you tell us how much longer you plan on being on a hunger strike?"

"I'm actually kind of hungry right now, so I think I'll just end it. Assuming you keep your end of the agreement."

They gave me sneaky-bastard glares. But they were as good as their word. I got a book as soon as I went back to solitary. The rest were in the barracks when I returned there.

About those books: a bunch were Westerns. I didn't realize Louis L'Amour wrote so many novels.

Alexander Nikolaevich and I settled into a routine. I'd refuse to work. The warden would find some violation other than that to put me in solitary. I'd go into solitary for whatever random sentence he set up. I'd be released back to the barracks, where I could use a mafya cell phone to talk to my parents or Lina, catch up on sleep, eat slightly better food.

Then we'd cycle back. Now he would give me two or three days back at the barracks instead of one, something Samir and Grisha had told him might relieve some pressure on him. We'd reached an informal, unstated understanding: He had to confine me and I had to complain, but we would both ease up.

A little. We still had our moments.

The weather had turned and it was starting to get really cold. The guards didn't allow you to have more than one layer of clothing, so the only way to stay warm was to pace back and forth. I would sit down and read for an hour, then walk for an hour, sometimes two.

I'd thought the FSB would be interested in interviewing me, if not outright torturing me for information. But they never really tried. Maybe they knew everything about me already and decided I wasn't worth the effort.

Their representative at the prison, a "curator," mostly ignored me after a heart-to-heart.

"We need to talk," he told me one day.

"What about?" I asked.

"You didn't fill out any of this background information on your intake," he pointed out. "What addresses have you lived at?"

"I don't remember."

"What's your mother's phone number?"

"I don't know."

"What's your sister's birthday?"

"Dunno."

He harangued a bit. Apparently, he was quite fond of his own sisters, or at least their birthdays.

"I've been in prison for like two years," I told him. "I forgot."

He moved on to my military background.

"What units were you in?" he asked.

"I'm not telling you that."

"You're going to give me—"

"*Zalupa*," I said, finishing his sentence.

"Zalupa" is Russian slang. It has two meanings. One meaning is "head of a penis." The other is "problem." So I was telling him I wasn't giving him anything of value, *and* I was going to be a pill about it.

"What did you say?"

I told him again I wasn't cooperating.

"Show me your tattoos."

I did.

"What does that number mean on your tattoo?"

"It's my cat's birthday."

Something I'd heard in a movie, I think. I added a suggestion on what he might do to himself.

The FSB guy picked up his briefcase and left. That was the last time anyone asked me about my military record. Maybe the warden did once, trying to make conversation, but I blew him off.

The administration could mess with me, but they had to play by certain rules. They could not beat me. The one time someone did—when I was kneed after my first time in solitary—I complained to the Ministry of Foreign Affairs. The ministry apparently got on the warden about it—I was of no use to them dead, and beating me up wasn't going to improve my health.

After the ministry balled him out, Alexander Nikolaevich came to my cell in solitary to ask why I'd complained.

Duh.

Alexander Nikolaevich didn't seem too interested in my side of the story, to be honest, but no one did that again.

The warden didn't like any of my complaints, but the one that really set him off came after I decided to grow a beard.

They had a rule at the prison that no facial hair was allowed. But Russian law said a prisoner could have a beard, as long as it measured one centimeter or less. So I started growing one.

The guards had a problem with that. They complained up the chain of command, and soon the warden himself came and threatened to shave my face.

"I don't think that's a good idea," I told him.

"Why not?"

"Because I'll have to defend myself and fight your guards."

He looked at the other prisoner with me in the cell and said, "What? This American is actually rioting!"

The prisoner looked at me and smiled as Alexander Nikolaevich stormed off.

I composed a protest against the warden and his threat to use physical force against me for growing a legally permissible beard.

I saw him only a few days later. His head looked like it was about to explode. He had a piece of paper in his hand: my complaint.

"What the fuck is this?" he demanded. "This says 'Alexander

Nikolaevich, head of IK-12, threatened to use physical force against me, Trevor Reed, citizen of the US, if I don't shave my beard!'"

"Yeah, well, you did say that."

"I didn't mean it!"

I shrugged. He went away mad.

If the circumstances had not been so dire, I guess I might have started to feel a little sorry for him. A punk prisoner was making his life terrible, and enjoying it. I wouldn't be surprised if his intake of vodka doubled because of me.

But give Alexander Nikolaevich credit. When he finally realized bullying wouldn't work, he tried bribery. He offered to make me a trustee, which would mean easier work and pay . . . I think the equivalent of twenty dollars a month.

I said no. He sweetened it by saying I wouldn't have to do anything, just sign the paper claiming that I was working.

I didn't go for that, either.

"Eventually," he told me, "you're going to give up."

"No, I'm not."

"Well, eventually this prison will break you."

"No," I told him. "Eventually I'll break your prison."

That was my attitude. But the reality was different. The prison *was* breaking me—not my will, not mentally or emotionally, but my body. I had developed a cough that rattled across my chest, slowly getting worse each day.

One of the prisoners—"Cuban"—got very sick and was shipped out to a hospital prison. He came back a few days later, looking even worse. He got shipped back. When I didn't see him, I asked another inmate if they knew when he was coming back.

"He's not coming back," said the prisoner. "He's in the tuberculosis ward at the hospital."

Anyone who had come in contact with him was to be given special rations to boost their strength. This generally amounted to some eggs, along with some milk and butter for our crusts of bread.

More Russian miracle vitamins, but better than nothing, I thought. Since I had spent hours with Cuban, I asked for the supplement. They wouldn't give it to me.

"How would it look if you got TB?"

It would look worse if I died of it, I thought.

Tuberculosis is rampant in the Russian prison system. At the time, though, I didn't think it was a threat to me. I'd heard that TB was very hard to get. I also had a Western view of illness: medicine can cure anything, and we've got plenty. I thought it was something less urgent, but still potentially dangerous. You can die of pneumonia, after all.

Sickness aside, prisoners in solitary confinement were entitled to medical checkups every six months. Grisha urged me to go for my exam, which would be at a hospital prison. It would feel like a vacation.

I should make it clear that the prisoners universally believed there would be no medical treatment at the hospital, or at least none that was effective. It was hard to prove that the staff even looked at X-rays, since they had missed what was going on with Cuban. They could cure no disease.

Well, one—hemorrhoids. They were said to be good at removing those.

I'm not making a joke.

Our "hospital" was LPU-21, a section of IK-21, another prison in the region. Like all prison hospitals, it was just another prison section with a few medical personnel, some diagnostic equipment like X-ray machines, and much better food.

And no solitary or work assignments.

I was sent there for my semi-annual exam. After my initial triage, I was given an X-ray, presumably to check for pneumonia or tuberculosis. I was then sent to a wardroom. It was similar to our barracks, with about twenty patients in each room, bunk beds, some chairs. The walls were a lovely shade of puke, a color somewhere between yellow, black, and blank.

Two guys came up to me with clipboards soon after I arrived. They were mafya guys, doing their own intake.

"Name?"

"Trevor Reed."

"What's your mafya name?"

"I don't have one. I'm American."

Double takes.

"Your Russian is native," said the one holding the clipboard.

I shrugged at the compliment and told them my criminal article. They asked about solitary. I told them I refused to work or do anything the administration wanted. I was wearing the black uniform, so they understood that I was an otkaznik.

A while later, an older guy—probably forty, though he looked far older—came around and started chatting me up. He had a way of carrying himself that told you he was important, but he didn't lead with the fact that he was the head mafya guy at the hospital prison. In fact, I only learned that later, from someone else.

He had a mafya name and a call sign, but let's call him Mentor. He headed the mafya's prison organization, and was a solid guy.

He asked a bunch of questions, and congratulated me on not cooperating. He asked if the mafya was taking care of me, and I told him it was. Then he moved on. Afterward, though, he introduced me to others in the hospital.

I was there for only a few days. Whatever was causing my cough didn't get any better, which wasn't surprising since I wasn't treated for it or, as far as I knew, diagnosed.

I should mention that many Russians I met, including medical staff, believed you got tuberculosis not from prisoners who had it but from being in cold, damp areas—like solitary confinement, I would assume, though that didn't prevent them from putting prisoners there. I tried to explain that TB doesn't waft in from the stones; you get it from being exposed for long periods of time to someone who has it. I don't think they believed me.

The second time I went to the hospital was more dire, but more interesting, too.

By now the prison was really winning. My body was wasting away, eating through muscle and everything else. The cough was near constant. I noticed blood when I spit.

My stays in solitary had been shortened, and then stopped completely. I'd been planning to "riot" with Grisha and the others with another hunger strike, but had to postpone that because I wasn't being sent to solitary.

I don't know why. Maybe because there were rumors about a prisoner exchange, maybe because there had been an intervention from Moscow, or maybe . . . unlikely, but maybe . . . Alexander Nikolaevich thought I was sick and felt some real sympathy toward me.

Nah.

Not possible. Though he may have started to fear that he would lose his job if I died.

I already looked like a corpse. My cheeks were caved in. My eyes were ringed like a raccoon's. My ribs stuck out through my clothes. That's what eating barely a thousand calories a day will do for you.

Coughing and spitting up blood was just a bonus.

The guys in the barracks hounded the nurse, yelling at her to get me to the hospital. They were afraid I had TB, and that they were going to get sick as well.

I was back in the barracks between commissions when, for stupid reasons, another prisoner and I began wrestling, horsing around. At some point I managed to break a rib off my sternum.

Stupid wrestling move.

I went into the little closet out of range of the cameras, and made a loud noise, pretending to fall. Then I went to the nurse. My rib was sticking out of my body.

This proved a lot more persuasive than coughing or spitting up blood. The nurse immediately arranged to send me to the hospital prison.

Before I left, I was given a note to deliver to the head of the mafya at the hospital. I hadn't realized it on my first visit, but the mafya often used the hospital prison to pass messages back and forth. I was given a note and instructed to give it to Mentor, whom I had met on the last visit.

That was the easy part.

The hospital was used as a way station for transporting contraband. I was given two massive duffle bags full of cigarettes, which I had to carry with another bag of my own clothes. These represented a kind of tax or assessment known as *obschak* in the mafya, goods or money collected from each prisoner. (There are set amounts for men convicted of certain crimes, but the general population gives according to their means.)

The guard receiving me at the hospital was amazed that I smoked so much. He started to confiscate the bags, grabbing them from me, but I wouldn't let go. As we started to play tug-of-war, Mentor happened to arrive. He smoothed things out with the guard, who scurried off.

A little later, Mentor introduced me to a prisoner higher than him in the overall hierarchy, though as I understand it, his function was more like a consigliore in an Italian mob than a direct commander. I'll call him "Brother."

Brother and I talked for a bit, him asking the usual questions: Why are you in solitary? And so on. Brother was impressed, and offered to take me under his wing. He asked if I thought about moving up in the hierarchy.

He said he believed I was quite possibly the first and only American otkaznik in a Russian prison. I'd definitely be the first brodyaga if I joined and was promoted.

I had to tell him I wasn't interested. We had similar methods, but our goals were different. And I wanted to get out, not run the place.

He told me he understood.

The hospital was a nexus where you might run into prisoners you knew from other camps, or guys who knew those guys. Whenever I met someone from IK-17, I'd ask about Paul Whelan. If they knew him, I would write a little note for them to deliver.

The notes weren't much:

> Hey, I'm also an American and a Marine. I'm also in here for bullshit. I heard that you were resisting the Russians, and I've been doing that, too. I just want you to know I really respect you for doing that. It helps me to know that I'm not the only one. Keep fighting. Semper Fi.

I never got anything back, but I did see one guy who told me he'd managed to deliver a message for me earlier. Even the hint of connection made me feel less alone.

There weren't a lot of Americans in the system. The only one I remember meeting was Jimmy Wilgus, an American musician who was detained in 2016 and sentenced to twelve and a half years in prison for indecent exposure, a crime his family says he didn't commit. As we're writing this book, he remains in prison.

The medical staff at the hospital took some X-rays of my ribs, trying to figure out what was going on. The only problem was, the technician took it of the wrong side.

I protested, cursed, swore—but all they did was send me back to IK-12.

I told the staff there what had happened, and demanded I be sent back. They put me in solitary instead.

I went on another hunger strike.

It didn't last long. By evening, I was on a transport headed back to the hospital.

This time, they got films of the actual problem. A doctor examined me, and said I had a separated rib.

"Can you fix it?" I asked.

"No."

The injury, he told me, was likely to heal on its own. Later, I would be told in the US that immediate surgery might have put the rib back exactly where it belonged, as opposed to where it is now, a little off-kilter. But it feels okay, as long as I don't get kicked there.

I returned to a bit of drama in the barracks, partly due to my rib. The guy who'd wrestled me had been ratted out, though we were never sure who the rat was, which made for anxiety as well as caution. Along with that, tension developed over a leadership issue within the mafya ranks. It didn't directly involve me, so I stayed as aloof as possible.

The mafya has some strict rules about forfeiting membership. Ratting on another prisoner is an obvious violation. But there are others that don't really make sense. Performing cunnilingus, even with your wife, somehow labels you homosexual, and you're kicked out.

For all its power and organization, the mafya never seemed able to institute real reforms in the camps. Simple things like improved food or real health care for prisoners would have been easily obtainable if the prisoners went on strike together. They wouldn't have to do something as dramatic as a hunger strike: simply refusing to work would cripple the corrupt system. But the mafya leaders I spoke to never seemed interested in using their actual power.

There were a lot of reasons, I guess. But to me, a lot of it came down to a serf mentality—most Russians expected to be treated like peasants.

That applied in and out of the prison system. Russians were constantly lied to by the media, let alone Putin and the rest of the government. There were people and publications that pointed out the lies, but most Russians simply took the lies in stride. They might not believe the obvious bull they were told, but they didn't go out of their way to disprove it, let alone argue against it. It would pop up in their conversations all the time.

All the months I'd been in solitary, I had never seen, let alone met, Grisha and Samir. I imagined them being some kind of superhuman beings. These guys had been in for years; I think seven by the time I left. They were hardcore, and so they must be giants.

They were, but not in the way I thought.

I was in a small room in solitary where some of our things were stored. I turned and saw two skinny, emaciated skeletons staring at me. They looked so frail and thin they could barely stand upright. A stiff breeze would topple both. They had deep scars on their wrists where they had cut themselves during protests, and cheeks hollowed by months of hunger and deprivation.

One of the skeletons walked over. "I am Grisha," he said, smiling.

Samir was the other.

That's when I realized they were just men, not the supernatural gods of resistance who had supported me.

Just men. Hard-asses to be sure. Men whose flesh and blood were withering into dust, but whose spirits would continue to propel me, and others, until resistance no longer was necessary.

I love those men.

FIFTEEN

HOPES AND FEARS

From my father:

This was the second Christmas and holiday season Trevor had missed. We hadn't lost faith or hope, but spontaneous joy was not a thing around the Reed household.

While Trevor's lawyers continued to make their appeals, Paula and I worked on the home front, trying to increase awareness in the general public and make inroads with politicians. The Trump administration had been less than supportive; we hoped to do better with the new president, Joe Biden.

The fact that Biden was a Democrat and our local representatives were Republicans could have complicated things. But we'd already gotten bipartisan support in Congress. And with Republican leadership backing our efforts, the possibility of Biden being criticized for an exchange seemed lessened.

While we had hope the new administration would help, our friend

Jonathan Franks warned us it would take time for the Biden people to get up to speed. In the meantime, Jon helped us increase our efforts with the media.

We found one of our biggest allies because of Twitter, the social media app now called X. I'd adopted a strategy of commenting on journalists' tweets, hoping that would lead to a connection somehow. It was truly a longshot strategy, and I was surprised to find a direct message one day from Jake Tapper, the CNN journalist, asking if we could talk about Trevor's case. When Jon and I gave him the details in a call a few days later, his response was simple: "What do you need me to do to get him out of there?" He interviewed me on CNN a short time later. After that, other journalists took more interest in our story and the networks began covering it.

Jake is an awesome human being. He started doing regular reports on Trevor, talking to us and to members of Congress. Texas congressman Michael McCaul, a prominent Republican and eventual chairman of the House Committee of Foreign Affairs, became an important ally as awareness built.

Whenever we spoke to the press, we made sure to mention that Trevor was only one of the many dozens of Americans held. I also constantly reminded people of Paul Whelan.

I think Paula was more effective at the television interviews than I was, but she hated doing them. My wife claimed to feel awkward and nervous every time she was in front of a camera. Sometimes she'd clam up, turn red, and maybe start to cry.

"I don't want to cry on television," she told Jon.

"You need to cry on television!" he replied. "They need to see Mommy!"

I was on television more than she was—Paula claims I'd love a second career as an actor—but it's Paula whom people recognized around town. That didn't just come from television. She had created and put up posters all around the community, referring people to our website and generally trying to make them aware of Trevor's plight. She even had bumper stickers made, which of course we put on our cars as well as those of our friends. We realized that effort had gone viral one day when she found a pickup with a bumper sticker she hadn't made. A man who'd started helping us pass the word to veterans' organizations had started designing and handing them out himself.

When she saw the sticker, she chased after the pickup, literally cornering the driver in a parking lot. The driver surely thought she was crazy, until she pointed out the sticker.

"See, there's this guy named Trevor Reed—" the man started.

"I'm his mother!" she burst out. "Thank you!"

The driver's wife turned out to be someone Paula had known back in grammar school. It's a small world.

Trevor called us the day before he was moved to the labor camp, letting us know he'd heard rumors that he was going to be moved very soon and that it was likely he'd be out of touch for a while. The embassy called SIZO the next day and found out he was moved, though Russian rules kept his destination secret, even from them. Finally we got a message from someone he'd met during his trip, letting us know he was okay and in Mordovia.

Eventually, he was able to communicate with us through the illegal system the mafya had, both with photos of his messages, which were in English, and then phone calls. I kept my phone charged and with me at all times.

He could be very demanding as well as terse. He'd communicate protests that he wanted filed. These weren't as easy to prepare as he seemed to think. We'd get an attorney to write them, and our interpreter to translate. They'd be notarized—there were hoops to jump through, ribbons of certain colors to be tied . . .

That last is a slight exaggeration, but time was always of the essence. And of course the complaints were often ignored.

Ambassador Sullivan stayed on despite the change in administrations. He had become an important advocate for us, and my now long-distance relationship with the embassy also improved.

Still, there were moments of friction with the embassy and the State Department. Probably the worst came a few weeks before I came home, when Trevor was still at SIZO. I heard rumors that the Russians were interested in exchanging Trevor and Paul Whelan, but that our government was against it.

I didn't know what was going on behind the scenes. We'd learn later that discussions about an exchange for Russian prisoners had happened even before Trevor was arrested—which probably explains why Trevor was targeted for prison: the Russians decided they needed another trading chip.

The Russians had suggested trading Whelan for Viktor Bout, a man the news media dubbed "the Merchant of Death" for his alleged role in delivering arms around the world. Bout had been convicted in 2011 of conspiring to kill Americans, helping terrorists, and illegally selling anti-aircraft missiles.

There had been exceptions, but official US policy for years was strongly against prisoner exchanges. Politics aside, they were thought to encourage hostage taking. There had, however, been a few trades over the years, most notably with Iran, where Jon Franks had first worked with former New Mexico governor Bill Richardson and Mickey Bergman of the Richardson Center for Global Engagement. Governor Richardson and Mickey, his righthand man, had been working to free Paul Whelan when Trevor was arrested, and became involved behind the scenes with Jonathan as the two imprisoned Marines became linked by the Russians in negotiations.

The political fallout of trading anyone for Bout was thought to be massive because of his crimes, and both the Trump administration and later the Biden administration flatly refused to include him in an exchange. But two other Russians were mentioned during informal talks: Konstantin Yaroshenko, a pilot, and Roman Seleznev, a hacker.

Yaroshenko was a Russian pilot who had been convicted of attempted drug smuggling after an overseas sting. He was in an American prison. While conditions there were hotel-like compared to what Trevor was going through, we heard that he was having trouble getting dental care.

Jon Franks and I floated the possibility of contacting his wife and making a joint statement pressuring our respective governments to care for our loved ones. Truth be told, she wasn't about to make a statement that could be interpreted as criticizing her government.

But our government didn't know that. So when we let it slip to State Department officials that this might happen, some feathers were ruffled. I got two angry emails from the embassy demanding that I contact them immediately. They were hot.

I delayed answering over the weekend.

Which of course made them more concerned.

When Monday came, I received a long email criticizing the plan and essentially stating that it had been Lina's doing. She of course knew nothing of the idea; State seemed always to blame or criticize her, having gone so far as to accuse her of working for the Russians. Ironically, she had been far more helpful to that point than they were.

I vented full blast.

We managed to patch things up, and as I said, a new official began to follow the case, or followed it more directly. In retrospect, I have a lot of praise for the embassy and State Department officials; without them, Trevor might never have been released.

In October, Paula, Taylor, Jon, and I went back to Washington and had meetings with members of the National Security Council, Department of Justice, different offices within the State Department, and Roger Carstens and the Special Presidential Envoy for Hostage Affairs staff.

One of the biggest common criticisms families of prisoners overseas had with the government was that it was difficult to get any information. I can't take any credit for this, but the complaint obviously registered with some members of the media, who began criticizing the Biden administration for not talking to us and others. Soon, Jake Sullivan, Biden's National Security Advisor, responded by holding a video call with many of the families of imprisoned Americans that December. He was extremely compassionate, even as we peppered him with questions:

What is being done to negotiate Trevor's release?

Is a trade being considered?

What level is it at?

He gave us a lot of answers, more than we'd had to that point. A trade was being considered; yes. Trevor and others were priorities. The president, he told us, was being kept informed. But as compassionate as Sullivan was, he could make no promises.

Trevor's isolation and physical condition worried us. And as the days went on, world events gave us a new fear. There were rumblings of increased conflict between Russia and Ukraine.

Russia had occupied Crimea and other areas of eastern Ukraine in 2014. The two nations and some separatists allied with Russia had fought continually since that time, though mostly in small engagements.

In late fall of 2021, Russia began massing troops on the border. Vladimir Putin's rhetoric escalated, and it became clear to me that there was going to be a full-scale invasion. It was also clear that the US and its allies would not respond passively as they had in the past. A war there would definitely hurt the chances of an exchange.

The video conference with National Security Advisor Jake Sullivan led to a personal meeting with him two weeks later, but Trevor remained in prison. It seemed like little progress was being made. If we didn't get him home before the war started, we might never see him again.

SIXTEEN

RUMORS

I wasn't back at IK-12 for too long before my coughing and ill health convinced me I had TB. The staff tested me, claiming I was negative. Not convinced, I told them they had to send me back.

When they refused, I used my only weapon: another hunger strike.

Alexander Nikolaevich was livid. This time, he was stubborn, determined not to give in.

I was determined, too. I also had an advantage: the sicker I got, the more pressure was on him.

It took six days before he was finally convinced to send me back to the hospital. By then, the embassy had been complaining and publicizing my condition.

The medical staff blamed my rib for the blood and the tuberculosis-like symptoms. They decided I didn't have TB. I have no idea how they arrived at that diagnosis. But it was surely convenient.

This visit felt different than the earlier ones, and not only because my cough was getting steadily worse. They didn't ship me right back to IK-12, leaving me instead in one of the wards. I could move around the barracks freely.

A day or two after getting there, I was outside in the hospital yard when I recognized Jimmy, the American musician I'd met during an earlier stay. I went over to say hello.

"Is it true?" he asked. "The rumor that we're getting out?"

"What rumor?"

"All American prisoners are going to be released," he said.

I must have looked doubtful, because all of the hope drained from his voice as he finished the sentence.

"I don't think so," I told him.

They weren't released. But whatever rumor he'd heard was based on at least a thin fact: the negotiations to free me had ramped up.

I wasn't involved in the negotiations, of course, and I only learned what was going on after the fact. My parents' campaign to raise awareness of my case had started slow under the Trump administration, despite the support of some important Republican federal legislators. Things dramatically improved under the Biden administration for several reasons. For one, my parents kept at it, getting publicity and gently but firmly prodding legislators for support. They had some very good advisers, especially Jon Franks.

Like previous American presidents, Joe Biden was extremely reluctant to trade wrongly convicted Americans for legitimate foreign criminals, fearing it would encourage other countries to take and hold our citizens. To this point, he had not made any trades to bring wrongly detained hostages home.

The few times American presidents had gone against this policy since the Iran Hostage Crisis in 1979–1980, there had generally been considerable backlash. But Biden had good political cover here. There was bipartisan support for bringing me home, so there would be less criticism from Congress. More important, his political base was far more sympathetic to such trades. The administration therefore had less to fear politically if it made a deal.

There was another factor, probably more important than any other: Biden himself.

Perhaps because he had lost a son, the president sympathized on a human level with the obvious distress of the parents and loved ones of wrongly detained prisoners. And I think when he finally started talking to my parents, he decided he would help them.

According to Mickey Bergman, the Russians had proposed a deal to trade Konstantin Yaroshenko for Paul Whelan under Trump, only to be rebuffed. Informal negotiations—more like suggestions by people outside both governments—had kept the possibility of some sort of trade alive after Biden took office. Roger Carstens, a former Special Forces lieutenant colonel, had been appointed by Trump as Special Presidential Envoy for Hostage Affairs during the last year of his term. He stayed on during the Biden administration, and became an important advocate for me and other wrongly detained prisoners.

The politics involved—globally and nationally—lined up in favor of a simple one-for-one swap. Both countries would get back a person they wanted. With Republicans in Congress already supporting my return, there would be little criticism nationally.

I don't know the exact play-by-play—there are different versions of what happened, as you'd expect, some with players I haven't mentioned, including the CIA. What I do know is, there was more truth to the rumors than I could have hoped.

The funny thing is, while all this was going on, I didn't see myself as valuable enough to be traded for someone. That only happened to really important people, like spies. So if I was going to get out, it would be more as an auxiliary piece to something larger.

•

Things happen in the gulag that make sense only in the gulag. A prisoner came into the hospital one Friday with scissors stuck in his gut. Because it was Friday, the medical staff told him he'd have to wait until Monday for surgery to remove them.

The scissors looked to be incredibly deep, and yet not life-threatening. He walked around with them poking out of his belly for three days.

He and I ended up not getting along. He bragged about not liking America. I was doing my business at a urinal once when he came up behind me and claimed he could kick my ass.

I growled something in response and he ran off. He never seemed to find the courage to confront me to my face, or when there wasn't more important business to attend to.

The Russian propaganda machine went into overdrive on February 24, 2022, when Russia invaded Ukraine. Many of the reports I saw on television were clearly fake. The hyperbole about Russian advances was comical. Newscasters would claim Russia had wiped out the Ukrainian air force in one day, then talk about shooting down a hundred planes the next.

Occasionally I would point out some of the illogic. A few guys would understand what I was talking about, but mostly they'd make excuses to believe, or at least pretend to believe. It was the oddest thing: They were victims of a system that lied constantly. They recognized and called out those lies. And yet, they couldn't accept that the government was lying to them about Ukraine, let alone the US and NATO. Ukraine had somehow threatened Russia, and had to be neutralized.

It became clear very quickly that the war was not going well for

Russia. Even the constant propaganda couldn't hide the fact that the country was taking sizeable casualties.

Not that long after the war started, prisoners were recruited to join the Wagner Group, a private contractor used as a military force in Ukraine. I later learned that Wagner had recruited several prisoners from IK-12, including two I knew well.

Neither came home alive.

One day at dinner in the barracks, one of the prisoners mentioned that the government had decided to give prisoners a chance for clemency if they volunteered to fight.

"If Russia gives you a rifle," he asked, "will you go?"

"Absolutely."

The others stared at me. I'd been arguing with them about the war, which they seemed to support.

"For us?" he asked.

"It's better not to ask me that."

An Uzbek prisoner smiled at me after they left. "These idiots. If they gave you a rifle, the first ones you would kill would be these guards. I can see it in your eyes."

SEVENTEEN

DESPERATE MEASURES

Back home, my parents knew things were happening, but didn't know of the specifics. My father found his patience running thin:

Christmas came and went. The new year dawned and still Trevor remained in prison. We began to hear reports that Russia might invade Ukraine.

In late February we received a call from Jon and Mickey Bergman. Mickey informed us that he and Governor Richardson were flying to Moscow via FedEx CEO Fred Smith's personal aircraft, loaned to them for their mission. They planned to visit Foreign Minister Sergey Lavrov. Trevor would be a topic of discussion, though they could not negotiate directly as representatives of the US.

They arrived on February 23. After meeting with Lavrov, they were directed to a wealthy friend of Putin's. They met with that individual, but then hastily flew home as Russia launched its invasion of Ukraine. Mickey called us a day or so later to let us know that they were waiting to hear if Putin would agree to an exchange of Trevor for Yaroshenko. Soon after, he called to let us know Putin would agree, and that they had notified the White House. But they couldn't get past the National Security staff. Even though Governor Richardson had known Joe Biden for decades, he was not put through to the president. But the White House was informed of the deal—and also became aware that we knew about the offer.

In late February or early March, we heard that the president was coming to visit the Fort Worth VA Hospital. After administration staff turned down our requests for a meeting, we decided to take our plea directly to him, staking out his motorcade with signs asking for Trevor's release.

Of course, we'd make sure the media knew what we were doing. If he didn't see us or our signs, he would see the news reports about them.

Advance details about the president's visit were skimpy. We realized there were only two paths into the facility he could take. I went to one; Taylor went to the other. About an hour after I arrived—Biden was still hours away—Taylor called and told me that the Secret Service had just searched her car.

Hmmmm . . .

Another hour passed. Her mom had just arrived, rendezvousing with Taylor. Her car had been searched, as had Taylor's a second time.

That did it. I packed up and drove over to them, followed by a small pack of reporters.

Meanwhile, a group of protestors began raising a ruckus just as Paula was about to give a TV interview.

"Trump, Trump, Trump!" they chanted.

"Oh hell no," said Taylor, beelining to confront them.

"I'm asking you to please not do this right now!" she told them. "My brother's in a Russian prison."

That didn't make an impression. The protestors marched on toward Paula.

Taylor stopped in front of the group and waved them to a stop.

"Stop! Back the fuck up!"

One of the men unfroze himself and went over to her. "What did you say?" he demanded, towering over her.

My daughter told him succinctly what was going on. "We need the president's help," she added, "and my mom's about to be interviewed."

The man told the others to move back around the building, listening respectfully as she explained what was going on with Trevor. Paula's interview went off without an interruption.

More time passed. Finally, the president's limo drove by.

He pointed at us.

Paula waved like crazy. The reporters got their footage.

We figured we'd wave again on his way out, but Biden did us one better.

Paula pulled up her phone as it started to ring. The caller ID said she was getting a call from the "Situation Room."

Huh?

She answered.

"Paula?"

"Yes?"

"This is Joe Biden. Was that you I saw standing out there on my way in?"

"Yes, Mr. President."

He said, "Oh, please call me Joe," and then he asked us how we were doing. He said he was being kept informed of our son's situation. The president, a Catholic, said that he and Jill kept Trevor in their prayers every day. Just that morning he had said a rosary for Trevor before getting on the plane.

We were all crying at that point.

The president said that he wouldn't be able to stop on the way out because he was running late, but promised his staff would set up a meeting.

"I've got to go over to Europe," Biden told us before hanging up. "I'm trying to stop that SOB Putin from starting World War III."

A few weeks passed without the White House setting up that meeting. Those days went slowly. Paula fretted about everything Trevor was missing—small things like birthday parties, big things like his education, and starting a family. The delays added up to a life stolen, possibilities turned to ash.

It wasn't the president's fault. But couldn't he move faster? When was our meeting going to take place?

Was there going to be a meeting at all?

Finally we decided to take matters into our own hands. Paula, Jon, and I went to Washington, intending to demonstrate outside the White House to remind the president of his promise to meet with us.

My plans were simple: I wasn't going home until we had that meeting. I would chain myself to the fence in protest if we were ignored. A chain, a lock, and several dozen news crews. That would do the trick. From five thirty a.m. till about noon we held up banners outside the West Wing and had news interviews and a press conference in front of the White House.

It happened that the president was getting vaccinated against COVID that day, and had invited the press along as part of his campaign to increase awareness of the vaccine. CNN journalist Kaitlan Collins, there to cover the vaccination, asked the president if he was meeting with us, since we were in town and, not to mention, had been interviewed by CNN and others earlier in the day.

"They're good people," he answered. "We're working on it."

The White House called us around three thirty, telling us the president would meet with us in the Oval Office at six.

We were escorted to the Oval Office with Jon and Alexandra Miller, a member of the National Security Council with special expertise in hostage issues as well as intelligence. After meeting the president and Deputy National Security Advisor Jon Finer, Biden explained what he knew about the situation and how negotiations had been going. He promised to have Finer get back to us in thirty days. We told the president that we knew about the deal proposed by Governor Richardson and Mickey Bergman. We spent some time talking about Trevor: his personality, his service as a presidential guard, and what he had been going through in Russia. Biden was impressed with Trevor's defiance, his refusal to work for the Russians, and his insistent silence about his military activities.

We emphasized his declining health. And I have to confess that I cried when telling the president about letters we'd gotten from Marines he'd served with relating how Trevor had helped them through tough times.

The meeting lasted forty-five minutes. Besides pledging to do everything he could to get Trevor back, the president shared some photos of his family, children and grandchildren, and spoke briefly of the loss of his son. By the end of our meeting, he wasn't talking as president; he was speaking as a father. He then directed Finer to get back to us in fourteen days, not thirty.

We came away from that meeting more hopeful than ever that Trevor would be coming home, even though we didn't know when.

EIGHTEEN

DO YOU FEEL COOL?

All of this political maneuvering was going on while I coughed up blood at the so-called hospital in the bowels of the Russian gulag. I had no idea how far along the negotiations were, and little hope that I was going home or being exchanged.

I was sinking. I'd lost a lot of weight, and just walking began to feel like a struggle.

I wasn't giving up. I did think a bit about my death. There would be some bitter consolation in it. It would embarrass the Russians internationally, though at that point I don't know how much lower world opinion of them could go.

More important, it would tell the bastards that Americans couldn't be broken. At least not this one.

A day or two after seeing Jimmy, I was called into an office and handed a document to fill out. It looked to me like a standard form they gave to prisoners who were going to be paroled. It had questions like *What job are you going to take when you get out? Where will you live?*

I had a little fun answering. I thought the whole thing was ridiculous, and not just because I didn't think they were going to release me.

I came to a form telling me that after I was released from prison, I wouldn't be able to visit Russia for the next several years.

Not sure why they'd think that would be a big deal.

The guard walking me back to my room asked me if I was going somewhere.

"Not that I know," I told him. "Why?"

"We don't have people fill out that paperwork unless they're about to be released. So I think you're getting released."

I'd already experienced my share of lies in Russian prisons. I thought the papers and the guard's comments were part of a psychological game to mess with me, for what I didn't know. But the next day, I was called to the administration office.

Alexander Nikolaevich, the warden from my prison, was there, along with the FSB curator.

"Ah Trevor," said the warden. "Come on in."

He wasn't just being nice; he was being ridiculously nice. Like I was his nephew and he was there to give me a special Christmas present.

"Take a seat," he told me.

I sat at the desk. A pile of papers sat in the middle.

"I have some excellent news," Alexander Nikolaevich told me. "President Putin has decided to pardon you."

Right, I thought. *Like they're going to pardon their critic.*

"I don't need a pardon," I told them. "I didn't do anything."

Their smiles flattened a little. The curator spoke some. The president—*the president! President Putin!!*—was going to pardon me, and I should be insanely happy, genuflect, and sign their damn paper.

I declined.

They were disappointed. Very.

I'd spoken with my parents maybe two weeks before on one of the mafya cell phones, so I knew they'd met with President Biden. They'd been very hopeful. But they were always hopeful, always optimistic, trying to keep my spirits up. I didn't think this was related to an exchange. Instead, I thought it was a trick. The Russians were going to video me signing, and broadcast that I'd admitted doing wrong, then charge me with something else to hold me longer.

But . . . maybe . . .

No, I couldn't afford to hope.

I looked over the form. I spoke Russian fluently by then, but there was one word I didn't understand.

I pointed it out to the warden. "What does this mean?"

"Oh, it means that we're going to pardon you."

"No, *this* word."

"You are requesting a pardon so that we can release you."

"Don't bullshit me." I took a guess. "Does this word mean 'regret'?"

"Yes."

"So this—" I pointed to the end of the document. "Does this say that I regret my crimes and I promise not to commit further crimes in the territory of the Russian Federation?"

"Yes."

I drew a line through the form.

"Why are you doing that!" Alexander Nikolaevich practically screeched.

"This says that I regret committing a crime, and the only thing I regret is that I came to Russia."

"There was a crime!"

"There was a crime that the FSB fabricated and framed me for," I told him. "I'm not going to admit to committing a crime that I didn't commit."

His face fell. "Trevor, don't you want to go home?"

I went back to my room without signing, still thinking it was an elaborate trick. A while later, I was taken back to the administrative offices, where one of the hospital's intelligence officers gave me a piece of paper with a phone number.

"Go back to the barracks and call this number. It's your embassy."

Maybe . . .

At that point I started thinking it might be real. Because this was really elaborate, far more involved than anything the Russians ordinarily did, even to me.

I called and got one of the embassy people who'd been tracking my case.

"Did the Russians try to get you to sign something?" he asked.

"Yes."

"Did you sign it?"

"Nah."

"Why?"

I explained. He didn't try to talk me into signing, nor did he say that I would definitely be released if I did, but he did steer hard in that direction.

"You won't be disappointed if you sign it," he told me.

I figured, I better sign. So I did.

The ambassador checked on me some time later, worried that I hadn't signed the paper, prepared to convince me that it was the right thing to do.

I told him I already had.

Sometime later, a prisoner told me I was getting transferred to Moscow in two days.

I told him that wasn't likely. But the information turned out to be correct. It had probably come from a prisoner with some sort of task that brought him into the administration offices where he saw paperwork or overheard a conversation about me. The next day, the guards came to my cell and told me to get my stuff.

"You're leaving on a convoy," one of them told me.

They searched me, then had me take my stuff to an office where my personal items from IK-12 were waiting.

Some of them. My clothes and most of the rest had been stolen. My Nikes were gone; ditto my jacket. Surprisingly, they'd left me my court clothes—my dress shirt and duct-taped pants, which by now were way too big thanks to the weight I'd lost.

I was given a paper to sign attesting that I had received my belongings.

"I'm not signing this. You guys stole all my stuff."

They hadn't stolen my books. But that was a different problem. I couldn't possibly carry all of them. So I donated them to the prison library. I sometimes wonder what prisoners will think of the parallels between Orwell's *1984* and the system that's imprisoned them.

The warden of the hospital prison came over and asked if I wanted to go on a trip.

"It depends on where it is," I told him.

"How about home?"

I didn't say anything, but he must have detected a faint smile. He nodded at me, as if silently admitting how badly I'd been abused, how evil his government had been, how horrible their conditions were.

Probably not. He certainly couldn't actually say any of that, and I doubt he could have admitted it, even to himself. It's difficult to acknowledge hypocrisy and evil when you depend on it for your daily bread.

The warden asked if I wanted to smoke and gave me a cigarette. I took it and lit up, even though I don't smoke. I figured they might be taking me to kill me, so why not.

●

There was some logic to my fears that I was being set up. Everything I'd experienced showed that the Russians couldn't be trusted. The timing for an exchange was terrible, given the war. In fact, if anything, I thought it would have made more sense if the Russians used me to send a message to the US and the world: they'd agree to an exchange, then kill me, demonstrating how ruthless they could be if the West didn't stop helping Ukraine.

Two vehicles waited for me outside, both with armed guards. I got in the second—I was the only prisoner being transported—and we began the seven- or eight-hour drive to Moscow.

About halfway there we stopped to refuel at another prison. They took me out and put me in a cell to wait. Once more I became deeply paranoid, fearing they would just kill me there. I didn't eat the food, or even drink anything, worrying that I'd be poisoned.

My paranoia increased as I was walked out to the van. There were windows at the top of the vehicle, too high to see out of, though I strained to get glimpses of something more than tree branches or the tops of buildings. I had no idea where we were. Then I heard someone in the front say something that included the word "Lefortovo."

Damn.

I wasn't going to an airport, let alone home. They were taking me to another prison in Moscow. A very notorious one.

Lefortovo was constructed in 1881; during the Soviet Union, it was a place for mass executions. Aleksandr Solzhenitsyn was also kept there at one point during the Cold War. In more recent times, it has housed high-level prisoners, including Paul Whelan and, after me, *Wall Street Journal* reporter Evan Gershkovich.

They gave me a medical exam when I arrived, standard protocol, then put me in a cell. A guard came and brought me to a shower. I was in for ten minutes—a comparative luxury—all the time expecting that they'd come in and kick the crap out of me. But nothing happened. I went back to my cell and slept.

Normally in prison, you see other prisoners in the hallway. You'll exchange a few words of camaraderie. Voices will rise above whatever mechanical din vibrates against the walls. Even if you can't see anyone, you can hear them. You sense you're not alone.

Here, everything was stone quiet, even the walls.

The cell was small. It had a TV, but either it didn't work or I was just too baffled by its controls to figure how to get it on. The furnishings were sparse: cot, metal sink, toilet. A pair of cameras were angled to capture most of the space, monitoring my every breath. They gave me a bar of soap, a toothbrush, and toothpaste. No paper, no pencils, no pens. I'd taken one book with me—a novel about a shipwreck—and after a bit of argument the guards let me keep it.

I managed to pull myself up on the bars and look out the window. All I could see was the side of a factory building in the distance, not even sky.

Food came. It was better than I expected. Way better. So much better, it freaked me out. I thought surely the quality meant it was intended as my last meal on earth.

A guard came, and told me it was time for my walk.

I told him I wasn't going.

"You have to."

"No, I don't." I quoted him the prison regulations that said I *could* go for a walk, but that I wasn't required to.

"If you don't go on your own, I'm going to make you."

"I hope you have some friends out there because you're not going to be able to do it by yourself."

He stormed off, but returned a short while later with the warden.

"According to the law, you don't have to go on a walk," the warden agreed. "But we do make everyone go on a walk here. So, can you just go? You don't have to actually walk or anything."

That's Russia, where the form of things is always more important than the substance, and where there is an art to following rules without actually following them.

I did want to walk. I didn't want to give in. So I played the game myself, telling him that the law allowed me two hours to walk, since I'd been convicted. And that's what I should get.

"Fine," he said.

I was taken upstairs to an empty concrete room on the roof covered by sheet metal. I walked a little bit, sat down, walked some more, until finally the guard came back to take me down.

Rather than going back to the cell, we went to a medical office for some blood draws. My paranoia returned. Once more I thought I was going to be poisoned, this time by injection.

The doctors wouldn't talk to me. The nurses wouldn't say why I was being tested. I let them take my blood, then was led back to the cell.

The lights at the prison are on 24/7, so the only way I could get some sleep was to put my shirt over my face.

I was there for three or four days, alone except for the guards who took me to walk or brought food. Then one came and led me to an office, where I was handed a phone. The ambassador was on the other end.

"How are you?" he asked.

"Oh, I'm doing just fine here at Lefortovo prison," I said, carefully naming the prison so he would know if something was off.

"Everything is ready on our side," he told me. "You should be leaving tomorrow, so get ready."

I had a ton of questions, but with all the guards standing around, and the line undoubtedly tapped, I kept them to myself.

Maybe now, I could hope?

No. No weakness . . .

But . . .

No.

The next morning, I got up early, waiting, waiting, waiting.

Breakfast.

Nothing happened.

Would it?

Did I talk to the ambassador or imagine it?

No, it was real.

But . . .

Finally, guards came and told me to get my things.

An FSB team, fully outfitted in combat gear, led me out of prison. My pants hung down against my hips, the waistband looped into place thanks to tape. Instead of shoes, since they'd been stolen, I wore furry Ugg knockoffs, more slipper than boot. They'd been my winter prison boots.

On the way out, the warden walked over to me.

"You're going home to America," he said kindly. "Have a nice trip."

Goodbye, I told him, using the Russian term that literally means *until our next meeting*.

"I hope not." He laughed.

I didn't.

You might be surprised, I thought to myself.

They brought up a van. I sat between two guys in the middle of the bench seat. Our vehicle was wedged between two others. The actions and routine reminded me quite a bit of our convoys in Afghanistan. My escorts were tight, well-trained, and equipped much like Western forces might be: fire-resistant outer garments, war belts with Glock pistols, some baseball caps. I asked one of the guys next to me if his uniform was made by Crye Precision, a well-known and generally revered American military clothing and gear brand.

He nodded.

"But is it?" I asked, knowing from prison that it was common for the Russians to counterfeit Western goods.

He showed me the tag. Legit.

So were their Glocks.

"Where are we going?" I asked.

"We're going to the airport," he said. "What were you in for?"

"Assault on police officers with a threat to their life."

"Oh."

"I didn't do it. I didn't assault anyone."

"Humph." He nodded. Probably he believed me, though I couldn't be sure. "Were you in the military?"

"I was in the Marines."

"Oh. They wanted some information from you."

"Something like that."

"What did you do in the military?"

"I'm not going to talk about that."

"Hey, no, no, nothing like that," he said. "Just curiosity."

Maybe.

These guys were members of FSB's Alpha Group, a tactical special ops unit trained for high-value, high-risk missions. I guess I should have felt flattered that I was important enough to be guarded by the elite. Instead, I was feeling unsure, paranoia mixing with hope.

Did they really not know who I was, what my background was? If so, why?

It shouldn't take this many people to guard me. Then again, it shouldn't take this many people to kill me, either.

The convoy stopped at the secure entrance to Moscow's Vnukovo airport. A guard slowly walked up to the van to request papers. The driver said they were Alpha Group, and the guard hopped to, racing to open the gate for them.

We sped to a hangar on the military side of the large airport. There we waited, apparently having arrived slightly ahead of schedule.

One of my escorts got out and went inside, returning with an armful of coffees. I hesitated when he offered me one.

He laughed, took a sip himself to prove he wasn't poisoning me, then handed over the cup.

I didn't drink it. Probably it was safe, I thought, but there was no telling at this point what lengths they might go to, and why take a chance?

A parade of officials, some in dress uniforms, some in camo, arrived. All for me. Maybe I *was* a big deal.

They chitchatted among themselves. I wanted to get the hell out of there.

A camera crew came up. I was taken from the vehicle—harshly, except not really. The guy who'd grabbed me was acting, trying to make it look like he was being mean, like he was handling a hardened criminal, but his grip was actually loose, gentle. He wasn't really an SOB, at least not at that moment; it was just pretend.

Very Russian.

My bag felt so heavy and my body so weak that my pace began to drag. My escorts realized it and slowed down. The man next to me angled his arm and body, making it look to the camera as if he were muscling me into place. In reality, he was helping me along. He guided me to the portable stairs that had been rolled against the jet, then helped again as I stumbled upward and into the plane, an An-148. Roughly similar to a Western regional jet like an Embraer E175, the Russian aircraft was outfitted exactly like a Western airliner, with a business and regular cabin section.

I was put in coach.

There were already twenty guys up front in business class, all wearing suits. Apparently they were FSB VIPs. A pair of stewardesses circulated through the cabin. Studying them, I realized I had seen them in the hangar, dressed in camo like the four guards sitting around me. They had changed for the flight.

Stewardesses equally qualified to offer you a pillow or kill you at thirty thousand feet.

After we took off, I tried working out where we might be going. The plane was too small to make it to the US without refueling. I suspected most of Europe would be blocked off to the flight, and we certainly wouldn't fly over Ukraine. Eventually I was able to look out a window and catch a glimpse of water below. I figured that might be the Black Sea. From that I guessed we were going to Turkey.

"Where are we going?" I asked the guard who seemed to be in charge of my detail. "Turkey?"

He glanced toward the curtain that had been drawn across the seats ahead, isolating us from the VIPs. Sure that they weren't paying attention, he held up a computer tablet that was tracking our position in real time on a map.

We *were* going to Turkey.

Assuming we made it. The plane looked like it had been around for decades, and it bounced like an old jalopy on a washboard road. Even if they weren't planning on killing me, the damn thing could easily fall out of the sky. I'd never been afraid of flying before that day, but that trip changed me; I'm scared of airplanes to this day.

Maybe it was the plane, or maybe something about not being in control, understandable after all those years of having no control in prison.

We started circling. And circling. Then some more, maybe waiting for clearance. Finally we touched down, trundling across the airport to a taxiway lined with security vans. Men decked out in dark suits and glasses stood near the trucks, brandishing rifles and looking like the guys in the *Men in Black* movies.

All right, let's go. Get me off this plane.

We came to a stop. A van drove up to us.

Just give me my airline ticket. I'll walk to the terminal.

The van zoomed away.

"Was that the State Department?" I asked the Russian team leader.

"No."

Some time passed. Another van came up, idled, then took off.

And again.

I'm just going to ask if I could walk to the airport and go on my own.

"How do you know this isn't the State Department?" I asked when another van approached and he made no sign of moving me.

"We are waiting on a jet," he said.

"Another jet?"

"Yes."

"For what?"

He sighed as if I had asked the dumbest question possible.

"We have a man on it," he told me. "The jet will park next to us. Our man and you will leave the jets at the same time. You will walk past each other on the runway and you will both get in your own jets."

"Are you kidding me?"

"No. I'm not kidding." He smiled. "It's pretty cool, huh?"

Uh . . .

"Do you feel cool?" he added.

"No."

"Well, you should. They don't fly us on these jets."

The whole idea sounded foreign, something snatched out of a movie like *Bridge of Spies.* And still I didn't believe I was particularly valuable, certainly not enough to be involved in some sort of espionage prisoner exchange.

"Is there another American being exchanged?" I asked, thinking of Paul Whelan.

"I don't know but I think you are the only one."

I was disappointed. If anyone was deserving of an exchange like this, it was Paul.

How much time passed after that, I have no idea. It seemed like a really long time. Finally, a Gulfstream crossed over the tarmac and came to a stop nearby. I pressed my head against the window, watching as a pretty jacked dude came down the stairs and began walking toward us. Honestly, I would not have been shocked if he'd pulled some martial arts moves and carried me out single-handedly, leaving a plane full of dead Russians in our wake.

Things went a lot more prosaically than that.

The FSB guys stood me up, holding on to me like they were holding a hostage—they probably got the same vibes I had.

"My name is Roger Carstens. I'm here to identify you."

"It's me," I said.

He turned around and walked back off the plane. Without me.

Damn. He didn't recognize me.

Quick—what was my isolation prep number in the Marines?

Needless to say, I couldn't remember that—it's a code number that is used during extractions from hostile territory.

My tongue was frozen, my brain fried. I couldn't even have remembered my phone number at that point.

I fell into despair. The Russians started talking among themselves.

"Are you sure America wants you back?" the Russian team leader asked me.

Within a few minutes, another American came on board. He told me he was a flight nurse, and after looking me over quickly, told me I could come with him.

I followed him down the aisle to the door. One of the guys on the plane held me back a moment, checking across the tarmac to see what was happening at the Gulfstream. Then he moved back, and I was walking down the steps, walking down from three years of detention, mental torture, and physical deprivation.

Across the tarmac, Konstantin Yaroshenko was walking with his own escort.

I knew who he was from Russian propaganda. I saw him stop to chat with some FSB guys on the tarmac. He didn't look like he'd missed many meals while he was in custody.

Everyone in the Gulfstream wore masks. The flight nurse took me to the back. Large sheets of plastic had been installed to form a containment area, a kind of bio bubble where I was to sit on a bench seat.

"Lay down and strap yourself in," the nurse told me, zipping the capsule closed.

At some point during my captivity, Russian prisoners had told me that I'd be tortured by the CIA when I finally was released. My government, they thought, would want to know if I'd betrayed the US, and would go to any lengths to find out.

I knew that was absurd, but it was hard not to think of those conversations as I lay down.

We took off. When we reached altitude, the flight nurse came back wearing a CBRN Hazmat Suit designed to protect him from radiation and other threats.

A decade and a half before, Alexander Litvinenko had been poisoned with what was believed to be polonium-210, a rare and highly radioactive element. Litvinenko was a critic of the Putin regime who'd defected to the West after working for the FSB. There were other stories about the Russians using radioactive elements to kill people. It occurred to me that I, too, might have been targeted.

"You think the Russians poisoned me?" I asked.

"No, no, no, this is for the TB," said the nurse.

"TB? You think I have tuberculosis?"

"Yeah."

He took my blood, swabbed my mouth and nose.

"You were in the military?" he asked.

"I was a Marine. And then I was a contractor."

"Where?"

"Afghanistan."

"No kidding. I was a contractor there, too."

Carstens and another State Department official, Fletcher Schoen, came back to talk to me. Fletcher had been in the 75th Ranger Regiment and had headed my case at State, along with Steve Gillen, who wasn't on the jet. They offered to let me talk to my parents. When the video call went through, I found out they were on the phone with President Biden, who was telling them I was on my way back.

The president graciously told them he was going to hang up, because he was sure they'd much rather talk to me than him.

I was served steak and a baked potato on the plane. My dad had told someone I was interested in the new mid-engined Corvette, which had just debuted, so they gave me a few magazines that had stories about the car.

We stopped to refuel in Iceland. Someone asked if I needed anything.

"Y'all don't happen to have any Copenhagen Wintergreen do you?" I said.

The pilot had some chew, but it wasn't Copenhagen.

"You think you can handle Grizzly?" I was asked.

I did.

"We aren't supposed to give this to you . . ."

They did anyway.

It felt like the first time I'd ever had tobacco.

The rest of the flight was uneventful. I tried reading, but I just wasn't in the mood. Mostly I spent the flight sitting and thinking. I prayed the plane didn't crash before I could see my family, and I wondered if this whole thing was actually happening. I was numb and full of adrenaline.

I wanted to get home. I wanted to get my strength back. And I wanted to plan out exactly what I was going to do next. Because I was getting the bastards back.

I just didn't know the details yet.

PART TWO

TRAINING UP

NINETEEN

HOMECOMING

My parents knew but didn't know. I imagine they went through as many contortions of hope and near hope as I did. There were rumors and back-channel communications galore in the weeks before I was actually returned. For my parents, though, I think things became really real on Easter weekend.

You'll notice our memories are slightly different. You can choose whose details to believe—I don't think either one of us thinks we're wrong.

My dad:

We were hopeful after we met with the president, but it takes two sides to make a deal, and we only had assurances from one side. But less than two weeks later, President Biden called Paula again, this time from Camp David, telling us he was thinking about us and they were working on something.

We didn't know how imminent "something" was until a few days later when I got a tip from someone to make sure I had my phone always charged and with me. I talked to Jon Franks soon afterward. He realized the transfer must already be underway. While he headed to our home several states away, we got a phone call from Roger Carstens, Special Presidential Envoy for Hostage Affairs, who was on board the plane with Trevor.

"I have someone who wants to talk to you."

It was the best call we'd ever had . . . interrupted by a call from the president, telling us that Trevor was released.

"We're talking to him right now," Paula told him, looking at me on the line with Trevor.

"Well, you'd rather talk to him than me. Congratulations and I look forward to seeing you and your son. I can't imagine how you must feel right now."

The representatives from the Defense and State Departments came to our house and the press arrived soon afterward. We did some interviews and a press conference, then left with Jon for Brooke Meade Army Medical Center in San Antonio, where Congressman Pfluger had found Trevor was being taken. It would usually take four hours by car to get there; I'm sure I cut the travel time significantly.

We were given all sorts of instructions on what we could and couldn't do, how close we could get, etc. They were still very worried about TB.

I wasn't.

"You know how many times I've come in contact with tuberculosis during my career as a first responder?" I remember saying to some official. "Plenty." I offered to wear a Class C Hazmat suit if necessary; I was not being kept from my son.

Nor was Paula. We plotted out a diversion so she could go and hug him.

In the end, it all got smoothed over and went well. Trevor looked exhausted and a little in shock. He was very thin, face sunken in with dark circles under his eyes. We had tears of joy, introductions, and a few photos. We did keep a reasonable distance of ten feet, saving the hugs and kisses for twenty-four hours later, when the doctors had done enough tests to be reasonably sure Trevor didn't have TB.

We stayed in visitors' quarters on the base while the medical people looked Trevor over. Adjusting to the outside world took him a few days. His apprehension was obvious the first time we went to a mall on the base. He had a tension about him that hadn't been there before. It would remain in place for quite a while.

TWENTY

LIFE AS A FREE MAN

I wasn't prepared physically or mentally for life as a free man.

It took several days before my body adjusted to normal amounts of food. Adrenaline kept me awake for three days straight. In fact, for months I was only able to sleep three or four hours a night. I often woke up thinking I was still in prison. Freedom was a dream I kept trying to wake up from.

The days were a rush of confusion, smiles, and other people's tears. There were batteries of tests those first few days at the Army's Post Isolation Support Activities program in San Antonio where I'd been taken to recover. High-level specialists checked me over. I didn't have TB. It turned out that, except for having lost an enormous amount of weight and strength, I was in decent shape physically.

They did some psychological assessments. Eventually I was asked how I had managed to survive mentally.

"I tried to not have any hope," I told the psychologists. "I knew that if I had hope, the Russians could take that away from me. And so I tried to deny myself having that so that I couldn't lose it."

My main "trick" was to focus on getting through each day. I would not think about my family or home until right before bed. It was a treat, dessert.

The other thing that had helped was hatred. I hated the government that had put me in the gulag. I took that anger and used it as best I could against their system. I'd studied their laws and cited them in protests. I'd refused to work. I'd made resistance my job.

That was all missing now. In its place was a desire to pay them back.

The war in Ukraine was the perfect opportunity to do that. They needed volunteers to fight the Russians. Volunteers who were trained in the art of war.

Like me.

There were some funny things those first weeks back.

I was worried about my teeth, given that I hadn't seen a dentist in three years. The man who came to examine me was pretty personable, and we got to talking. He confessed that, while he had gone to dental school, he hadn't practiced in like nine years.

"What do you do?" I asked.

"I'm a brain surgeon."

Among the psychologists and psychiatrists I saw was a psychologist who told me the last returnee he'd worked with was Bowe Bergdahl, the Army soldier captured by the Taliban and later court-martialed for desertion.

"Obviously, your case is different."

"I hope so," I said, trying to inject some humor.

The medical team was concerned about my mental state. I think I was pretty stable, and maybe that threw them.

"Have you recently had thoughts of suicide?" asked a nurse the first time we met.

"No."

"Have you been having any homicidal thoughts?"

"If you mean do I want to go kill the Russians who did this to me, I do. But I don't want to kill any Americans."

"That works."

A nutritionist worked up a meal plan to get my weight back up. I could choose from a wide variety of foods, but mostly ended up with steak: the nurses would ask me what I wanted for dinner, I'd tell them to surprise me, and inevitably they would order steak.

The physical therapist asked what my goals were; I told her I wanted to do a 300 PFT in three months.

"Doable," she said. "If you're extremely dedicated."

"I am."

For those of you who haven't been in the Marine Corps, PFT stands for "physical fitness test." A 300 PFT would represent a perfect score on that test.

Four or five years before, getting a 300 would have been child's play for me, and most likely every other Marine in the Presidential Guard.

Now it was just an ambition. To get a 300 PFT, a twenty-year-old recruit must do twenty pull-ups, one hundred crunches, and run three miles in eighteen minutes. (The requirements vary slightly by age.) Mercifully, we won't estimate here what my first scores in those categories would have been when we started rehab. The rehab specialist started me out with bands to get my muscles working again. She soon had me advancing. As I gained weight, I gained strength quickly. But full disclosure: I never did quite make the running time.

●

I was only in the hospital for three or four days before moving to a general's suite in nearby apartments at the base.

At least, it seemed like a general's suite, or a mansion even, after my cells in Russia. My visits with my family grew longer.

My father and I were alone one day when I decided to tell him that I was going back to fight the Russians in Ukraine. It wasn't so much a decision as an imperative: I needed to set things right, and the only way I could do that was by standing up to the bastards.

Call it "retribution" or "revenge." "Justice" might be a better word.

"A search for wholeness" would be an even better description.

He became quiet. I can only imagine the anger and disbelief that boiled inside him.

I tried to explain my need for revenge. The Russians had stolen nearly three years of my life. I was going to make them pay.

I'm sure that equation didn't make any sense to him. Neither did the knowledge that I'd be in a position to expose Russia's lies and propaganda, having experienced them firsthand.

Most people looking at me in that moment—underweight, undernourished, pale—probably would have thought it highly unlikely that I would be going to fight anywhere ever. But my father knew me very well, and he undoubtedly was sure I would go.

What he couldn't know or understand was why.

In a lot of ways, it was just a continuation of my life: not revenge so much as simply resistance. For the past three years, all of my energy had been focused on fighting my war against Russia. They released me, but my fight carried on. Resistance wasn't a hobby. It wasn't even a belief: it was everything.

It was part of me as a person. It had become my only reason to live.

When I came home, it was as a soldier still fighting a war. You can't turn off purpose by flicking a switch, or stepping off an airplane.

Until I could satisfy that purpose, I had no other. I was nothing, except mad anger.

I think my dad realized that, standing alone with me in the room. And it must have hurt him most of all.

I spent about two and a half weeks in "reintegration" after the hospital. I gradually got used to being with people in crowds. This was very awkward, even unsettling, at first. I'd go to a mall and pretend I wasn't freaking out. But I got better relatively quickly.

We went to Florida courtesy of CNN and Jake Tapper to do some media interviews, then home to Texas.

If my life were a Hollywood movie, the next scene would be a tearful reunion with Lina, followed by a big church wedding and a ride into the sunset.

But no life is a Hollywood movie, especially not mine.

I can't measure the depth of my gratitude toward Lina. I've barely scraped the surface here of all the things she did for me, how she was my soul itself, keeping me alive throughout the ordeal in court and in prison. Words only go so far to describe feelings; they can't replicate the electricity of touch, the jolting warmness of hugs, the reassurance of a whisper.

And yet, our relationship fell apart.

There was no climactic moment. We were passionate yet logical at the same time. We both realized that we would not have a future together.

Things came to a head when she delayed applying for her visa to come to the US. I asked why; she had no good answer. I think I'm sure she already knew that the romantic phase of our relationship was over, a realization I only came to belatedly.

We were now more like soldiers who'd been through a battle together than lovers. We shared a deep bond, but that bond no longer included romance.

Lina pointed out, correctly, that I had changed. In her eyes, I became more hardened, possibly more distant. My imprisonment certainly had a lot to do with that, but so did my need for revenge. At the same time, there were practical considerations. She didn't want to live in the US, and I didn't want to live in Europe or elsewhere.

She couldn't stay in Russia. Even before I was released, it became obvious that the FSB was watching her. She left the country for her own safety, abandoning her mother and family. Today she lives on her own, far from her homeland, an exile.

She's doing fine today. We still have a good, platonic relationship, though we don't talk too often. I owe her beyond the possibility of repayment.

It seemed ages ago now, but my father's prediction that we'd see *Top Gun* together as soon as it was released happened to actually come true: *Top Gun Maverick*, long delayed for various reasons, was released that spring. My father and I saw it together the first night it reached the local theater.

I'd been home for a few weeks when I got a message from Jose, my old team leader in Afghanistan.

"Saw you on the news," he said. "Glad you got out."

"Thanks, bro."

"I thought you might have PTSD, or something," he said.

"Nah."

We talked a little. Then he told me he was going to Ukraine. "We're going to go get these bitches back for you."

"What the hell," I said. "I'm going, too."

"You can go with us."

"Okay. I need three months to get back in shape."

He was all for it. He told me to let him know when I was ready. He'd tell me what to do, and how to join up with him.

A common misconception is that the Western volunteers who went to fight for Ukraine did so for the money, as if the Ukrainians were handing out bags of cash to anyone who could hold a gun.

Maybe a few volunteers thought there was good money to be made, but if so, they soon realized that wasn't the case: getting paid was a big problem, even when I went there.

Some men went because they wanted to prove something. They were civilians who thought they were the next Rambo, or had a military background but hadn't seen action. A lot lied about their experience, only to be found out, with luck, as they went through training.

This biggest group, though, at least among those who were successful fighters, were motivated by outrage. They were realists about war, but they were also idealists, adamant about fairness and fighting for what was right.

Jose was typical. He'd heard accounts of Russian soldiers killing civilians, raping women, stealing.

"Before that, I thought the Russians were soldiers like us," he says. "They turned out to be doing things from Genghis Khan's day."

Jose had been in Ukraine twice before the war, which may have reinforced his sense that he was needed there. After seeing videos in early April of the Bucha massacre, he and a group of friends put together a plan to join the fight. Not long after our talk, they snuck over the border with Poland and found a group to train with. By the time I met up with him later, Jose would be famous among the Russians, who put a bounty on his head. (They seem to only know his call sign, though, which for obvious reasons I'm not using.)

●

Joining the fight was not as simple as going to a recruiting station, taking a physical, and being sent to boot camp. There were an array of groups and organizations with formal and informal relationships with the Ukrainian military and government. The biggest and best known was the International Legion, which is part of the Ukrainian army. It had a number of units, which generally though not exclusively operated under the army's chain of command. Volunteers with the Legion underwent a training program, which varied depending on their prior military experience. The Legion was the government's official program, and had the largest number of foreign fighters at the time.

Jose became a team leader with a Legion unit that took part in the Kharkiv counteroffensive in the fall of 2022. Over the course of a month, the Ukrainian forces he fought with liberated a large portion of territory in the region that had been taken by the Russians in the early days of the war. Apparently unprepared for a counterattack, the Russian forces had not dug in, and were slow to bring up artillery to stall the offensive.

Jose describes the initial days of the fight as being something out of a World War II liberation documentary. Civilians cheered them as they rode toward the enemy, waving flags and often giving them food and drink.

Eventually, though, the fighters reached a river that stalled the attack. Air-dropped mines indiscriminately blew up civilians, as did an increasingly voluminous bombardment of artillery and missiles. The violence only escalated from there.

Jose wanted me to be a part of his team. It wasn't just that he knew me. The fact that I could speak Russian would be a major asset.

Translators were few and far between, and he felt his team's lack of a Ukrainian speaker had handicapped them during the fight. While I couldn't speak Ukrainian, most Ukrainians could speak Russian.

I started running to get back in shape. Within a week or two I graduated to running with a plate carrier, and then a weighted backpack. My endurance, as well as my strength, was returning.

One day I was hanging out with some friends at a Texas Ranger baseball game. The guys had served with me as Presidential Guards and gone on to other leadership positions before going into civilian life; two had been contractors in Iraq as well. They'd helped keep my spirits up in the gulag, writing consistently and checking in with my family to see how I was doing.

I told them I needed their help.

"I'm going to fight in Ukraine, but I'm out of shape. I need you guys to get me back up to speed."

I didn't have to elaborate, let alone ask twice. They instantly and unanimously decided to help. Each looked at his work schedule and arranged it so that I had a full course of drills and refreshers, everything from basic riflery to small unit tactics, most days of the week.

I—we—got better and better as the weeks passed. I ate everything I could, and added strength training to my cardio routines. A friend who had been a close-quarters-combat trainer put me through the paces with a Glock until I could outshoot him. Or just about.

All of this in the Texas summer, with the heat at 108.

My weight moved up past 195; it had dipped to 120 before coming home. I was strong again, and sharper as an infantryman than I'd been since leaving the Corps.

The one thing that didn't improve was my sleep. In prison I'd manage maybe four hours a night. I couldn't get past that here.

●

Autumn helped a lot.

I had known her, distantly, before going to Russia, an acquaintance of an acquaintance at the edge of a friends-group. After I got home, we started communicating online, back and forth. Nothing too serious; just friends.

At some point, she asked me a question about Texas, either through a message or a group chat. Working in Baltimore but hating the city, Autumn wanted to move back to the Dallas–Fort Worth area, where she'd gone to school. I gave her some advice, and offered to help when she came down.

Offhandedly, I told her I was looking for a place, too, and we could be roommates.

"Okay," she replied.

The first time we met in person was at the apartment I'd picked out. It had two bedrooms—our arrangement was entirely practical. I wanted to be close to my family but I wanted to be in my own place. I wasn't sure exactly when I was going to get to Ukraine.

She didn't have much furniture. We went out for drinks . . .

I don't know what the spark was, but there was definitely a spark. But again, life isn't a movie, and this wasn't a "meet-cute" moment in a rom-com. From my point of view, we both kind of liked each other, and didn't really want that much. We just kind of evolved into a relationship. I even liked her dog, Mooney, who moved in with us. I wasn't crazy about him sleeping on the bed—*No bed* became my one rule for him—but otherwise we got along very well.

Autumn had a tough exterior, not unlike a combat soldier: hard, even harsh, on the outside, gentle with me. Usually.

Most of all, never vulnerable.

That didn't mean she didn't care deeply about me, as I would eventually find out.

Soon after we moved in together, Autumn started helping me work out. Athletically minded, she trained alongside me, reviewed my cardio programs, made sure I was eating what I was supposed to eat.

Pizza was on the diet, at least on off days. Autumn and I were at a local pizza place after working out together when I got a call from Jose, asking when I was coming out to Ukraine.

"We're doing some real shit tomorrow," he said. He was serious, and joking at the same time. He knew it would take weeks if not months for me to get there.

"I can't make it by then. What do you want me to do?"

"Just sit tight," he told me. "We don't have any slots. But we will, soon."

I'd ordered a bunch of gear, but until that phone call, my plans were still a bit blurry. I could tell from his voice that he wanted and needed me, and that helped me bring everything into focus.

I didn't hear from him for two weeks. He didn't answer texts. I started worrying that he was hurt. Finally he called me again.

"I'm in the hospital" was his opening line.

"What happened?"

"Oh man, it was crazy."

Jose's unit had been following a column of retreating Russian troops, destroying their BMPs (Boyevaya Mashina Pekhoti, "military vehicle of the infantry," aka armored personnel carriers). When their vehicles were destroyed, some of the Russians managed to escape to a nearby village. Jose led his team into a building where they were holding out. After making entry, they were chased back by fragmentary grenades. As they regrouped, Russian artillery began hitting the building.

Rory, a team member from Ireland, was killed. Everyone else on the team was hit, including Jose, who took shrapnel in his chest. He kept fighting, pulling his wounded men out of the building to be medevacked. At some point, a Ukrainian T-72 tank came up and finished off the building and whatever Russians were left inside.

Videos of the action still circulate on the internet.

"My whole team was wounded," Jose said. "So we're going to be in the hospital for a while. There's no point in you coming out yet."

I was disappointed, but it bought me three more months to get into shape.

Some of the guys who were training with me wanted to come as well. But they had families and jobs and commitments: pregnant wives; little kids.

All I had was a burning desire for revenge. And that wasn't keeping me in Texas.

You can hear a lot about war, but you don't really know what it's like until you're actually there. You can imagine things based on your experience, but you don't really comprehend until you're in the middle of it.

While I was waiting for the word from Jose, I drove out to Oklahoma to visit a contractor who'd been with me in Afghanistan. He was just back from Ukraine. I asked him what it was like.

"This isn't like Afghanistan," he said. "This shit is straight up World War I."

I heard the words. They wouldn't really make sense for months. Then I'd understand all too well.

Autumn and I had some great times. Every day was something new. We went to the zoo, the botanical gardens. We even flew out to Hawaii for a few days before she started a new job.

I continued to rehab and practice my combat skills. I got a list of gear from Jose that I'd need or that would be valuable for the team.

It would eventually fill two duffle bags. I had high-quality clothing, body armor, combat knives. I tried to get the best I could find, or at least afford.

All the gear was legal to transport to Europe. It didn't include rifles or the like. Believe me, I would have brought them if allowed.

Finally, I got the word from Jose that he had recovered and was putting a team together. I made my final arrangements, but kept putting off one of the most important: telling my mom I was going. I knew it would hurt her.

Finally, a few days before I was supposed to leave, Autumn and I went over to the house to pick up some things.

I walked up behind my mom when we were alone in the kitchen.

"Mom," I said, putting my arms around her waist. "I have something to say."

She cut me off. "I know. You're going to Ukraine. You think I'm dumb?"

I'd made the mistake of having packages of gear delivered to their house. Between that and seeing how hard I was working out . . . well, my mom's not dumb.

She wasn't enthusiastic. Not at all. But she didn't try to talk me out of it. I told her and my father, flat-out, to prepare themselves: I'd never be taken alive. My mom said later that she understood it was something I really needed to do.

"I didn't like it one bit," she admits now. "But I understood. And I can't be angry anymore."

My sister could, and was, and maybe still is. She was never one to hold back her feelings, and she let me know exactly what she thought.

I was still going. As much as I love her.

Autumn, of course, had known from the beginning that I was going. She'd helped me train; she'd listened to my conversations with Jose and others. She'd watched videos of the fighting; she'd listened to me talk about what I would do when I got there.

To this point, she'd been accepting, or at least stoic.

She volunteered to drive me out to the airport. The ride was fine until I told her to be sure to let Mooney sleep on the bed while I was gone.

She glanced at me and asked if I was joking. Break the one rule I had for the dog?

She choked up a bit, then started to cry.

"I don't want you to go," she sobbed.

The words shocked me.

I thought—I'm not sure exactly what I thought. I thought—I knew—that she knew I had to do this.

I thought—I knew—that she was in favor of this.

I knew she cared for me, but not so much that my leaving would tear her up.

I was wrong, especially about the last. Very wrong.

"Are you sure you have to go?" she said tearfully. "You could get hurt. I love you and you could be killed. I want you just to stay here. I'll miss you. Mooney will miss you, and your family will miss you. We all love you so much."

It hurt, terribly, but my mind was made up.

How had I imagined saying goodbye?

Not with tears, not from Autumn. I realized then I deeply loved her, but I had to do this. And that pull was stronger than anything else.

We kissed and hugged, and in the end I tore myself away.

PART THREE

REVENGE

TWENTY-ONE

UKRAINE

This being real life and not a movie, the scene with Autumn at the airport was not actually our last goodbye before I left for Ukraine.

Inside the airport, I found out my bags were oversize for the flight. I ended up having to buy an extra pack and get a new flight the next day.

I landed in Warsaw, waiting for some documents and instructions from Jose. The documents were to show that I was a volunteer for a non-governmental organization, a private nonprofit that does humanitarian work, which would make it easy to get across the border.

A few days passed. Finally, Jose called and told me it was taking too long.

"Can you just get across the border yourself?" he asked.

It wasn't an unreasonable question, at least as far as he was concerned. After all, he had done it himself months before, with even less prep than I had.

Okay, I thought. If he did it, I could, too.

Poland shares a long border with Ukraine, but the capital is some two hundred miles away. My destination was Lviv, where two of Jose's guys would contact me. The best way there was by bus, with several operating between the countries.

I don't speak Polish, and the people at the hotel didn't seem to speak English. But I managed to get by with Russian. Russian came in handy at the bus station as well, though I didn't understand the directions and station layout well enough to get on the vehicle I bought a ticket for.

After a bit of wandering, I found another bus heading for Lviv and got on in the middle of a large group of women. They were all Ukrainian, and said exactly nothing to me or anyone as we boarded and headed out. Their sudden silence felt odd, and I was afraid I'd interrupted some sort of convention. Their occasional glances toward me didn't seem particularly friendly, and I wondered if they were planning to stick daggers in me if I fell asleep.

Finally one of the women asked if I wanted to move my pack across the aisle. She said it in Ukrainian, but it was obvious what she meant, and I gladly agreed.

"Do you speak Ukrainian?" she asked.

"No. But I speak Russian."

Her face brightened. So did those of the women nearby. I was peppered with questions and candy.

"I'm a volunteer," I told them. "I'm going to fight the Russians."

"Oh, thank you, thank you!" The women couldn't have been kinder, pulling out food and treating me as if I were a favorite nephew.

In between saying I wouldn't have any trouble at the border, Jose had suggested I say I was a medic if anyone asked. That was supposed to be a get-over-the-border-free card.

Or so he implied.

I worried about that the whole bus trip down. A medic? With magazines and all sorts of non-medic gear?

Right.

I was dressed in civilian clothes, but my gear and bulk probably made it clear I was there to fight. I wasn't sure how that would be viewed. The US government was on record saying its citizens should not go to Ukraine; hopefully no one else would mind.

There was a long line of vehicles at the border, mostly trucks carrying supplies. Buses were ushered to a separate lane. We moved up quicker than I thought we would. I got out my blue American passport, which of course made me stand out just a little more.

I took a deep breath as the border guard climbed onto the bus, asking for passports. The guard put her hand out, and I handed mine over.

"What are you going to do in Ukraine?" she asked in perfect but stern English.

"I'm a humanitarian aid volunteer medic," I told her.

"Yes, I'm sure." She took the passport, and continued down the line, then off the bus.

I'm going to get pulled off. I know it.

Contingency plans rolled through my head. None of them were very good. Finally the border guard came back on the bus, and I prepared for the worst.

She handed my passport back without a word or a second glance.

We rolled across the border to the Ukrainian side, where the only notice I got was a brief glance and a look away.

I was in.

Officially, Lviv dates its founding to 1256, but people have lived there since at least the fifth century. The Rus, the Mongols, the Tartars, the Lithuanians, the Poles all fought over it, seizing the city and its strategic castles throughout the medieval ages. The Swedes tried to take it but were repulsed; the Ottomans laid siege but made peace before forcing it to surrender. As part of the Habsburg Empire, it was an important cultural center with a significant number of Jews. Some sources say that by 1910, it was the fourth largest city in the Austria-Hungary Empire.

Russia captured it in World War I, but Austria-Hungary soon won it back. Lviv served as the capital of the post-war West Ukrainian People's Republic, even though the majority of its population were ethnic Poles who preferred their traditional ties with Poland. Poland moved troops against the Republic, holding on to Lviv during the 1920 Polish-Soviet War.

Lviv was part of Poland until World War II. Many of its Jewish residents and refugees who'd flooded the city died either in the fighting or in the concentration camps after the Germans invaded. Soviet troops took over the city toward the end of July 1944.

It became part of the Ukrainian Soviet Socialist Republic following the World War. Like all of Ukraine, it remained tied to Russia and the rest of the Soviet Union through the Cold War, but fissures in that relationship gradually grew. The People's Movement of Ukraine, the first political opposition group working to free Ukraine from the Soviet Union in the early 1990s, was extremely active in the city, with its members winning a majority on the city council in 1990. Along with similar results in Kyiv, the elections were a key moment for Ukraine's independence movement, as well as the eventual breakup of the Soviet Union.

When I arrived in 2022, Lviv was a way station for volunteers like myself, looking to join the fight. It had also become a kind of R&R place for soldiers looking to take a few days or weeks off from the battle. Being in western Ukraine, it was over five hundred miles from most of the heavy fighting. Even Belarus, a Russian ally, was over a hundred and fifty miles away.

That doesn't mean it was immune from attack. Missile and air strikes began on the region soon after the initial Russian invasion, and continued sporadically throughout the war. In October 2022, the Russians managed to briefly cut off the city's electrical supply. Residential buildings near the railroad station in the center of town were destroyed with significant injuries and at least seven deaths in an attack in September 2024.

Unfortunately, that all passes for light casualties in the context of that war.

Before the Russian invasion of Ukraine, the center of the city was a pretty mélange of cobblestone squares marked by statues and colorful plantings of flowers. I didn't see any of that, partly because of the war, and partly because it was already night. On the way into town, Jose sent me another message. My contacts weren't going to make it to town until the next day.

"Can you figure it out?"

I guess.

The bus left me off in the parking lot. Two Ukrainians walked by as I was trying to get my bearings.

"Hey, are you a foreigner?" they asked.

Or something like that. They were speaking Ukrainian, which I didn't.

I told them in Russian that I was.

"From where?"

"America."

"Fuck yeah."

They walked on. I took out my phone and did a search, looking for a hotel. The first thing that came up was the Hotel Lviv.

Has to be good, I thought. I don't know anything about the hotels here, but they wouldn't name it that if it was bad.

Right?

I found a taxi and gave him my destination. Off we drove. And drove. And drove some more, until finally I was convinced he was going to kidnap me.

He wasn't. And at least according to the map, Hotel Lviv is only about two miles from the central bus station, though that doesn't seem possible. It's possible my sense of time was distorted by adrenaline and fatigue. Or maybe the cabbie got lost. Fortunately, the hotel lived up to my expectations, maybe even a little beyond, with a fancy marble foyer and clean rooms.

I checked for bugs in the room. Electronic bugs. Didn't find any.

I slept fairly well. The next day Jose sent me instructions on how to use an app similar to Uber, along with instructions on where to meet my contacts, whom I'll call Stiffler and Cola.

I was pretty psyched when I met them. They seemed a cross between combat heroes and TV stars. I'd watched some of their fighting thanks to social media posts and videos over the past several months. But what really surprised me was their reaction to me. Jose had told them about my stay in Russia, and while I don't think they were in awe, they were certainly enthusiastic and welcoming.

Stiffler was a South African mercenary. The reality of the war was evident in his face: part of it was missing, blown off somewhere in Ukraine on an earlier mission with Jose. Despite the scars, he looked younger than he was. Cola had been a Ranger, served in Africa, and fought in Mogadishu, the Somalia city made infamous in the movie *Black Hawk Down*.

We talked for a bit, then headed to another place they called the Casino. I thought that was the name of a bar, but it turned out to be literally a casino outside of town. Dozens of pretty girls walked around the place—not prostitutes, Cola assured me. "There's a strip club for that."

I didn't go, nor did they while I was with them.

The games at the Casino looked pretty shady. I did a few hands of what seemed to be Texas Hold'em, played by rules that didn't exist outside of that building. That was more than enough for me. I can't really say I gambled, though. When you gamble, you at least have a slim chance of winning.

Both of Jose's guys got pretty drunk that night. I crashed with Stiffler, then left him and Cola to enjoy the rest of their R&R while I headed to Dnipro to meet up with Jose.

Dnipro is in the center of Ukraine. It was a lot closer to the fighting than Lviv, though still a good distance from the front. It's also a good distance from Lviv—my best option was a twenty-hour train ride. For the equivalent of twelve dollars, I was able to buy a spot in a deluxe cabin: a closet-size double with bunk beds.

Soldiers packed the train. I'd say most were drunker than a dog in a whiskey barrel. My compartment may have been deluxe, but to get my gear inside involved considerable contortion by myself and the other occupant, a Ukrainian army officer who was heading back to the front after leave.

By this time I realized that the best way to communicate was in Russian, since so many Ukrainians spoke it, and it was relatively rare to find anyone who could speak English comfortably. Occasionally, I would get the cold shoulder if I started speaking in Russian, until the person I was talking to realized I was an American and only using it to communicate. Especially at first, my nationality was pretty obvious once someone got a good look at me.

"Why do you speak Russian so well?" asked my compartment mate soon after the train left the station.

"It's a long story." I didn't feel like going into detail, and changed the subject to him. He told me he'd been home with his wife for the first time in a year. I didn't ask him about his experiences in the war; somehow it felt out of bounds.

He got off after a couple of stops. His replacement was older, harder, and more energetic. He was a weapons officer, and when he realized I was American, started grilling me about what I planned to do. I asked him to keep his voice down and not tell anyone I was from the US. I was getting tired, and feared that I'd spend the rest of the long trip being "interviewed" by curious Ukrainians.

I might have escaped that fate had I stayed in the cabin, but eventually I got hungry and went out to find something to eat in the commissary car.

I have to pause here to give a plug for the Ukrainian hot dogs I had on the train. They were the best hot dogs I ever ate. Not just those dogs, but every hot dog I had in Ukraine, including the ones I snagged at a gas station, were first rate. Rather than being plopped into a slit bun, the Ukrainians cook the meat inside the dough, so that it looks and tastes like a long, fat hunk of freshly baked bread.

That's the basic bit. It can be dressed up with toppings, different fillings, and, of course, several variations on the sausage inside. But however they were fixed, Ukrainian hot dogs were my go-to culinary food away from the battlefield.

A side benefit: many were free for soldiers. But back to the train.

I made my way to the commissary car and scored one of those hot dogs. Wending my way through the crowd, I sidled around two very large, completely jacked soldiers. They looked ready for a bodybuilding competition. It's rare to see guys that jacked in Ukraine, or Russia for that matter. Even stranger was the tattoo one of them sported: a Nazi swastika.

Both of them were also way smashed, even compared to the rest of the train.

My companion in the train compartment made a face as the pair approached down the hallway outside, pausing every few feet to share some booze with everyone they met. He shook his head as they leaned into our compartment, warning me not to engage.

Too late. They asked how I was. My reflexes kicked in.

Good. Yourself?

Blah-blah-blah. Until one of the Nazis asked where I was from.

"The United States," I confessed. It didn't make sense to lie.

"You're fucking American?"

"Yeah."

"Fuck yeah."

That was followed by a "Sieg Heil!" and a full Hitler salute. Which, you know, felt more than a little weird.

"Uh, no," I told them.

"Why?"

"My relatives fought the Nazis in World War II," I explained.

"Oh. But you want to kill Russians?"

"Yeah."

"Yeah! Fuck! Have a shot with us."

I had a shot. They hung around for a bit, then went to the next car, apparently continuing their quest to share a drink with every human on the train.

Things were peaceful for a while, at least in my part of the train, until I had to go find the men's room.

"American! Hey!"

You would have thought I had come to win the war single-handedly. As much as I insisted that the Ukrainians were the brave ones, the soldiers crowding around wanted to congratulate me, thank me, and get me drunker than they were.

They didn't quite succeed, but I did drink enough to have a decent nap.

We stopped briefly at one point, and a bunch of soldiers went out to have a smoke and get some fresh air. I got off myself, stretching my legs.

"Hey, is it true you're an American?" asked one of the soldiers.

"Yeah."

"What are you doing here?"

"I came to fight Russia," I said. "I know you guys need help."

"It's not Iraq or Afghanistan here. It's fucked up."

"I know."

"There's a good chance all of us will die." He stared at me, suddenly stone-cold sober.

"I know."

"You knew that, and you still came out here?"

"Yeah."

"Just to help us."

"Well, I would like to help." It was true, but a little bit of a fudge as well. I was mostly here for revenge.

The Ukrainian started crying. "There's Ukrainian men hiding in Poland who won't even fight for their own country," he said between sobs. "Thank you so much."

"You don't need to say thanks. I have my own reasons."

Tears slid down his face as he stepped forward and hugged me. "Whatever your reasons are, thank you."

"Sure," I muttered, choking up as I got back on the train.

I hadn't seen Jose for years, but he was easy to recognize when he met me around the back of the train station in Dnipro. He wore the same serious yet easygoing expression he'd had in Afghanistan.

His apartment happened to be nearby, and he shouldered one of my heavy bags as he led the way. The exterior of the building wasn't particularly special, not for Europe, but the apartment itself would have commanded a premium rent in most US cities. The kitchen had granite and top-of-the-line appliances; the furnishings in the living room and bedrooms were new and included a large TV. We started catching up as I unpacked some new Gore-Tex tops and bottoms, assault packs, a combat knife, and other basic gear. They were for Jose and his team, replacing personal things that had been stolen or lost after he and his guys were hurt on the battlefield. He apologized that he couldn't pay for a month at least.

I told him not to worry about it.

He thanked me, then hooked up his GoPro to the TV.

"Watch," he said.

I'd seen a lot of combat videos from Ukraine already, but these were different. They were immediately more intense. The explosions were unrelenting. Even the most chaotic boss fight in the most exponential video game couldn't compare to the adrenaline packed into the snippets of fighting flashing across the screen.

I'd been prepared for something worse than Afghanistan. This was beyond even that.

"Beer?" he asked.

I drank the first in maybe two minutes. The second couldn't have taken three.

The war the Russians had intended to fight when they invaded Ukraine in February 2022 was very different than the war I had come to join. The conflict had actually begun a decade before, when Ukrainians succeeded in ousting then President Viktor Yanukovych and his government's pro-Russian policies following months of protest and bloodshed. With his removal, the Ukrainians turned back toward Western Europe, where economic ties had been steadily growing since the end of the Soviet Union and Ukraine's subsequent independence.

Strongly allied with Yanukovych—he was often described as Putin's puppet—Russia encouraged separatists in the eastern part of the country to break away and form their own nation. In February 2014, the Russian army invaded Crimea in southeastern Ukraine, taking over the city and installing a pro-Russian government there. Russia subsequently annexed Crimea and sent troops into portions of two Ukrainian oblasts or regions, Donetsk and Luhansk, where separatists had gained control. Fighting continued on and off after the annexation, with the legitimate Ukrainian government and most of the world refusing to recognize Russia's actions.

Except for the occupation of Crimea, the action in the eastern provinces were primarily small-unit conflicts. Heavy weapons like artillery and missiles were used, but the forces tended to be small and the fights sporadic. The separatists received backing from Russia, with Russians manning sophisticated weapons systems, though no division-size Russian military units were committed directly to battle.

That war ended with the February 2022 invasion. Russia launched massive attacks against Ukraine, aiming not only to seize territory but to decapitate the government. The Ukrainians mounted a heroic defense. Key battles saved Kyiv, and the rout of Russian forces effectively turned the tide of the invasion in north-central Ukraine. Russian forces made significant gains in the east, occupying and expanding from the breakaway areas. The Ukrainians launched a series of counterattacks that fall, taking back large swaths of occupied territory. Jose had been involved in those battles.

The invasion and much of the counteroffensive stages of the war were relatively mobile affairs, with large units maneuvering quickly on the battlefield. With allowances for vast differences in technology, this phase of the fighting could be compared to some of the classic phases of World War II, featuring rapid advances and strategic slashes. As the year went on, however, the battle began to change to a more defensive one, with forces entrenched on both sides. To greatly simplify, the Russians had dug in, and the depth of their defenses made it difficult for the Ukrainians to break through the lines. Artillery, always important, became a primary weapon, making the battlefield resemble something from World War I, albeit with drones instead of biplanes. The carnage was horrific.

Ukraine had retaken considerable land from the Russians by the time I arrived. Their overall strategic aim and to some extent their tactics remained the same as at the start of the counteroffensive in September. But their rate of gains had drastically slowed.

Casualties are always a matter of conjecture in the middle of a war. The lowest credible estimates at the point we're writing this posits 60,000 Ukrainian dead, 250,000 wounded (US intelligence estimates); 700,000 killed or wounded (British estimates) on the Russian side.

Civilians have been purposely targeted by the Russians as part of their war strategy, aiming to destroy the country's ability to survive. Those casualties are even more difficult to estimate; the Ukrainian government in June 2024 listed 12,000 civilians as confirmed dead. That number is surely too low, and doesn't include the thousands of civilians forcibly moved from their homes and brought back to Russia.

As intense and horrible as they were, the videos Jose showed me could only hint at the ferocity of the fighting and the damage that was being done. They chilled me nonetheless. The idea that so many civilians were being killed in the rubble angered me. I didn't need any motivation to fight, but it would have been easily stoked by everything Jose showed and told me that night.

Dnipro reminded me a lot of Russia. Gray buildings, a lot of concrete. Jose's building was older, so it had more charm, but the overall feel of the city was very Soviet. A lot of people spoke Russian here, so many that they never frowned when I used it.

The city had remained well removed from the frontlines since the start of the war, but it had hardly been unscathed. Russia periodically sent missiles, striking random targets, mostly if not all civilian.

The nearby train station itself had been targeted several times. The airport, an oil depot, a school, random apartment buildings—all had been hit.

Residents were defiant, and morale, to the extent I could tell, remained high. There were stories of people attempting to loot businesses during the early days of the Russian invasion. The looters were caught, beaten, and held for the police. Crime did not appear to be a problem.

I spent a few days getting acclimated to the country and gathering kit that I didn't have. There were a lot of military stores in Dnipro—like maybe one out of every ten businesses. The selection was wide: clothes, plate carriers, all manner of gear for weapons. Munitions, artillery shells especially, were a problem at the front, but buying support gear at the rear was not.

Another thing that wasn't a problem: finding food. Shawarma stands were everywhere.

Shawarma dates to the Ottoman Empire. Lamb primarily, but also chicken, beef, veal, falafel even—thin slices of any of these are melded together and roasted on a spoke. They're sliced off and placed in a wrap, usually with some sort of sauce. The most common version in the US has traditionally been found in Greek restaurants, made of roasted lamb with a pita bread cone and a tzatziki dressing. Here there were a lot of varieties made by Azerbaijanis, Georgians, Turks, guys from all different nationalities. The only thing they lacked was true spice; if you wanted to go extreme, you had to ask for as much hot sauce as they had.

Pizza was another popular food. We ate at a place with an American vibe. The décor was a cross between an American diner and the Hard Rock Cafe, with a bit of old school muscle car on the side. A Harley hung from the ceiling; random car parts lined the walls.

Jose was recruiting a new team, aiming to rejoin the fight. He had become disillusioned with the Legion, and was hoping to find another

Ukrainian command to work with. His idea was to join as a unit, and to be assigned special-ops-style missions. He felt a small spec ops team could make more of an impact on the war than standard infantry, if used properly. He wanted English speakers, American or British, so team communications would be easy. He wanted guys who had already served in Ukraine, if possible, so they would know what the war was really like. Ideally, they had served in spec ops in their home countries as well.

I didn't have a special operations background; I'd never been Marine Recon or a Ranger or a SEAL or a Green Beret, etc. But my ability to speak Russian made me valuable, since it meant I could communicate with whatever Ukrainian command we dealt with. It would also give us an advantage if we found ourselves operating behind the lines among the enemy.

After a week or so in Dnipro, Jose and I traveled to Kyiv, the nation's capital. While we were on the train, who did we run into but the two Nazis I'd met earlier.

They were considerably more sober, but still recognizable.

"What are you doing here?" I asked.

"Our mission is finished," one of them explained. "It was supposed to take three weeks, but we did it in three days."

"Yeah, we killed them in three days." The other one laughed.

The mission had been to attack a Russian outpost across the border. At least that's what I gathered. Apparently they had taken no prisoners.

My two Sieg Heil "friends" (yes, let me underline the irony; they were anything but friends) told me they'd been in mafya before the war, and apparently were still part of it. They offered to get me whatever I wanted—girls, guns, whatever.

I thanked them, but passed. Jose and I were glad when they left; neither of us was particularly fond of Nazis.

Jose's search for a Ukrainian force to hook up with didn't go particularly well in Kyiv until we met an American I'll call Tex, mostly because I don't know his real name. Or anything about him, except that he's actually from Oklahoma.

We were referred to Tex by an American who'd been in the war but was heading back to the States. According to him—hearsay entirely—Tex was supplying the Ukrainians with rifles, small drones, and various munitions. He didn't seem to speak Ukrainian or Russian, or at least didn't do so when we met. But he spoke Spanish well. He hinted that he had worked in Colombia, South America, but what he did there was left to our imaginations.

He was a cheerful, friendly guy, and after looking over our resumes told us he'd be happy to help us make a connection. Within a few days, Jose, myself, and two of Jose's friends met him at a high-rise in downtown Kyiv. Upstairs, we followed him into a fancy office where two Ukrainian officers were waiting. One was a colonel, the other a lieutenant colonel; both were with Ukrainian military intelligence.

An assistant brought in some steaming Turkish coffee. I felt underdressed, if not totally out of place. Jose quietly studied the two Ukrainians, sizing them up. That's his MO. He goes real quiet at the beginning, figuring everything out. Apprehensive, though not showing it.

I generally joke. There wasn't much opportunity for that here, though.

The Ukrainians spoke flawless English. They started asking questions about the team's qualifications. That went smoothly enough, until they got to me.

"It says here you can speak Russian," said one of the colonels.

"Yeah. I spent some time there."

"Let's speak Russian a bit."

We did. My accent impressed them. They started smiling. We'd apparently made a good impression.

"I just want to make clear that these guys are not going into Russia," said Tex.

"Oh no," said the colonels.

I was thinking, hell, I'd love to go to Russia and kill some of those bastards. But I kept my mouth shut.

They asked us if we wanted to do assaults as a unit with Kraken, a volunteer group under the Defense Intelligence agency. (The agency's Ukrainian name is Holovne pravlinnia rozvidky Ministerstva oborony Ukrainy. While many sources abbreviate it as HUR, it's also abbreviated and better known to American volunteers as GUR, which sounds like "grrrrr" or "gore" to an American.) The Kraken units generally work with the Ukrainian army; their command is separate. In a way, they are similar to the American CIA paramilitary teams that worked with Special Forces and other units in the early days of Afghanistan. Reconnaissance and special operations are among their specialties. The units I was familiar with were commonly used as elite shock troops or the "tip of the spear," working ahead of a main force or charged with a particularly difficult mission that enhanced or even made possible the larger attack. In that way, they're more like Rangers, say, than Green Berets.

Truthfully, what we wanted to do was fuck shit up; reconnaissance was more secondary. But we agreed. We exchanged contacts, and were told to wait for a few weeks while they checked out our resumes and backgrounds.

TWENTY-TWO

ON THE WAY

It occurs to me that I haven't explained the relationship between Ukraine and Russia. This isn't the place for a deep dive into what is a very complicated history, but to give a very brief background:

Most Americans are probably aware that Ukraine was part of the Soviet Union before its breakup. We tend to think of the Soviet Union and Russia as synonymous, but they're not. While Russia dominated the USSR, it was only one of a number of states, albeit the largest and most influential. Ukraine was one of the founding components of the Soviet Union in 1922, following the victory of the Communists during the Soviet-Ukrainian War at the tail end of World War I. The republic suffered immensely during the early 1930s, with four to five million people dying during famines caused by Communist policies launched by Joseph Stalin. Those policies featured collectivization of private farms and the relocation of millions of small farmers from their land. Soviet planning called for heavy industrialization in Ukraine, which had had a largely agrarian economy. Stalin violently repressed opposition, purging political leaders, intellectuals, artists, and anyone even suspected of opposing his rule.

Ukraine suffered massively during World War II, bearing much of the brunt of the German extermination campaign against Jews in Eastern Europe. An estimated 1.5 million Ukrainian Jews were killed in the Holocaust. At the same time, a large portion of non-Jews sided with the Nazis against the Soviets. Nationalists desired an independent Ukraine; besides opposing the Soviets, many also supported the Nazis' genocide.

Putin's narrative of Ukrainians as Nazis derived in part from this history. What Putin left out is the famine and destruction of Ukraine by the Soviet Union in the years before the war. The Soviets also attempted to ban the Ukrainian language multiple times and destroy any part of Ukraine's history and culture that diverged from the Russian narrative. They purged local leaders and intellectuals, sending thousands to the gulags.

Russian influence in Ukraine remained strong even after the breakup of the Soviet Union. Many families had Russian roots and relatives in Russia. Nonetheless, a majority of the country backed politicians who sought closer ties with the West. Among the politicians' aims were membership in the European Union, which would facilitate trade and economic development. A significant number viewed NATO membership as a balance against future Russian interference.

The Russian government under Vladimir Putin viewed Ukraine's turn to the West as a threat. In the eyes of Putin and his allies, Ukraine was necessary, at a minimum, as a buffer to the West. In the eyes of the Ukrainians, Putin wanted their country as a vassal state, and was willing to go to any length to secure it.

Prior to the breakup of the Soviet Union, a considerable number of nuclear weapons were kept on Ukrainian soil. Those weapons were removed. Russia, the US, Great Britain, France, and China subsequently agreed with Ukraine that it should remain a non-nuclear power. An agreement signed by Russia, the US, and Great Britain promised that those countries would aid Ukraine if it was attacked.

Following the Russian invasion in 2022, America and other Western allies began supplying weapons and other goods to Ukraine. The amount of aid has fluctuated over time. At the time I went to fight, Ukraine was receiving significant assistance, though there were shortages of some munitions, and not every request for weapons systems—F-16s, for example—had been answered affirmatively.

The Ukrainian authorities took a few weeks before arranging for us to start training with them. I believe they were checking our bona fides, making sure that our resumes were actually accurate. They'd had quite a lot of trouble with wannabes claiming to be more than they were. Finally, they told Jose he could bring what was now a twelve-man team to Yavoriv to train.

GUR gave us several names to choose from for the team. We selected "Hydra" after the mythical beast of many heads.

West of Lviv and close to the Polish border, the training base hosted a variety of foreign volunteers. Not everyone got along. In our case, a group of gnarly Georgians were camped nearby, and there was often grousing back and forth about who was going to use what facility. Jose had to break up a near fight one time when some of our guys wanted to use part of the bathroom to shave and the Georgians objected.

A lot of the training was very basic, stuff we could already do in our sleep. But it was important for us to practice small-team tactics, since we'd never worked together before. There are subtle differences between how the US Army and Marines work in the field, to say nothing of how a British or New Zealand soldier does things. Those differences were smoothed over with practice.

One area of training that was all new to me involved the use of drones. Back when I'd first been a Marine, the US military generally relied on forward observers to find and identify the enemy. Traditionally this involved small, highly trained units operating behind the enemy lines.

Ukraine did that, too—once.

By this point in the war, they were using an army of drones to accomplish most of that mission. They taught us how to launch and recover the unmanned aircraft. It was a revelation: you could sit in a bunker on your side of the front line, directing artillery miles away, striking an enemy that had no idea where you were. There were various techniques to lessen the chance the enemy could find you, even if they tried tracking the drone.

We spent weeks training, practicing recon, close quarters combat, and foreign weapons proficiency. We learned to work advanced systems like Javelins and Stingers. We rehearsed with drones. We perfected our teamwork and craft.

Then Command suggested we become a mortar unit.

What they wanted was a mobile attack force that would insert around the battlefield. The idea was this: a small team would arrive at a position off the frontline, set up some portable mortars, fire off a few rounds, then zoom away before the Russians could figure out where they were.

It wasn't a bad idea, except that we had trained to act as scouts on the leading edge of the fight. And none of us were mortarmen.

Mortars are relatively simple weapons: at their most basic, a tube and a projectile. But getting them to hit a target is a difficult skill to master. It is very easy to hit friendlies in the area.

It's also rare to see the enemy you're aiming at. Which all of us wanted to do.

We had rudimentary mortar training, but we all wanted to fight in the way we'd practiced, not risk others' lives perfecting our skills on the job. Or to put it another way: we wanted to shoot people face-to-face.

I was frustrated, and not just because by now I'd spent months without seeing any action. We were without contracts, which meant we weren't being paid. The Ukrainian government didn't dole out large wages; being a volunteer was nothing like working for the State Department as a contractor. But it was enough to live on there. I was spending my savings, and they were rapidly decreasing.

I decided to take a break. Autumn agreed to meet me in Poland, bringing over some more equipment that I needed.

Our time wasn't idyllic. She truly wanted me to come home. I didn't understand the depth of her love, or how great her fear was that I would be hurt. I couldn't understand why she wouldn't accept that I needed to fight. The trip probably left us both more frustrated than ever. Our relationship was heading downward.

Just before I got back to Ukraine, our team was offered the opportunity to work with Ukrainian marines who were preparing an assault in the southeast. It looked like a good opportunity . . . except that it called for a couple of months of more training before getting into the fight.

That turned me off. There was another catch: my security clearance from Ukrainian intelligence had not come through.

I couldn't officially join the group until it did. I couldn't fight, and I couldn't get paid.

I don't think the hang-up had anything to do with me personally. I don't think my "stay" in Russia was the problem. I think my paperwork simply got lost, a not uncommon occurrence in Ukraine.

It happened to other guys I knew who didn't have the same background.

All armies are bureaucracies filled with paper pushers. The only variable is where the paper they push ends up. In the case of Ukraine, the paper often got pushed into a black hole.

Figuratively. Although, given that they were under constant attack, it's possible it was literal as well.

While Jose worked to get me hooked up with the team, I hung out in Ukraine, trying to fill my time. The days dragged on. Solitary had been infinitely worse, but this wasn't particularly fun.

I happened to see an Instagram feed from someone who called himself Rogue Warfighter. The page had some pretty sick combat videos. I liked a couple of the videos; soon after someone messaged me from the account.

"Hey bro," he said. "We're all Marines here on the team and we're really big fans. We know who you are, and we're in Ukraine and we're fucking these dudes up. Just wanted to let you know."

"Funny thing," I replied. "I'm in Ukraine. You guys have any open slots on the team?"

"Let me talk to my team leader."

That message came at a point where I almost gave up.

I had a plane ticket to America booked for a trip in a week or so. Mickey Bergman, who had done so much behind the scenes to get me out of Russia, was to be honored at the James W. Foley Freedom Awards dinner in Washington, DC, and my dad had lobbied me heavily to be there. I was also feeling bad about my relationship with Autumn. I'd realized there was more to it than I'd thought, and I hoped to repair it if I could.

I didn't understand why she didn't understand me. I wanted the chance to somehow explain it.

But most of all, I was disillusioned. I didn't think I'd get a chance to fight. I felt the Ukrainians were so disorganized that they were their own worst enemy.

Was revenge worth it? Was it even possible? I had real doubts.

I still wanted it, though. Badly.

The IM from the Rogue guys a few days later was simple, without promises, yet filled with hope:

"Can you get to Kyiv and meet our team leaders?"

"Sure."

We met at a coffee shop in the city. There were two guys, both huge dudes. They gave me a rundown of Rogue Team: ten men, mostly US Marine veterans. A former Army Ranger, a Uruguayan infantry officer, a Ukrainian combat medic.

Nice.

The guys I met were there to see if I was the real deal. I gave them a little of my background, then started to vent.

I've been here forever. I've done all this training. I didn't get a clearance, so I've just been waiting.

"That's how it always is," said one of the Rogue members. "No one has ever gone to a team without waiting around for months. Our own clearance can take months."

He asked for my resume. I told him I'd been an infantry squad leader, martial arts instructor, Presidential Guard. I'd worked for State in Afghanistan on a mobile team. I'd done the GUR training. I spoke Russian fluently.

I don't know that they were impressed, but they did give me an address, a date, and a time. I was to show up there. GUR, the Ukrainian intelligence service, would look me over. If GUR approved, I could get my clearance taken care of and join the team.

On the appointed day, I got in a taxi and set out. The directions took me to a flower shop.

Huh?

I took a quick look. It was definitely a florist. And a busy one.

I went down the street, where I spotted two dudes in camouflage.

That's probably it.

"Hey, I'm looking for the headquarters of GUR," I told the guards.

"There's no military base here," they told me.

"No, I'm supposed to report there."

"Well, there's no base here."

I went back to the flower place.

"I'm an American," I said at the counter. "I'm looking for GUR."

Maybe one or two of the people working behind the counter glanced in my direction before going back to their business.

Everything about the place said florist rather than special operations until someone tromped down the stairs. He had a thick beard, a pistol in his belt, and the exact mannerisms of an ex-SEAL I knew in Afghanistan.

Not him, but close enough.

"I was told to come here," I said.

"Yeah. Come on."

We went upstairs.

"Wait here," he said, pointing me to a couch.

A few minutes later, he brought over Super Dave.

Super Dave had been an Army Ranger, then worked as a contractor for Blackwater during its heyday. Somewhere in there, he'd also graduated from Columbia and worked on Wall Street—something I wouldn't know until our very last mission. He was smart, tough, calm in combat. When you saw him in civilian clothes, you could tell he was in decent shape, but you probably wouldn't figure that he was a badass. You had to see him in combat to realize what a warrior he was.

The same was true of Teddy, another team member I met that day. Teddy had been an infantry officer in South America. He'd been to airborne and commando school, and was well squared away.

After our introductions, Super Dave told me to fill out some more forms, similar if not exactly the same as the ones I'd done at the training camp.

At that point, Dave was not yet the leader of Rogue. They were definitely a stacked team, made up mostly of Marines. They would get involved in a major action before I was cleared to join them; devastated by a large number of casualties, the team broke up. Super Dave took over the leadership and he and Teddy began rebuilding when my clearance came through.

That was all down the road. The woman I handed the documents over to said my clearance would come through in six to eight weeks.

I didn't feel great about that. I was impressed by Super Dave and Teddy, though. They took me out to a McDonald's and gave some background on what they'd done, what they expected to be doing.

The stories were similar to what Jose had talked about before I'd come over. The delay sucked, but these guys were the real deal. I knew once my clearance came through, I'd get my chance to do what I'd come for.

Pay the Russians back.

Given that I had time on my hands, I went back to the US to see Autumn and my family, and to attend the awards dinner. I'm not big on formal events, but there was a side benefit for me: the dinner was a public event, and any Russian who was looking for me would probably catch some social media or maybe news clip that showed I was there. That would make it unlikely they would suspect I was in Ukraine.

Things with Autumn went . . . not too well. I think she really hated me by the time I left. But she loved me, too. She cried and begged me not to go.

I did anyway.

I was too far in, too dedicated to revenge not to. Retribution meant everything. More than love. More than life itself.

TWENTY-THREE

LETTING GO

My dad:

Trevor came back from Ukraine the first time, in our opinion, mostly to pick up gear and bring it back, not so much to see us. He still hadn't been in combat.

Which was a good thing, from our point of view.

We didn't want him to go. We'd made no secret about that. Over and over, I thought, Why? Why would you want to do that?

It was the same question I'd asked him when he announced he was going into the Marine Corps.

But the thing with Trevor: if you argue with him too strongly, he digs his heels in.

The Russians learned that.

We convinced him to attend the 2023 James W. Foley Freedom Awards dinner with us, honoring efforts to bring American hostages like him home. He used this as an excuse to come back and pick up more equipment for his team.

He did go to the dinner and meet many people like the Foleys, who work behind the scenes and publicly to bring innocent Americans home, along with Mickey Bergman and Governor Richardson, who'd helped push the administration to act. He also met the Special Presidential Envoy for Hostage Affairs staff and other freed hostages.

He was still very withdrawn, but he did open up a bit, talking to fellow former hostages and the people who'd helped get him released.

He was still wrapped up, though. His mind was elsewhere.

Ukraine, to be exact.

He'd been so adamant about doing this, there was no talking him out of it. By this point, it was senseless to try.

TWENTY-FOUR

FIRST BLOOD

Night's falling. Artillery and mortar rounds blast in the distance, exploding in the direction we're taking. I'm bouncing in the back of a Toyota Hilux pickup, hauling ass down a highway southeast of Donbas. The Hilux—think of a Toyota Tacoma modified slightly for military duty—whips past a row of tanks on the back of low-rider trailers. We pass other military vehicles headed in the direction we're going, speeding confidently in the dark because there's no reason to suspect anything coming from the other way. Certainly there are no civilian cars.

Without warning, our pickup veers off the highway onto a dirt road, sending me against some of the stacked gear and ammo.

It feels good.

It's taken several weeks, but my clearance has come through and I've been officially accepted as a member of Rogue Team. I'm about to get my combat cherry popped.

I'm excited, and more than a little nervous. Ready and unprepared at the same time. Like everyone going into the real part of war for the first time.

I'm dressed for combat, plates in my vest. My rifle is a CZ Bren, short-barreled variant. The Bren is a Czech-designed automatic rifle, chambered for NATO rounds. To a civilian, it's not all that different from an M4 or M16, though I would compare it more closely to an FN SCAR, the Belgian creation that has seen some action with American special operations troops. Given a choice between a 14.5-inch and 11.5-inch barrel, I went with the shorter, favoring the slightly lighter weight and easier maneuverability. I'm unlikely to be encountering anyone beyond three hundred meters, so the longer barrel isn't important. I'll end up not liking the gun all that much, but that lies ahead.

Everyone else on the team has either a Sig Sauer or Bren 2 rifle. We use strips of tape, in this case blue, to tell other Ukrainian units that we're on their side. There are more elaborate friend-foe procedures, radio details and such, but as I'll soon find out, the difference between life and death on the battlefield can easily come down to a few inches of colored duct tape.

The call to go on the mission came only a few hours ago. We'd scrambled to get ready, to go and gas up, get briefed, get underway. Our destination is along the Siverskyi-Donets Canal, an area where the Ukrainian army is pushing against the Russian occupiers.

A series of canals run through south and east Ukraine, dating from the 1950s and '60s, built for irrigation and fresh water supply. The Siverskyi-Donets section here is wide, deep, and mostly dry. It's somewhere between seventy-five and one hundred meters across, and when full looks more like a river than something man-made. Where it's empty and shorn of vegetation, it looks like an ugly scar in the earth.

That's it now.

The sides are cement and can be difficult to climb. Get stuck in it, and you're an easy target, as many Russians have found out during the course of the fighting.

Donbas is sometimes called an industrial part of Ukraine, but the area we're driving through is exclusively farm fields. Empty.

There's no sign that they've been farmed since the war began. By now they should be filled with crops, all decently high. I'm no farmer, so I don't know what they'd be growing here—wheat, corn, and sunflowers are the country's major export crops—but I do know a fallow field when I see one. And that's all I can see as the sun sets.

It's pretty, the sun setting in an orange haze at the horizon. It's only when you think about it that you understand the beauty is born from ugliness: the haze comes from smoke, things burning, things exploding, people's lives being incinerated.

There are dark clouds to the north, on my left. It looks like a thunderstorm. Which makes sense, because there is a constant rumble of thunder in the background. But it's not thunder, and those aren't clouds made by nature. The area to our north is being hit by artillery shells, landing with the rapidity you sometimes get in a Texas hailstorm. The shelling is part of the battle for Bakhmut. Forces around and near the city are being pounded by the Russians as they try desperately to hold their gains there.

Bakhmut itself is too far away to be seen. The war, though, is very close.

There are flashes of light in the dark cloud ahead. These, too, look natural, like a storm bank, but they're man-made: flashes of explosions as a Ukrainian village is pulverized.

To our east are the villages of Kurdyumivka and Ozarianivka; to the north, Andriivka and Klishchiivka. None of these places, or dozens just like them, actually exist anymore. They are, for me, obscured names on a tombstone, indiscernible embers on the ground. War has consumed them.

The truck jerks to a stop near some trees. Super Dave gets out and goes to a nearby bunker, which serves as a command post for the Ukrainian unit we're tasked to help. He needs to get an update on where we're going and what we're dealing with.

I've only been with the team a few days, but already I like them. There are just four of us for now: Super Dave, Teddy, and Yan. And me.

Yan had served in the US Army as a combat engineer, deploying to Iraq. He was older than the rest of us, in great shape, easygoing. Yan had come to Ukraine barely a month after the war had started, weathering a lot of the confusion as Ukraine scrambled to defend the country and organize volunteers. Cruise missiles had rained down on his training base soon after he got there, sending a large number of would-be volunteers back to their home countries. When I met him, he was on his second deployment.

They call me Gulag. I'm not sure who came up with that. It's an obvious call sign, granted, but I would have preferred Captain America or Winter Soldier or something to do with America, something positive. But they tagged me with Gulag and it stuck. Like any good nickname, once it was there, it was there.

The Russians are peppering the area nearby with artillery. Most of it feels far off, but every so often a shell manages to arc closer. Finally a good-size blast convinces us we ought to take cover. I move over behind the trucks.

Rogue Team is, in theory, a long-range reconnaissance and sabotage team, trained to work behind the lines. At this point in the war, there isn't much opportunity for those particular assignments, so we're tasked to assist units on the frontline. On this mission, we're going to look over defensive positions, maybe take over some positions for a bit so the Ukrainians could rest.

Briefing at the bunker finished, Dave comes out and we start driving again. When we drove through villages on the way out, people waved flags and cheered us on. There's a lot of patriotism in Ukraine, a spirit that they were all in it together. At times, you could feel as if you were truly a liberator.

Now though, there aren't any villages left. The first houses we see are mostly just walls without roofs. We pass rows of wood piles, as if the structure squatted into the earth.

A surprise ahead: an intact house.

As we get closer, I see through my night vision that it has a hole in the roof. But the rest is still there, including the front porch.

Four old people sit in rocking chairs, staring at us as we pass.

I wave. They don't wave back.

They're the first people in Ukraine who haven't done that. I wonder if they're collaborators. Or ghosts.

Most likely they're just people who are very tired of war, who have lost everything, and who look at us not as liberators, but as men causing them more suffering.

They're gone in a blink.

We pass another bunch of wrecked buildings, then a third. They make me think I'm seeing the world through a dystopian video game. It's hard not to think of the people who would have been here just a few years before. It's hard not to think of my home in Texas devastated the same way.

Past the houses, we turn onto another road, this one in the middle of a field. We don't go very far before our driver realizes he's made a mistake. He backs up; the other truck backs up, and we bounce back to the main road, which I call a main road only because we were on it first.

There are craters everywhere, some but not all filled with water and mud. The more the truck bounces, the more it hurts my back.

We've been in the truck for quite a while. One of the things you don't want to do in Ukraine is drive too long. The longer you drive, the greater the odds the enemy will find you. They tend to target vehicles, since hitting them not only kills the occupants, but ties up resources and burdens whomever the vehicle and unit was supporting.

Both sides use drones to spy on each other. I can see them buzzing overhead with my night vision, but I don't know whose they are.

A bunch fly in from the north. I decide they're Russian, since that's where the enemy is.

Artillery shells begin to fall. They're not especially close: six hundred yards. But that's near enough for us to realize we're being targeted. So yes, those are enemy drones overhead.

We pick up speed.

And then we're there, a tree line and trenches where we are to dismount. Someone shouts to move quickly, but I'm already out. I don't have to be told to hurry up.

Empty, our Hilux backs up to leave. It gets stuck in the mud. Eventually, the other truck will come up and take our driver back. The pickup will have to wait until the next day, when a BMP will arrive to haul it out of the mud.

We wait in the trench line for ten minutes, getting our bearings and making sure we're not being targeted. Ready, we run to a line of trees, then work down to a field we need to cross to get north to the canal where the troops we're to help are waiting.

The field is six hundred yards across, dotted with mortar and artillery craters. A trail has been worn through the brush.

We start across. There's movement ahead, in a second set of trees at the far end.

Soldiers.

Russians?

No. Definitely not. They're moving in the open on our side of the canal.

Ukrainians, probably exhausted from a day of fighting, exfiltrating from the front.

I'm relieved, then alarmed. There's nearly a platoon of them, all bunched up, moving slowly through open ground—they're a sure target, several times more obvious than we are. They're too close together. One artillery shell could kill them all.

A miss could take us.

Run!

I push faster, knowing we have to clear the field before the Russians see the Ukrainians or us.

There are craters everywhere. I'm not sure if the field is mined.

It must be mined.

It can't be mined if we're going through it. It would have been cleared.

We need to get across.

I manage a few hundred yards before the shells begin to land. Fortunately, the first salvos are far off. Teddy, bringing up the rear, makes it to the trees before the enemy finally zeroes in on the path we took.

Sweat flies off him as he reaches us, muttering something like "that was close" before ducking down amid the woods.

We cross to the canal. Most of it is protected from the enemy's sight by a high berm, but ahead there's an exposed part. We can see across it to the enemy's position, which means they can see us as well.

Someone shouts instructions to crouch as you run.

Maybe we are shot at. I can't tell.

I find out later the Russians often fire machine guns and the occasional tank round at anything moving there. But I don't hear anything as I run. All I think is, I don't want to stop.

I'm at point; everyone's spread out behind me, following as fast as they can.

A shell arcs down ahead. I throw myself down. It lands a hundred meters away.

I move out again. Soon I won't even flinch when I hear the shells, I'll just run.

We make it to a point where the berm gives us cover again. The Ukrainian positions are just ahead, up a hill.

Teddy and I break off from the others and go up the hill, heads as low as we get them. We run straight into the trench network, finally protected by decent cover.

There's a guy standing at the position ahead. We've reached Dupont, our objective.

"*Spetznaz?*" He's asking if we're the special operations troops he was expecting.

"Yes." I take a breath.

Teddy asks the guy if he speaks English. He doesn't.

I talk to him in Russian. He begins showing us where everything is, how the defenses are laid out.

The Ukrainians have a PKM machine gun, covering the Russian side of the canal. The PKM is a Russian machine gun. The design is old—the newest model dates to the late 1960s—but it's a deadly and generally dependable weapon when handled properly.

The Ukrainian takes us back around to a long-roof bunker at the right side of the trench that his team is using to rest in when off rotation. It doesn't look very comfortable, but we're not the ones who are going to be using it.

The next machine gun position has a German-made MG 3 machine gun that I've never seen mounted on a bipod before. The MG 3 is an old weapon, first fielded in the late 1950s to early '60s. Heavily based on the German World War II MG 42, it looks like it belongs to that war, not ours.

Its operator continually scans his sector, swinging the gun back and forth. Good. Very good. But the position isn't dug out real well. Have to fix that.

We look over the rest. They did a really good job of top cover. Camouflage netting and foliage and whatnot, enough that if you were looking at us from the other side of the canal, you wouldn't be able to tell there was a trench here. But there are a few things they need to fix, improving the field of fire, angles, making sure that there are no open sectors. There's one spot where a rut in the front of the canal makes the trenches vulnerable to a surprise assault.

We explain the problems. The Ukrainians understand and get to work fixing things.

The trenches are muddy. There are spent shell casings everywhere. The bottoms of the trenches are lined with them. There is a constant noise that I can't figure out until maybe an hour passes; it's the sound of an army of rats scrummaging through discarded rations and trash.

Along the footpath behind the fighting positions a crumbled body wearing a plate carrier lies on the ground. It looks like a skeleton, twisted and forgotten. I can't tell what side he was on when he was alive, or how long it's been since he died.

There are other bodies. And rats eating them. At least the rodents have the grace to scurry as we near.

The warhead of an unexploded rocket-propelled grenade (or RPG) launcher is stuck in the ground nearby.

"Do you have any rockets here?" I ask the Ukrainian commander.

He doesn't understand until I ask about RPGs.

They don't.

"Do the Russian have any armor?" I ask.

He tells me a BMP comes by once an hour. While there are no RPGs here, the other positions have rockets. As long as the BMP does not come directly at them, which seems unlikely, they'll be okay.

We go over the fields of fire again. Once that's taken care of, I tell him he can get some rest.

He looks doubtful.

"There are two extra guys here now, so you guys can sleep more and we'll take over the machine guns."

He agrees, finally.

I take one of the positions. The shelling hasn't stopped. It's less than during the day, but it's still brutal. Both sides. As I'm watching, one of our shells hits something big on the Russian side of the canal. I don't know if it's an ammo stockpile or what, but the explosions light up the night. Things start cooking off. I'm treated to a small fireworks show.

It's said that you don't hear the bullet that kills you. Shells are different. If you hear an incoming shell whistling toward you, it may be too late. I reflexively duck with every whistle. Eventually, I will grow used to the sound, but the idea that I could be killed or maimed at any moment never goes away. It hovers around the edge of my consciousness, content to let my mind focus on more important things, showing itself just enough to keep me uncomfortable.

A little before false dawn, the real shelling begins. Shit explodes everywhere. The artillery is firing well over us, but the mortars land close. For two hours, there's an explosion nearly every sixty seconds, maybe quicker. They pause for a few minutes, then begin again.

There are more mortar rounds fired in those two hours, I think, than the average Marine mortarman fires during his career. But they don't hit anyone.

An SU-25 Frogfoot, a close-air support Russian attack plane, flies over their line and starts a gun run on some of our friendly forces on the left flank.

The SU-25 is kind of the A-10A of Russia. It's built to fly low and relatively slow. This air attack is something American soldiers haven't experienced in decades. The US has operated exclusively with total air superiority since World War II. No enemy aircraft has blown up our forces since before I was born.

That's the thing about this war. I'm fighting on the side of the underdogs. The enemy is the one with the superior firepower and all the advantages that brings. They don't have full control of the sky, but they have a clear advantage.

My side doesn't come close. Not on paper, at least. Not in anything you can put a number on.

I chat a bit in Russian with the Ukrainian soldier who comes to relieve me.

"Is it like this every day?" I ask.

"Every one."

"How long have you been here?"

In this position, two months. In total fighting in the area, eight.

"This is our house now," he tells me.

It's one thing to be shelled, and another to be shelled all day. To be shelled every day for two months?

Five a.m. comes and we move out, hoping to reach the rendezvous point with the trucks before the sun fully rises. Our artillery is sending shells overhead as we run back down the trenches and then along the canal.

As I start down from the fighting positions, the path disappears. My night vision flashes white, and a shockwave pounds my ears. In that same moment I hear this crazy loud crack, the sound a two-by-four might make if it was ten times thicker and whacked by Paul Bunyan's axe.

An artillery shell has exploded in the trees I'm running toward.

I take a knee.

Am I dead?

I look back, unsure whether I was hit. I see the rest of the team running across the field toward me, completely unfazed.

What is that smell?

I glance at the ground and realize I've knelt in a pile of trash.

Except it's not trash. I've knelt on a dead man, eviscerated by an explosion.

My leg is in his rib cage. His uniform shows he was Russian, though by now nationalities mean nothing to him.

I move a few feet over to pee.

Another dead Russian lies farther down the path. Whatever killed him took away half his skull, leaving his brain exposed in his helmet like a cup of rotting custard.

We get back to the Hiluxes just in time to see the BMP come up and haul the stuck pickup out of its hole. The BMP crewman yells at us to move faster.

Go! Go! Go!

Russian artillery has followed us across the woods to the field and to the road. We jump in the back of the trucks as the BMP pulls away. Ukrainian soldiers watch from a nearby hole, waiting for the artillery to move on so they can continue to the front.

The world continues to explode around us.

I'm exhilarated, fried with adrenaline, excited to be alive, thrilled, and fearful, all at the same time. We speed through the ghost villages to the fields and dirt road. The old people are gone, their porch empty.

The sun is up as we reach the highway and I can see the fields. Rather than the brown weeds I imagined, the rolling acres are filled with flowers—beautiful, gorgeous flowers that have sprouted in the midst of war; blue, orange, yellow flowers spreading out along the ground, gorgeously defiant in the face of war's insanity.

TWENTY-FIVE

ROGUE TEAM

That was my first mission.

I remember it vividly, that first time in hell. The other missions, though, blend together. Different details come back. The shapes sometimes change. Directions reverse. I remember a left where I once thought right. I can't precisely picture where a machine gun was, or how far we had to run across the field. But the bodies of the dead men are always the same.

At the end of that mission, we turned in our gear and went off for food. That became something of a post-mission ritual.

It may seem surprising, but there were a large number of restaurants operating despite the war raging only a few miles away. There was a pizza parlor in Kramatorsk we'd go to regularly. Eventually, the Russians targeted it with a pair of missiles. The attack killed Ian Tortorici, an American who was on our sister team. Three other team guys were wounded. A dozen civilians also died in the attack.

I don't think any of us spoke the entire day after we found out.

It's believed the Russians targeted the restaurant because they knew foreign soldiers ate there, thanks to information from an informer who was arrested by the Ukrainians. But plenty of sites that were hit had not been deliberately targeted. That was the thing about Russian missiles. They were indiscriminate, and poorly aimed. Even if they weren't explicitly targeting civilians, the Russians didn't care much if they killed them.

Russian propaganda, incidentally, claimed that the restaurant was a secret NATO headquarters. It somehow failed to mention the children who died in the strike.

After the pizza parlor was attacked, we found a restaurant that specialized in Jordanian food, and ate there instead.

Rogue Team was assigned a safe house in a village called Druzhkivka. We were in a little neighborhood of tract houses, not too unlike what you'd find in America, adjusting for the fact that the roads were dirt and the buildings smaller.

The neighbors all had gardens, though most were untended now, weeds growing amid flowers and vegetables. There was a cherry tree in our yard, some apples, and a few berries. Sunflowers, roses, and shrubs grew wild, oblivious to combat's disorder.

There were three stories to the house, with bedrooms, a kitchen, and a living room, just like in the US. The family had signed the house over to the Ukrainian army, leaving most if not all of the furnishings and even a few knickknacks and books on random shelves. My room had been a kid's room, judging from the animal-themed sheets on the bed.

The house was a crazy mix of civilian and soldier décor: a stereo system and old TV, kids programs on video tapes, medical supplies, boxes of dried food, MREs. I'd eat breakfast off what had been the family's good china. Their refrigerator was stuffed with food we'd either buy or get from local volunteers. Ammo and weapons filled what had been the family garage. Our vehicles sat in the driveway. Besides the two Toyotas, we had a utility vehicle that looked kind of like a Suzuki Trooper, but honestly I'm not sure what it was. It had tape on the side of it that said "Anna" in Russian letters. So we called it the Anna.

We had a satellite link in an open room upstairs. Starlink gave us a way to use the internet and communicate back home.

We were far enough from the front line to feel relatively safe from attack. Still, I slept with my rifle next to me at all times. There were still civilians in the town, a decent number of them, but they were all very much pro Ukrainian, and as far as I could tell, uniformly appreciative of the soldiers and volunteers in their midst.

"Safe" did not mean the town was beyond Russian reach. They had long-range artillery systems aimed at the village, and they occasionally demonstrated their destructive capabilities. But the worst, for me, were the sporadic cruise missile attacks.

The first time I heard a cruise missile overhead, I dove to the floor next to my bed, sure we were about to be blown up. The sound faded, then was replaced by a loud explosion that shook the house. I got up and went to the window. A black plume rose from the center of town. I'm not sure now, and probably wasn't then, what was hit, or how much damage was caused. Whatever it was would have been civilian.

Cruise missile attacks were random, and thankfully comparatively rare. Every single time, though, I thought the missile was coming directly for us. The missiles came to be the scariest sound in Ukraine for me, worse even than the dirge of mortar and artillery rounds on the battlefield. There was something very ugly about the pitch of the fan-jet or whatever the hell engine pushed it through the air. I'd listen and wait, hoping the sound would fade.

When that happened, I knew someone a mile or two away was going to die. That sucked as well.

Fighter jets occasionally flew low and loud overhead. Those were probably Ukrainian, since they didn't seem to be bombing anything. Air raid sirens constantly went off. In Kyiv, an alert would sound well in advance of a missile arriving; you might have an hour before it arrived. The missile might even be intercepted miles away. Here, you had two minutes to find shelter.

We used a basement room below the garage as a bunker. I don't know how safe it would have been with all the ammo and explosives we had stored above it. Fortunately, I never had to find out.

Each team kept its personal weapons—rifles, machine guns, grenades, etc.—at their safe house. Specialized weapons were kept at a base in a nearby town. There, an underground basement held things like Stinger anti-aircraft missiles, Javelin anti-armor missiles, and all manner of different ammo and explosives. Our administrative offices were also located there.

Nearby, another army base had barracks and buildings used for briefings and classes. Early on I helped give a briefing on Russian mines, translating from Russian to English for our team and other volunteers. Not far away was a camp we called Hawaii, a regular army base with a chow hall, showers, and a motor pool. We'd gas up there, get some water, and occasionally eat.

Rogue had been organized as a special reconnaissance team, training to go behind enemy lines to scout, attack high-value targets, and wage general havoc. The Ukrainians had made good progress here a few months before, but by the time we arrived, things had settled into an uneasy stalemate. The Russians had been wedged into positions on the north side of a large canal system. During my time, we were attached to units tasked to an area on the south side of the canal, with Russians now on their flank as other units pushed east. That meant we would have no area to scout until the brigade joined an offensive planned for some point in the near or distant future.

In this war, the future was always like that: tomorrow or never.

To put us to use, the brigade commanders had us periodically relieve some of their frontline troops, reviewing their defenses and suggesting improvements: exactly what we'd done on the first mission. Most of the area was open farmland, crisscrossed by irrigation ditches and segregated into plots by narrow tree lines. We'd usually get to the fields in the pickups, though there were light armored vehicles and even ATVs available at times.

The ATVs were kind of cursed, I think. Our sergeant major, a Brit, got blown off one during a shelling. Concussed, he had to be medevacked out. We never used them ourselves.

Vehicles close to the front were readily targeted by the Russians, who used drones to watch for them. Because of that, we'd typically be dropped near but not at our assignment. We'd move from concealment to concealment, occasionally racing through open fields, praying we were too puny a force for them to bother targeting.

Occasionally our prayers were answered positively. More often, the powers that be decided we were worth at least a few mortar rounds. The barrages tended to miss by decent margins, though, and in any event we felt safer on foot than riding in artillery magnets once the big stuff flew.

My time in Ukraine mostly blurs into a chaotic jumble as I look back. I remember the parts that scared the hell out of me, or were crazily, darkly funny, but the stuff around them blurs into the background. Before we went into action, I made it a point to send my parents and Autumn messages saying I loved them. I don't know if the messages had much impact on them, Autumn especially. But if it happened that I died, I wanted the last thing they heard from me to be love.

Typically we'd be sent to the canal area to check defenses and give the soldiers there some rest. Dave and I would go together, splitting out from Yan and Teddy, moving through a trench system and bunker complex until we found a group of Ukrainians holding the positions. We'd check out their machine gun positions and take some of their turns on watch. We'd make a few suggestions, but by and large they did a good job setting things up.

It was obvious that we were foreigners, which made the Ukrainians curious about us. Conversation inevitably began with *Where you from?* Saying "America" continued to impress.

No matter how well positions had been camouflaged, the Russians always seemed to have their eyes on us. One time we were with a Ukrainian unit when a shell hit near the position where Teddy and Yan were, to our east. A wounded Ukrainian was carried up to our trench line, where he was met by a mine-clearing vehicle that evacuated him from the battlefield. Russian artillery immediately targeted the vehicle, following it as it drove off. Fortunately, they weren't very accurate, and the vehicle escaped without a hit.

In that case, the mine-clearer had no special markings, and it could be argued that it was a legitimate target, even though anyone watching would have realized what it was doing. But the Russians seemed to love going after our medical vehicles, even when marked and obviously carrying wounded.

Our rules of engagement prohibited us from doing that to them. Though to be honest, I can't swear I wouldn't have aimed at a Russian ambulance if the opportunity presented itself.

Do that to us? Then it's good enough for you.

I'm sorry. That's how I felt on the battlefield. I doubt I'm alone.

My deepest fear was not that I would be killed, but that I would kill someone I had known in Russia—another prisoner, or, God forbid, Lina's brother. I argued with myself that their presence would surely be a result of their own decision. But I knew too much of the Russian government to pretend that they'd have much free will.

I shot at every Russian I could nonetheless.

Things tended to be relatively quiet during the night, but soon after the sun came up, the Russians would always send mortar shells in our direction. Then artillery. Then whatever.

One day the unit we were with was given orders to support an attack on the north side of the canal.

Dave and I joined machine gunners at their positions. They began firing; the Russians answered. The Ukrainians fired rockets. The Russians did as well.

The gunfire quickly became so intense that standing was out of the question. Overhead, drones picked up Russian positions, and Ukrainian mortars began pounding them.

The battle had only been going for maybe two minutes when the Ukrainian manning the PKM machine gun where I was looked over at me and nodded, inviting me to take a shot.

I'd never fired a PKM, certainly not in combat. It was a thrill.

Yes, that word. A thrill. In combat.

After a few rounds, a spotter relayed that my shots were too low. I corrected, aiming to scorch the tree line.

Russian rounds landed all around us, mortar shells mostly behind, rockets mostly in front. *Whistle, boom. Hiss, boom.*

The Ukrainians brought up rocket-propelled grenades and began firing toward the enemy positions. They didn't seem to do any damage. The mortar duel continued. In the meantime, Dave had the PKM moved to a different spot, and we set up our own MK 48 machine gun. Dave started firing, aiming for a clump of soldiers in the middle of the trees.

"Yavin, this is Rogue," I called over the radio, contacting command with their call sign. "Be advised, troops in contact. Enemy SPG-9 with infantry in the open directly north of our position."

"Roger."

I translated the spotter's corrections with difficulty—his Russian wasn't that good—but Dave finally laced his target.

I took over. I wanted to get the bastard who was firing the rockets at us, but I couldn't pick out the actual target.

Then a round from a recoilless rifle hit about thirty yards in front of us.

"Where's that from?" I shouted to Dave.

"Uh, it was at us," he yelled.

"From where?"

"I don't know."

I lit up the tree line.

"It's gonna be farther," said Dave.

The Ukrainian spotter started giving me directions. I adjusted my aim.

"You're hitting them!" he said. "You're on target. Keep firing right there."

I did.

"Finish the belt! We're going to hit them with the rockets!"

The MK 48 clicked dry. I picked up the gun to move back as the Ukrainians began firing rocket-propelled grenades.

Something big landed close enough to shake the ground, nearly knocking me off my feet. The gunfire continued for a while longer until the Ukrainian commander radioed to cease fire.

"How'd the attack go?" I asked one of the Ukrainians. "Did we get the objective?"

"They didn't attack yet."

"We didn't attack?"

"Not yet."

To say I was deflated is an understatement. We'd just been in an outlandish firefight, started by ourselves, one that extended probably for a good mile along the front and used a ton of ammunition. The way I'd been taught, that kind of firepower kicked off an assault.

"We didn't attack?" I asked again.

"There will be an attack," answered one of the soldiers. "It could be in five minutes, it could be tomorrow."

"What?"

"Well, they were supposed to attack," explained the Ukrainian. "They were supposed to assault those positions when we started firing, but for whatever reason, they didn't."

I just stared at him.

He shrugged. "It's Ukraine."

Attack or not, the results were bloody. The spotter told us that we had hit the Russians in the position and they were calling for casualty evacs. We also had one Ukrainian wounded, though not at our position.

I asked if he was going to make it and he said he didn't know.

Our rockets had mostly missed. The mortars did some damage, but many shells had missed. They'd had trouble finding the enemy.

That was the reality of the war. Uncertainty, hesitation, ferocious action. Bravery. It all mixed together. Not just for us, I imagine, but for everyone.

I suppose for all wars.

The Ukrainians we worked with were generally pretty good, welcoming, and—considering that we were in a combat zone—easygoing. They welcomed volunteers and special ops guys. The soldiers were happy to shoot at the Russians, and took pride in killing them. The men were all a little older, many past what would have ordinarily been considered military age. And they hated Russians.

But there were other areas along the front where that wasn't so. The problem was this: spec op units like ours would sneak through the lines, cross behind the Russians, and raise havoc. By the time they crossed back, the Russians would know where they were and begin firing at them. The Ukrainians manning the front line would be the ones who caught the brunt of it, not the special ops guys, who would exfil out to their safe houses behind the lines.

Occasionally we'd work with other teams that were part of GUR. One was a heavy weapons team designated "Bravo." The first time we met them they were our QRF—Quick Reaction Force, the guys you called in for help when crap came down in buckets. That's where I first met Speedy. He was actually an attachment from a direct-action team he led, Black Maple—temporary assignments or attachments were a constant thing, especially for us, since our core team was so small.

Speedy ended up working with us a lot. He was a former soldier from Canada who'd volunteered to fight soon after leaving his own army. He hadn't seen combat until he got to Ukraine. (Interesting factoid about Speedy: the Russians claim to have killed him four separate times now.)

A lot of our attachments were there for specific tasks, like driving. We worked a few missions with a pair of Dutch snipers I'll call Pim and Vim. They worked at night, aiming to pick off enemy soldiers with precision shots near or behind the front lines, the classic sniper assignment. Our job was to provide security, making sure they weren't vulnerable to attack.

These two guys had known each other before the war. They were funny, but unintentionally so: they would constantly argue about crediting kills. On one mission I remember them going back and forth about whether a man they saw fall was truly dead, or just wounded. We weren't in a position to check—the Russian had fallen a good ways off.

I don't think the sniper got credit. Not that the tally made any difference to anyone but them.

The Ukrainians had spent the winter of 2022–2023 planning for a major offensive across the eastern front. Originally scheduled to kick off in the spring, it had been delayed for various reasons. Small attacks had started around the beginning of May, testing Russian defenses.

Those defenses had been greatly beefed up during the winter, as we'd seen firsthand.

Ukraine would attack all across the fronts, winning back considerable territory but not quite breaking Russian defenses. Retaking Bakhmut to our north was among their significant objectives, as was chasing the Russians from the canal areas close to us.

We didn't know all the details, of course, but we were well aware that the Ukrainian army was preparing for a major push. As June approached, we were tasked to assist Third Assault Brigade, a Ukrainian grouping of several battalions of infantry, armor, artillery, and assorted smaller units. (Third Brigade would be considered roughly equivalent to, though much smaller than, a traditional corps command in the US military.) Their primary objectives were in the Bakhmut area to our north.

Our task, as eventually briefed, was to assist attacks near and across the canals. Once the Ukrainians reached a specific phase point, we would assault, poking a hole in their lines. The brigade forces would follow, penetrating the lines and flanking the adjacent positions.

We began a series of training exercises, reviewing our small group and infiltration tactics, brushing up on things. We were set to be the vanguard of a major assault.

That was great. But . . .

Our time at the front was now limited.

GUR units were on a strict rotation schedule. While our part in the assault was due to happen soon, we were also scheduled to leave the combat area a few days afterward. And Command refused to change our exit date.

The assault date approached . . . then passed. A new date was set. We staged our gear, went to the tactical command center, got comms set, drove to the staging point . . . then got word that the date had been pushed.

Repeat.

We waited, sweating, hoping to get into action before being given mandatory leave.

And then it happened: Our replacement team showed up. We weren't getting in the assault at all.

We turned over the safe house, and were given temporary quarters in a bombed-out elementary school with some hope that the Ukrainian army would reach the phase line and we could join the battle.

But they didn't. Ordered to stand down, we reluctantly loaded the trucks for the trip to Kyiv and the end of our deployment. It was likely that leave would be permanent, the unit disassembled.

To be honest, by that point I welcomed the break. I'd planned to leave at the end of the month anyway, so I could go to college at the beginning of the upcoming semester.

We packed up our two trucks and set out for Kyiv. I was supposed to sleep the first half of the drive back, resting up before taking the wheel. But I couldn't. I was too awake, still buzzing on adrenaline. My experiences had been more than I'd hoped for. Truthfully, though, I wanted more. I was ready to go home, but also sorry to have missed the battle we'd trained for.

Maybe I'd tasted revenge, but not the full measure.

Super Dave called us to turn around a few hours into the drive.

"We're going back," announced Dave, explaining that the advance forces had finally reached the phase line and our mission had been reinstated. "Third Brigade specifically requested us."

Hell, yeah!

We whipped around and hit the gas.

TWENTY-SIX

ONE LAST MISSION

Earlier, Rogue Team had been augmented with two members, Rauta and Pele. Rauta was a Swedish combat engineer, had been in Afghanistan and Iraq, and was a solid guy who knew his stuff. Pele . . .

The thing about Pele was that he *really* didn't care what you thought about him. And he had a very dark sense of humor.

At least, I think it was humor. He'd joke about taking my stuff when I died. Or maybe he wouldn't wait for the Russians to kill me.

Nice guy. But I think that was his way of saying I was okay.

"Pele," by the way, is not his real name. He's named here after the Brazilian soccer star, or the Polynesian goddess. More or less at his request. He'd been a contractor in Afghanistan after serving his country's military.

We added a couple more members for the final mission. There were two machine gunners borrowed from a heavy weapons squad, Austria and Greek. Austria and Greek's call signs were not especially creative, since both came from those countries. Austria had been in his country's elite light infantry. Greek had served in the Greek army, then joined the French Foreign Legion and later volunteered to fight in Ukraine. He was already in the country when Russia invaded Crimea, and had fought the Russians in Donbas before the second invasion in 2022.

Last but not least were Belka, a Belarussian who had joined the volunteers to fight Russia and earlier had headed his own team, and Speedy, who'd worked with us earlier.

We rendezvoused back at the elementary school, dusted ourselves off, and got organized. Things in the sector had developed quickly. A sudden surge by the Ukrainians led to a few tweaks in the plans, as well as an objective farther into what was currently occupied territory. The basic idea remained the same, though: we would spearhead an assault on a Russian position for a regular Ukrainian army unit, which would push up behind us.

The Russians had mined the area we were attacking through. Engineers had been called out to clear a path using mine-clearing vehicles. These would shoot out a line of explosive cord. The line would then be detonated, exploding the nearby mines to clear a path. The engineers also used more painstaking methods, searching for mines and disarming them by hand.

Originally we were supposed to take an infantry-fighting armored vehicle to attack a line of trenches on the Russian side while covered by the vehicle's mounted machine gun. But the vehicles were deemed to be a major risk, easily spotted and targeted. So instead, we'd be driven to a position on the south side of the canal and dropped off, possibly—no, almost certainly—under artillery fire.

From there we had to head west up the canal about two and a half kilometers on foot to a bunker complex. We'd wait there for word from Command that the regular troops had reached the mission's phase line. Once that came, we would cross the canal, head east on the north side, and assault the Russian positions. There were two villages there, both occupied by the Russians, as were the tree lines in the area where we would operate.

Third Brigade's main force would be to our rear and to the west. On our right flank, to the south but still on the north side of the canal, were Belarussians. They had assaulted our objective the day before, lost a Ukrainian scout, and retreated.

Our part of the operation would launch pre-dawn.

I didn't get much, if any, sleep before getting up and loading our gear in the French Roshel tasked to take us to the drop-off point. The Roshel is an armored personnel carrier; think of a Brinks armored truck with a lot more armor, badass tires, and military gear. It has a cool vibe and is relatively protective, but it's very cramped inside when you're kitted out.

Dave interrupted our nervous chatter as we got underway. "Okay guys," he said. "Don't forget the most important part."

Everyone went dead silent, trying to figure out what that part was.

"Have fun."

We laughed. It was the first time he'd broken the tension like that on the way to a mission.

We were working with Third Brigade, but we couldn't talk to them directly. Instead, we had to talk to them through our own command due to comm issues. Belka and I had separate radios to do that, along with the team radios everyone had.

Team members carried at least thirteen magazines for their rifles. I think I had fifteen for my Bren. I also had four hand grenades and two charges of C-4 explosive. My combat vest was loaded full with plates, front, back, and sides. My assault pack was stuffed with food and four and a half liters of water. The team had a couple of AT-4 anti-tank weapons. We also carried a Bulgarian Bullspike, a small anti-tank weapon developed from the Soviet-era RPG-22, and an MK 48 machine gun.

Pele was packing a revolving grenade launcher, which looked like something out of *Rambo.* It had six chambers, which in theory meant you could fire salvos in quick succession. The reality was short of that. In the field, the weapon had a disappointing tendency to jam.

Three UAVs were assigned to work with us. One drone was from GUR; the others, Third Brigade. They would provide intel from overhead. GUR also had access to real-time radio intercepts, which would prove vital during the operation. There was also a Bayraktar drone following us during the daylight portion of the mission.

I don't remember the code word for the phase line we headed toward. The words "hole in the ground" keep popping into my head. That wasn't it, but it was the literal description of our first marker.

We headed up a dirt road with what looked like a jungle on each side. The truck turned off the trail, parking in a bomb crater so wide and deep it held the entire vehicle.

We waited there for a couple of hours. We reviewed our mission plans, ate some MREs, drank some water. Guys who smoked, smoked.

I had a cigarette, too, even though I don't smoke. I was that anxious.

As I was putting on my face paint, someone yelled that the personnel carrier was there and ready to depart.

"Looks like we didn't get all dressed up for nothing," I said jokingly in a Scottish accent.

It was a goofy, nervous thing. I sometimes used accents to lighten the tension. Super Dave called me on it today. "Okay, William Wallace," he told me, smirking.

(Wallace was a Scottish warrior during the First War of Scottish

Independence, defeating the English at the battle of Stirling Bridge. It's surprising what a Columbia University grad knows.)

An M113 armored personnel carrier drove up and we got aboard. Buttoned up, the carrier treaded forward.

It took forever to reach our designated drop-off point. Finally, it creaked to a halt and the ramp at the rear dropped.

"Ramp dropping!" I yelled, running out as it landed.

"Go!" yelled Super Dave. "Go, go, go!"

We ran to a nearby trench. Artillery shells were already bursting nearby—far enough away that the blasts couldn't hurt us, but close enough to vibrate our eardrums. The M113 reversed and booked out of there.

We hauled butt to the bunker, taking artillery fire. There was a firefight directly to our right, with small-arms machine guns and rockets firing nonstop. By the time we reached the bunker I was out of breath, regretting my life choices. The shelling went on forever, rounds impacting near enough to shower us with dirt. I was pretty sure we were going to die in there.

Finally, the shelling stopped. Either the Russians had run out of ammo, or they decided we had to have been killed by now.

When the shelling stopped, Super Dave got us up and led us down the canal. The sky above us was open, in clear view of any UAVs. We didn't linger.

We reached a blown-up bridge at a spot on the canal where we could easily cross. I slid down the side of the canal, almost straight down on my butt, to a flatter area where I could hobble across the rocks and giant concrete slabs of the destroyed structure to get to the other side.

I spotted an anti-tank mine on a piece of rubble just in time not to trip it. I warned Teddy, and continued on.

Once across, we headed back east again, still in the open. The shelling had slowed but never completely stopped. Once more it kicked up. The shells inched uncomfortably close. But I was so used to mortar fire now it was almost like white noise.

If white noise were lethal, maybe.

We stopped for a breather in the shadow of a slope that protected us from the worst of the shelling. Yan yelled something over the radio I couldn't make out. I finally walked over to him to find out what he was saying.

"We're going to have to hustle," he told me. The explosions were starting to zero in.

"Okay," I said. But *No shit* was what I was really thinking. It felt like all of Russia was firing at us; the best way to survive was to run forward, out of it.

When I'd first seen action here, the amount of shelling had felt crazy. How could they expend so much ammo?

I was jumping on the ground and covering up at every whistle then. Now I just accepted the onslaught as reality. It wasn't aimed at me specifically. It was aimed at everyone who wasn't Russian.

That one's at least a hundred meters away, so I don't care.

That one's close. Damn.

I moved as quickly as I could, weighed down by my gear. Rather than thinking I was going to die, I focused on being tired.

I hope we get there soon.

We moved down a little hill, turning north. We started through foliage where Ukrainian sappers had marked a path with blue tape to show us the lane that had been cleared of mines.

The terrain around us at that point looked like a jungle. We climbed over trees sheered to the ground by artillery or the mortars. That took us to an open flat of sticks, tree logs, and debris, the ground having been de-wooded by explosions.

Finally we reached a Ukrainian guide who was waiting to bring us to the final coordination line, the point where we'd have a chance to get last-minute orders before crossing forward to the actual assault.

All that hell, and we weren't even at the starting line.

He brought us through the woods to a pair of shell craters maybe thirty meters apart in the trees. They had been dug out to form a crude defensive position. The team divided in half, filling each hole. Super Dave and Yan left to do a leader's recon; the rest of us sat and waited.

"Where's the next friendly position?" I asked our guide.

"This is it."

"This is the last friendly position?"

"Yeah."

I yelled over to the other crater that we needed to pull security. The Russians were very close, closer than friendly troops.

It began to rain.

Super Dave came back. He got a radio update from the tactical command center:

There's an estimated forty Russians in the position you're about to assault. They have rockets, RPGs, an automatic grenade launcher, and small arms.

Command also gave him locations for a number of machine guns. They would be targeted by artillery.

We got ready, waiting for the unit we were spearheading to get closer.

Command called again. The element that was supposed to push up with us had been forced back. We'd be on our own if we proceeded.

Damn.

All of us said we'd do it anyway. We're ten guys, but that's cool.

Dave went over our plans once more. "They're out there and we're going to kill 'em," he told us as he closed off the briefing.

Dave *never* talked about killing anyone.

They're out there and we're going to kill 'em.

Things were about to go from nasty to insane.

The odds were, in fact, against us. But they weren't quite as lopsided as they may seem.

The Russians had a reinforced platoon of paratroopers with low morale holding the positions we were going to assault. They hadn't had a food resupply for several days. Their water was low. Just recently a Russian unit of "volunteer" prisoners had stolen their water supplies as they fled the battlefield. A Chechen unit that had taken heavy casualties had bugged out, according to intel, taking whatever water and food the prisoners had left.

So while we were facing what should have been a unit of up to fifty or more men, it was a very good bet it was far smaller, that less than half of the men would be in shape to fight, and that far less than half would be very motivated to do so.

We counted on that.

We formed a line to attack. You may have seen that in old movies, but in the real world of modern combat, it's close to unheard of for even a small unit to advance in a line. But given the layout of the Russian defenses, as well as our small size and the terrain, it made sense here.

We split into two sections, five apiece. I was one point man, positioned on the far left of the line. The other point was Rauta, with his guys to our right.

"Ready?" I looked over at Super Dave.

"Yeah."

"Advance!" I yelled, giving the hand signal to the others.

We started forward, using the trees to partially cover our advance.

We went for maybe twenty minutes, until we came to an area patched with MON-100 Russian mines, anti-personnel weapons that spray hundreds of steel pellets and fragments when set off. During our class on Russian mines, the instructor had warned that they had a kill radius of a hundred meters, with a wounding radius at least eighty meters beyond that.

We halted and took cover in an artillery crater. Yan and Rauta moved up, located the mines and their trip wires, and detonated them harmlessly, sending shrapnel raging through the nearby woods. The team moved on.

We were still a good distance from the objectives when we started taking serious incoming fire. Light artillery and heavy mortars, maybe both. We soon realized the shells were far enough away that they didn't seem like an immediate threat. They weren't all exploding, either. One would hit in the distance. You'd expect a burst and a boom, but nothing would come.

A round whistled in nearby.

Blap.

Then nothing. A dud.

I glanced at Austria, the closest guy to me. He shrugged. We kept moving.

The shells may have been defective or just old. Or maybe the dirt, which was fairly wet, was too soft to allow a detonation.

I didn't spend any time trying to figure it out.

The radio barked.

"Gulag," I acknowledged.

"They have a drone flying over the body of a dead Ukrainian, do you see it?"

"I see the drone, but I don't see the body." I strained to see ahead. "There's some smoke in the trees."

It was a thin little wisp, barely discernible. I pointed it out to Super Dave. All I could think of was someone smoking a cigarette in the woods.

Yan came over. I pointed it out. "Is that cigarette smoke?"

"I don't know."

Finally I realized it was coming from a bunker that had been hidden from view. Yan and I moved up to frag it, formed a rough L so we could attack without getting caught in each other's crossfire. I approached the front of the bunker, trying to see who was there.

Why are they smoking? Are they retarded? Why don't they hear us coming?

Someone fired once or twice across the field in our direction. Yan started firing into the bunker. I began firing, too.

Not much. My Bren jammed after only a round or two.

Dude, are you fucking kidding me?

Tap-rack-bang—field procedure to unjam a weapon in combat.

I fired another round. Another.

The gun jammed again.

Fuck me.

I called to Austria and had him come up with his machine gun.

There had been no return fire from the bunker. Yan crept closer and tossed a frag in there.

The response was immediate: a fireworks display that would give some Fourth of July celebrations a run for the money. The bunker apparently had housed a stockpile of ammo. Bullets, grenades, God knows what else began cooking off. Nearby trees began to catch fire.

Time to move on.

As we moved up, I saw the body of the Ukrainian Command had called about. There was a tree line beyond him, with a row of bunkers.

We went forward gingerly and began clearing the bunkers. They were empty, of people at least. Whoever had been manning them had left hastily, abandoning their weapons.

The Russians had left some papers there. They contained the names of humanitarian organizations in Russia that were sending them supplies because their government couldn't manage to properly support them. Otherwise, all they left was trash, literally: old papers, care packages, food, documents, uniforms.

And the body of one of their own comrades in a trash pile not far from the bunker. He'd been there a while. How they slept with him so close is beyond me.

Once we had all the bunkers cleared, intel reported that we had Russian soldiers some two hundred meters in front of us in woods and foliage thick enough to be a jungle.

"They're prepared for combat."

So are we.

Austria went up with the machine gun, me right behind him. Pele and his grenade launcher followed.

"Aim out about two hundred meters," Super Dave told Pele. "We'll hit him with the grenade launcher, and advance on them as soon as we fire those rounds."

Pele set off a couple of rounds, and we launched. We'd gone more than a hundred meters when I realized we weren't being shot at.

Which was weird.

My ballistic glasses fogged as I ran, I guess from sweat. I finally had to pull them off so I could see.

I hope I don't get hit in the eyes by shrapnel.

I'd rather get hit by shrapnel in the eye than step on a mine or get shot because I couldn't see where I was going.

More than a hundred meters, and we still hadn't been fired on.

GUR radioed with the explanation: the Russians had heard us shouting to each other in English and retreated.

Super Dave ordered us to stop yelling and use the team radios instead. We found three machine gun positions, still equipped with PKMs and ammo belts. We followed the Russians' trail into the woods. They'd dropped a couple of AKs as they ran.

And something else: a pile of feces, still steaming, lay in the grass.

"They literally shit themselves," said Yan.

Farther on, we found body armor, plates, and carriers lying on the ground. They'd been shed so their owners could run faster.

By the time we find them, they'll be naked.

Another bunker system sat to our left off the trail. We stopped chasing the Russians and went to inspect it. All the positions were deserted. We cleared them and reoriented ourselves. By now, the Belarussian volunteer unit was coming up on us from the south. Command called and told us that we should continue past our tree line, trying to catch any Russian stragglers.

The woods broke into a Y, with an open field between them, spreading to at least three hundred meters. Bullets began flying through the trees as we went to the left.

I raised my rifle to fire across the field.

"Don't engage," said Dave. "We need to get close to them and kill them. Otherwise, they'll just keep retreating."

We were too far and the woods were too thick to see exactly who was firing and from where. Dave outlined a plan to have us circle around and take them from the rear.

We hadn't gotten very far when grenades began to fall. A group of Russians were firing automatic grenade launchers from a tree line ahead: not at us, but at our target.

The grenades were killing their own men. Maybe they thought their guys were us, or maybe they'd decided to fire at them because they were retreating.

GUR called in with more real-time intel: Russian artillery was about to aim salvos in our direction.

We ran for cover. Once more the abandoned Russian defenses provided empty bunkers to take shelter in. The last guy on the team squeezed in just as the first shell landed.

We inspected our new digs while the artillery barrage continued. The Russians who'd been here a short time earlier had abandoned their weapons, including some brand-new AK-12s, the country's latest assault rifle. There were also Russian cigarettes, watches, and condoms.

The shelling went on. A round hit so close and so hard that my nose started to bleed. I felt a sharp pain in my head. Light flashed behind my eyes—not in front of them; somehow the flash evaded my irises and went straight to my brain.

Metal filled my nose.

Oh, fuck.

GUR told us to sit tight. We didn't know it at the time, but the harder concussions were coming from a nearby Russian tank.

Ukrainian artillery rounds soon took it out.

We held on for about a half hour until the shelling finally started to taper.

We got out of the bunker and started north, running through some really tall grass, past blown-up trees. Every so often a mortar round would randomly screech in our direction, but it was always well off.

Until it wasn't.

I've thought about that round. It wasn't one of the scary ones. I've guessed it was an 82.

The Russians have a variety of light mortars firing an 82mm shell, so that makes sense. Most likely, then, it would have been fired from a tube first designed in 1937, based on an even older model made by the French. Effective weapons do not have to be recently made.

I've thought about the shell so much because I saw it explode. There was no flash of light; instead, a blackness erupted where it was landing.

I thought it was far enough away from us that it had safely missed.

But it hadn't quite.

"I'm hit," said Super Dave.

It seemed impossible that the explosion injured him. It seemed impossible that *anything* could injure him. But there was the wound, straight through the side of his right leg.

It was strange. Mortar shells had exploded much closer to us than that one and no one had been wounded. We'd later learn that the doctors treating Super Dave thought he'd been wounded by small-arms fire. Admittedly, rounds had snapped and whizzed overhead the whole time we fought, so it's possible. At the time, however, we were all convinced the mortar shell had hit him.

He was the first serious casualty we took, on the last mission of our deployment, days after we were supposed to leave the battlefield.

Belka put a tourniquet on him. I called for an evac and arranged the rendezvous.

Super Dave could hobble and, with Teddy's help, set off for treatment. Yan took over as team leader, and we began moving again. Soon we reached the tree line that had fired at us earlier.

The enemy was gone. The woods were ours.

A Ukrainian army unit with Ronin, a GUR team, was supposed to take the positions we'd swept through. The volunteers soon made contact with us over the radio. I gave the comms guy the layout, telling him where the bunkers were, where we were, and where we believed the Russians were. All of those details suggested how they could continue assaulting the enemy.

They started for us, then apparently stopped.

"The Ukrainians aren't going forward anymore, bro," the GUR volunteer handling the radio told me before using pretty strong language, implying they were too scared to continue.

Yan and a few guys went back to guide them forward so they could take their assigned position. Austria and Greek held our eastern flank with the machine gun; Speedy, Belka, Rauta, and myself moved west down the tree line.

We stopped and sat for a while, watching and listening. Suddenly we heard branches being broken in the distance. Then something louder.

A BMP?

"Speedy, you hear this?" I asked.

"What?"

"Listen."

"It's a BMP," he said. "Is it ours?"

"It's north of us, so I don't think so," I told him. "You have the AT-4?"

"Yeah, it's here," said Speedy.

"Give it to me."

Hitting the BMP with the AT-4 missile head-on from a distance might not disable it, and would leave the crew and whatever passengers they had to come and outnumber us. So I decided to wait until it was very close, when I could be sure of hitting the troop compartment from the side. That would fry the troops inside and hopefully kill the gunner on the top. As soon as the round hit, we'd charge the vehicle and get at the survivors before they could swivel the main gun toward us. Assuming they were still alive.

The Ukrainians began hitting the area with artillery. A large metallic *ping* clanged through the air, accompanied by an explosion that I've never heard before or since. The Ukrainians had taken the armored vehicle out with an Excalibur round, a GPS-guided artillery shell.

A few moments later, we heard scared Russian voices hurrying off, muffled by the distance. They were retreating.

I told Belka to call Command to see if they had a unit crossing in that direction, or if the vehicle was theirs. I didn't want to open up on friendlies.

"Not theirs."

A few seconds later, the voices began to fade. The Russians were gone.

The BMP had caught fire when it was hit. The gunner and commander died. The rest of the crew jumped out and ran for it. They turned out to have been much closer than we'd thought, less than a hundred yards, headed right for us when the guided artillery round hit.

We moved west, finding another tree line that ran north to south. Farther on, a Ukrainian unit from Third Brigade had taken over a trench system anchored by a good-size bunker. We helped them set up defenses, properly placed their machine guns and rockets, and made sure their rear flank was covered.

By now it was dark. The Russians fired illumination rounds from mortars and artillery, turning night into day. The battlefield became a collage of shadows and bright light.

It reminded me of Infantry School, but this was real life; the wrong shadow could kill you.

With the defenses finally set, the Ukrainians told us we could go get some sleep. In the morning a guide would arrive to take us back out. Our mission had been accomplished. Done.

And mine?

I was done, too. Ready to go back. I'd accomplished everything I came for.

Everything I *thought* I'd come for.

I knew I had a lot to do: return to the States, get back to school. I'd made the Russians pay, in a small way, for some of what they'd put me through.

But retribution involved more than revenge. For the past year, longer, I'd mostly thought of myself and my enemy. Even if that score was now settled, I had more miles to go, more things to feel and understand.

Two or three hours later, one of the Ukrainians woke me.

"The guide's here. You have to go."

I checked my watch. It was shortly before 0200, two a.m.

We weren't supposed to leave until very close to dawn, when there'd at least be a little light. But the guide had to be somewhere else then. We either left now or we went back on our own.

Even in the light, it would be easy to get lost.

We packed our stuff, then filtered out of the trench. The guide wasn't an actual guide—just a young soldier who'd been through the path once before—but he seemed to know what he was doing. Between him and our night vision, I felt we'd be fine.

We'd gone a fair distance down a trail in an open field when he abruptly stopped and began to backtrack. We waited until he found a new spot to the right, and began walking again.

We were spread out, watching the field and our flank, worried that some random Russian who'd been missed during the advance might be lying nearby, ready to ambush us.

There was an explosion, loud and sharp. It was followed by a bloodcurdling scream.

Belka had stepped on a land mine.

Somebody moved up to put a tourniquet on him. It might've been Austria or Speedy; at this point I can't remember.

We're taught to keep dispersion, to stay apart, to move only in the path that we already know is safe. It's against natural instinct, which tends to bunch people together for companionship and conversation. But in combat, you need separation. That's hammered into us in training. Every Marine knows it. Everyone who volunteered for Ukraine knew it.

I remembered it now. I willed myself to stay where I was. Someone was already seeing to Belka. My job was to call for medevac, not go to him. I had Austria bring me his radio.

"Bandito, Bandito," I called, using the Command call sign. "This is Gulag. Be advised we have a casualty patient. Belka. Method of injury, land mine. Severe injuries to the lower leg and possible femoral bleed. Tourniquet applied. Position roughly one click south of our last. Please advise."

Bandito responded in Ukrainian. I had to tell him to use Russian.

He caught on quickly. "I'll respond back to you when I talk to Third Brigade," said the GUR contact.

I hope this doesn't take a long time. We're pretty exposed in this field. Soon as the sun starts coming up, we're going to start getting butt fucked with artillery.

Belka's leg was mangled and he had to be in a lot of pain, but he was a hard SOB. He didn't act like he was in shock. We didn't have any painkillers, no little syrettes of morphine. All Belka had in the way of distraction was a cigarette, which he was smoking calmly.

Bandito came back on the radio with a coordinate for the medical evacuation. A vehicle would meet us a hundred meters to the south.

Straight ahead. Through what we now knew was a minefield.

"Sir, we're not going to move one hundred meters through a minefield where we already took a casualty," I responded. "We'll all be casualties."

"Okay." Bandito hesitated. "I thought you had a guide with you."

"We do. But apparently he's not a very good one, because he led us into a minefield."

"I'll figure something out," replied Bandito.

Angry, I went over to the kid who'd led us into the minefield.

"How do we get out of here?" I asked him.

He looked at me stone-faced.

"Do you speak Russian?" I demanded.

He didn't answer.

I grabbed him by the collar and yelled. "Hello!! Do you fucking hear me??!!"

"I think he's in shock," said Austria.

He must have been. He was just a kid, in way over his head.

I was mean to him, I admit. I was pissed because my buddy had just had his leg blown off. But I was meaner than I might have been. Than I wish I was.

A couple of scouts from Third Brigade arrived to help us over to the collection point. I gave one of them my radio so he could communicate directly with Third Assault Brigade, rather than having to go through GUR.

We began moving out. The trail was narrow. Pele started to take a step off for space.

Hey, don't step off the trail! There could be mines there!

Don't step off the trail!

Don't!

The earth erupted. Pele's leg blew into oblivion. Something whacked my own legs hard.

I started to fall, knowing I'd just been hit bad. So bad, I was sure to die.

TWENTY-SEVEN

READY TO DIE

Both my legs hurt, but my right felt worse.

Femoral artery.

I reached for the tourniquet on my belt, pulling it out as I started to collapse.

Cut off the bleeding. Stay alive.

I pulled the tourniquet over my leg, positioning it above the wound as I fell softly onto my butt, sitting upright.

I tightened the tourniquet. In training, we practiced to get that done within two minutes. Here it took seconds.

Tighter. Good.

Pele screamed nearby. Much of his leg had been blown off by the mine. Austria or Speedy got a tourniquet on him.

"My eyes!" yelled Greek. "My eyes. Do I have an eye? Check my eye!"

Speedy leaned over with a flashlight. Greek's eye was intact, though there was shrapnel all around it.

"My balls," Greek cried. "My balls. I got hit in the balls."

His groin was a mass of blood.

"Yan," I called. "Hey, Yan, can I get a little bit of help, buddy?"

I tried to be calm. Logical.

"Are you hit?" he asked.

"I think I need another tourniquet."

"Where are you hit?"

"I think in the femoral."

"Are you fucking kidding me, bro?"

"I'm sorry."

He put my second tourniquet a little bit above the one I'd put on.

"I think it needs to go higher," I told him.

"Higher?"

"I think so. I feel it higher. The pain."

Yan put on the second tourniquet. My leg was pretty shredded.

"Casevac on the way," he told me, indicating that Command had already been told we needed a casualty evacuation.

I don't know how long it took for the evacuation team to get to me; a couple of hours, maybe. In the meantime, the pain just kept coming.

Pele asked someone if he could get his leg back. They told him it was gone.

Yan tried to take my rifle away but I wouldn't give it up. In training, they teach you to take the rifle away from the casualty. They say a wounded man might go into shock and become combative, possibly killing friendly troops.

I soon learned, though, that another good reason to take the rifle is so they don't kill themselves. The pain is incredibly bad, and many a soldier has preferred instant death to something more drawn out.

I thought about it myself, but only for a moment. I'd already put my family through so much.

Hearing that I had killed myself . . .

If I was going to die, it wouldn't be because of weakness.

But I held on to the rifle. I was thinking that the Russians were nearby, that they might come and overrun us. I'd at least get one or two before they killed me.

As long as I had the gun, I could fight. I was going to fight. That's why I was here. Get the Russians back.

The pain kept building. Yan went off to help the Ukrainian soldiers take Pele to the rendezvous.

Maybe I should kill myself, I thought. I should just do that.

No. You already put your family through so much.

End the pain.

If you're going to die, just die on your own. Don't be a coward.

My fingers started to go numb. I thought maybe my plate carrier was cutting off my circulation, so I took it off.

The tingling continued.

My left foot started tingling as well. The sensation climbed up my toes to my foot.

What they don't tell you about tourniquets—your limb swells. My leg looked like it was twice as big as it normally was.

That's weird. Tingling and elephantiasis.

Weird.

Tourniquets also hurt. Another thing no one says.

My entire body started tingling. I couldn't move the ends of my fingers.

Something bad is happening.

I had the radio. "Hey, Yan, if it's possible, can you guys send two guys back? I'm going to try to help you hop out on one leg, but in a couple of minutes, I'm not going to be able to help."

Yan came back with Teddy. They stood me up, my arms around both their shoulders.

I was able to hop. More or less. By now it was daylight, and we could see that there were mines all over the place. We were in the middle of the world's thickest minefield. Or so it seemed.

We had to scoot past a bunker at the edge of the field. There was a mine there, inches from the path.

They don't see it!

"Stop!" I yelled.

We stopped. They thought it was because of the pain.

"There's a mine right there," I told them, pointing out a MON-50.

Yan looked at it. "Deactivated," he said.

We passed by carefully.

We got out to a stretcher. I was carried to the collection point under some trees. Greek was there, hobbling around—pockmarked with shrapnel, but stalking back and forth.

By now my fingers had stopped working completely.

"You want some water?" asked Teddy.

I tried to grab it, but couldn't grip. Teddy put the bottle in my mouth.

My body was shutting down. I felt my hands curling up, my wrists caving back to my chest. I had *T. rex* arms; I was a fossil dinosaur; I was one of the Russians I'd seen on the trail, curling up to die.

Trash.

I guess this is rigor mortis setting in. I'm dying.

The shrapnel probably spun through my leg until it got up higher and then cut my artery near the pelvis.

I'm going to die here.

I tried to ask for more water, but I couldn't talk right. My words slurred. I knew exactly what I was trying to say, but when I tried to speak, my tongue wouldn't work right.

The tingling vibrated in my face. Tremors ran across my lips.

I'm going to die very soon. Right here.

Ironic. The Russians manage to get me on the last day.

Ha!

I laughed out loud.

I should ask God for forgiveness for my sins.

No. I know I'm going to hell. I need to focus on what's important before I die.

"Greek, I need you to say something to my family."

"Oh come on, man," he said. "I think you're being a little dramatic."

Greek could be a jerk.

"Look at my hands." I slurred the words.

He grabbed my hand, then let it go. It retracted back into my chest, like it was on a spring. He could tell it was stiffening, and realized things were getting serious for me.

"What do you want to say?" he asked.

"Tell my family—"

"Tell your family that you died doing what you love."

"No—"

"Tell them you love them."

"No. Shut the fuck up."

They already knew all that.

"I want you to tell them I died a free man."

If it hadn't been for my family, I would have died on the concrete floor of solitary. I wanted them to know that even though I died, everything that they went through wasn't in vain. I died free.

No one could take that from me. I had freedom.

And retribution.

"Tell them you died a free man?" said Greek.

"Right."

"All right."

"Good."

Just then, the BMPs showed up. Artillery shells quickly followed. Soldiers jumped off the vehicles. It seemed like an entire platoon had arrived to get us out of there.

The sked or stretcher they put me on was a thick piece of plastic that wrapped around me as they double-timed to the back of the BMP.

A round whistled nearby. I still see it, landing ten meters away, closer, exploding, debris going everywhere . . .

Now I'm truly dead.

But I wasn't. Neither were the guys carrying me.

They tried to get me onto the bench in the back of the personnel carrier, but I couldn't move my body to help and the stretcher kept getting stuck at the hatchway. I wanted to yell that they should just throw me in, but my mouth wouldn't work. Someone screamed at them and they smushed me in there, diagonally, half on, half off the bench at the side. They rammed the door shut, knocking it against my head.

Probably it hurt. At that point, I didn't feel it.

I hope these guys aren't all going to die right now trying to save me. I'm already dead.

The BMP began grinding away. Pele and Belka were put in a second BMP nearby.

More explosions. And yet we didn't get hit.

That's the weird thing about artillery. It'll blow up right on top of you and you're sure you're dead. But you're not even hit. Then there's the shell, like maybe the one that hit Super Dave, where it's so far off it can't possibly get anyone, and yet it does.

We started getting bombarded by Grads, 122mm rockets fired in volleys. Rockets hit maybe every second. The BMP was struck, either by shrapnel from a Grad or an anti-personnel mine. The interior vibrated like a rectangular gong.

Please don't catch fire. I don't want to burn up. Let me die of blood loss first.

Thirty seconds later, something else hit us. The track propelling us banged, messed up somehow.

I'm going to get stuck in this. It's going to catch fire. The crew is going to bail out. They're going to forget that I'm in here and I'm going to catch on fire and die.

The BMP kept moving. More shells landed. Explosions.

Then nothing.

I threw up. Puke soaked my uniform.

After the shelling subsided, the BMP commander came down the hatch and looked at me.

He grimaced, and went back up.

Even he thinks I'm dead.

We drove down to a main road, where an armored ambulance waited. The rear opened. As they started to take me out of the BMP, I realized the Russians were now shelling the ambulance. They were missing, but they were definitely aiming at it.

"Hurry!" someone shouted. "Get him in."

They shoved me in, got Belka and Pele inside, too, and buttoned up. The medic began working on us as we hauled out of there.

Pele was pretty lost. He'd said something earlier about not wanting other people's blood, about wanting to be left. I told him that wasn't happening. Now he was close to delirious with pain.

I told him he was going to be all right.

"Shut up, Gulag," he snapped. That was Pele. Now I was sure he would survive.

The medic cut my pants, inspected the wound, then hit me with an injection. Pain reliever, I assume.

He went back to my leg. I think he took some shrapnel out. I didn't want to watch. Or even think about it.

They drove us to a field hospital, a small building that maybe had been an urgent care or medical clinic at some point in the past.

Now it was overwhelmed with wounded patients on stretchers and gurneys in the hallways, others walking everywhere in between. Men were missing limbs; others had their eyes or heads wrapped. Blood puddled everywhere.

They set me down in a hall to wait for treatment. Someone came by. I asked if I could use his phone, to tell my parents and Autumn that I was okay.

"Of course."

I texted my dad.

Hey, it's Trevor. I got wounded. But everything is OK. They said that I'll probably keep my leg and I'll update you more when I get my phone.

Waiting outside of the operating room, I watched as they brought a guy out on his gurney. He looked like he'd already died, pale, glassy-eyed. He was alive, though.

Why does he look like that?

They wheeled me in. Someone appeared in front of me, looking like the evil anti-hero of a slasher movie. He was dressed like a butcher, had a surgical knife in his hand and a tray stacked with more.

"You're not going to cut me," I told him.

"Yeah. I am," he said.

"But you're going to knock me out first."

"I don't have the anesthetics."

"Do you have a local anesthetic?"

"Yeah, I'm going to give you that. You won't feel anything."

"Are you sure?"

He raised his hands in a kind of shrug.

The surgeon gave me the local and started cutting. He opened the wound up with a spreader. He had scissors, and he started cutting away bits of my leg, clearing blood clots. Weeks later in a Ukrainian hospital, it would turn out that I still had a piece of shrapnel buried deep inside the upper part of my leg near my pelvis. It had entered my lower thigh and tumbled upward. Neither he nor subsequent doctors would be able to get it out. But he knew his business, and did what he needed to save my life that day.

And yeah, I felt it. I really felt it.

It was the worst pain I've ever felt in my life. I wanted to scream but it hurt so bad I couldn't speak. I felt all of the blood leave my face and I started shaking.

Finished working on the clots, the doctor applied an anti-bacterial. He cleaned and treated the entry wound. That hurt almost as bad as his scissoring.

"Can we cut your shirt off?" he asked.

"Hell no," I told him. "It cost three hundred bucks."

I pulled it off for him. It was covered with blood and vomit, but at that moment, it was the most precious thing I owned.

"Do you have a bag for this?" I asked.

They brought one.

Funny thing: a lot of guys do care about their gear when they're brought in for an operation. I ran into a guy who said he broke down and balled when the doctors cut his pants off him to operate.

They were Crye. I felt his pain.

As they wheeled me out of surgery, I caught a glance from a guy waiting to go in. I realized he was probably seeing how pale I was, and wondering why that was, as I had earlier.

He'd find out soon.

Pele was too badly off to be transported immediately. Belka and I were driven across country to Dnipro. Greek had managed to walk out and initially didn't even go to the field hospital. He even took his looted AK-12 with him. Eventually he would have surgery to remove shrapnel, including the bits near his private parts. He was very happy to send us weekly photos of the progress there.

That was his kind of humor.

I was at the hospital in Dnipro for a few days, where I had another operation. Super Dave and Yan visited me. Super Dave limped into the room: he'd been a patient here himself.

I called my father and told him what happened.

He asked if I wanted him to call the State Department to see if they could help get me home.

"No."

"The president?"

"No. Everything's cool. I'll be okay."

I don't know what the State Department or the president could have done for me at that point. Probably just be mad that I had gone to Ukraine after they'd gone to such lengths to get me home.

After a few days, they sent us to Kyiv in a train. Every compartment was full of guys with bloody bandages, missing limbs, eye patches. Some were in wheelchairs, some on stretchers.

We were met by a fleet of ambulances, which ferried us to various hospitals around the city and region.

When an American service member is wounded in action during a deployment, they're eventually transported to a hospital for treatment far from the battle area, and from there taken to a facility back in the States.

That wasn't about to happen here. I wasn't a serviceman, and the US had done backflips to keep volunteers at arms' length. I realized that I would have to find my own way home once I recovered.

While I was figuring that all out, I asked my father to call a foreign embassy in America to see if they could help a teammate who'd lost his foot on the mission. He didn't have anyone to help him and was in a bad way.

My father didn't have much information about him at the time, and couldn't answer all of the consular officer's questions. Fearing the worst, Dad asked if they would be able to help the wounded man.

"Sir, we are not the United States," snapped the officer. "We take care of our veterans."

Ouch.

But true, in this case. My teammate got home. In the meantime, the timeline for my own journey suddenly got moved up.

I still had shrapnel in my body, and it became obvious very quickly that I'd have to go to either the US or Europe to get further treatment; the hospitals in Ukraine were just too overwhelmed. I was trying to figure that out when Jonathan Franks got a phone call from a reporter who asked if I had been wounded in Ukraine.

And then added something like, "By the way, we're printing a story saying he is."

I don't know exactly how word got to the reporter. Someone in the State Department or Department of Defense leaked it, with the other agency then confirming it.

Jon managed to get the reporter to agree to hold off on publication for a couple of days, to give me time to leave the country. I wasn't worried about myself so much as everyone at the hospital. I thought if the Russians knew I was there, they would aim an attack on it. They really didn't need much of a reason to hit hospitals, but nailing me might give them special satisfaction.

Scrambling to leave within forty-eight hours, I reached out to anyone I thought might be able to get me out of the country. Jake Tapper happened to call my mom from his family vacation in Europe. When told of the situation, he offered to have a CNN news crew in Ukraine take me to Poland.

I had a misadventure with an American non-governmental group that honestly didn't seem to know which direction was up. They not only couldn't help me, but gave misinformation to an aircraft that had arranged to take me out of the country, blocking that chance to leave.

Finally, I found Dr. Janine von Wolfersdorff at Life Bridge Ukraine, who arranged for me to be evacuated by FRIDA, an Israeli-Ukrainian NGO directed by Mark Neviajsky. She also persuaded a German hospital to treat me. I'm very much indebted to them.

In the end, the US decided to allow me to go to a military hospital in Germany—most likely because they were embarrassed by Germany's offer of free treatment.

I was still in Ukraine the next day when *The Messenger* reported my situation.

Other publications quickly followed. Fortunately, I made it out without the Russians trying to stop me or take revenge on anyone who'd helped me.

My parents were immediately bombarded with press inquiries. Even though I'd been endangered by my own government, we limited our response and my public anger to minimize any effect it might have on prisoner negotiations. We didn't know if any were happening, but I certainly didn't want to endanger anyone because of some official's carelessness, vendetta, or pique.

Whatever.

I did find one thing very ironic. The media speculated that my decision to fight might endanger negotiations. But was that my fault or theirs, given that Russia had not known about it until they blasted it to the four corners of the world?

The media was pretty critical of my decision. Not that I remember asking their opinion.

My treatment at the military hospital was very minimal. They didn't even do an MRI on my less-injured leg, even though it, too, had been riddled with shrapnel. I still had metal in my body; in fact, I have it to this day.

After their precursory treatment, they told me I was free to go. And in fact, should do so ASAP.

"I can't walk," I told the staff. "I've got shrapnel in my legs. I have nowhere to go till I can get someone here to help me."

Fortunately, an officer found an empty barracks where I could stay.

As usual, my parents had offered to come to Poland or even Ukraine to get me and drive me to Germany. They both got international drivers licenses and packed their bags.

I warned them off; I didn't want them to come here or spend any more money on me. Besides, I had my own agenda.

Autumn met me in Frankfurt.

I was sure our relationship was over. But here she was.

Which isn't to say we fell into each other's arms instantly. For one thing, I was hobbling around on a cane, and letting go of that would have been dangerous. But she did dress my wounds, and in general took better care of me than a team of doctors would have.

For another, real life is not like movies. I felt awkward around her, still closed up, cautious about showing my feelings. And she was still very, very mad.

But loved me anyway. And I loved her.

We spent time in Europe, going to Prague, then Krakow, then back to Frankfurt, gathering up gear that was on its way back to me from Ukraine. I slowly recovered both my health and our relationship. By the time we returned to the US, we were a committed couple again, closer together than before I'd left.

EPILOGUE

My parents say I'm back to my old self since I came home from Ukraine. "He laughs again" is how my dad puts it.

Maybe.

I do feel like I've healed something that had been badly broken. Before I went to Ukraine, I didn't sleep well, I obsessed about killing, about getting revenge. I sleep better now. Mostly.

I was not myself. Now I am.

Medically, I have issues. My back, the shrapnel deep in my body. But I carry on.

Since I've been back in the States, I've gone back to school and am currently enrolled in an international studies program. Eventually, I hope to work for the State Department or find some other capacity where my experiences and education will be useful.

I've spoken out about Russian cruelty, and the conditions in Ukraine. On October 9, 2024, as we were working on this book, media reported that a Russian court found me "guilty in absentia" of having fought against them in Ukraine. I was placed on an international wanted list and given a fourteen-and-a-half-year sentence in their prison system.

Russia accused me of being a mercenary, which of course wasn't true, but that wasn't their biggest lie.

They claimed I'd been killed there.

I don't know how that quite squared with the prison sentence. Maybe they planned to resurrect me before incarcerating me.

My parents' lives are a lot calmer. While I was the one in prison and then at war, they experienced an outrageous amount of stress. They spent a lot of money getting me home. I don't know exactly how much. They've never shared the figure and refuse to do so. I'm sure however much it was, it affected not just their present lifestyle, but their future retirement as well.

Still, neither expresses regrets.

"If it took living in a tent and eating rice and beans every day," says my mom, "I would still have done it."

It wasn't quite that bad, but they both work pretty hard at a time when many people their age are fully retired. I can never repay them financially, let alone emotionally, for what they did.

"The shock of seeing your kid in a cage never leaves you," says my mom. "And then there's the toll of trying not to let him see how it's affecting you."

I did see. Then and now.

My mom was approaching menopause when I was arrested, and the stress may have made that transition even more difficult. She began stress eating as a way of coping. "Eating my feelings," she explains. Donuts, sweets—they helped her cope, and added something like fifty pounds to her relatively small frame. Thankfully, she's been able to lose that, eating better and walking every day. At the worst times, her doctor prescribed a mild antidepressant as well as drug therapy to cope with the midlife hormonal changes. She's beyond both now.

Talking with her sisters and close friends helped her get through many of the darker days. Her real buoys were my aunt's two small grandchildren, whose energy and open love was like a tonic every time she saw them.

My parents have continued to help the people they met while I was imprisoned. Though he has now left for other commitments, my dad was deeply involved with a group called Bring Our Families Home, which was just forming about the time I was released from prison. As of this writing, there are more than sixty Americans officially detained overseas, though we believe the true number may be in the hundreds.

The government tries to limit the number of people they recognize as wrongfully detained, let alone those they try to help. If you ask my father, he'll tell you he believes the only people the United States government will help in a foreign country are those that are very wealthy, very famous, or are related to or know someone high up in our government.

Or like me, they gain enough publicity that the situation could negatively impact the next election.

That's where Bring Our Families Home comes in. By increasing public awareness and continuing to prod elected officials, the organization works to increase the odds that all families will get the help they need.

Pele and Belka recovered from their wounds. Both received prosthetics. Both returned to Ukraine to continue the fight.

Jose and the bulk of his team worked with the Ukrainian marines for several months. When they finally saw action, their unit was pushed into an unplanned assault against prepared Russian positions. Ambushed, they were struck by helicopter gunships and an artillery barrage. Devastated, they fell back with severe casualties.

Jose and his team escaped serious injury. He has since returned home.

Rogue Team reconstituted itself, gaining additional members after I left. In late October 2024, Super Dave led them through Russian lines for an operation in Russia's Bryansk Oblast. Attacking a bunker manned by Russian FSB border guard troops, they encountered an unexpectedly large force. Super Dave and Rauta were hit as they began to withdraw. Corey Nawrocki picked up the machine gun and laid down suppressive fire for the rest of Rogue Team to withdraw until he was killed by a sniper. Super Dave, Rauta, Corey, and a team member named Poet, whom I didn't know, all died in the engagement.

The rest of the team managed to make it out, traveling some twenty-five kilometers back to the Ukrainian lines.

A few months later, Austria was also killed.

I owe my life to those guys. Super Dave was one of the bravest and best leaders I've ever known. Rauta and Austria dragged me off the battlefield when I was wounded; they never blinked, even when it seemed the whole sky was falling down on us. They were the greatest warriors I've ever known. It was a privilege to have known and fought alongside them.

I can't help but think I should have been there for them, as they were for me.

Until Valhalla, brothers.

ACKNOWLEDGMENTS

I owe many people thanks. First and foremost is Lina, for being a wonderful human being, and putting her own life at risk to help me and my family. She never gave up on me even when I was tempted to give up on myself. No matter how dark the tunnel was, she found light in it. I will never be able to repay what she has done for me.

Thank you, too, to Autumn, who has stayed by my side as I have recovered.

After the prisoner swap, my parents released a statement thanking some of the many people who helped get me home. It was heartfelt, and remains a good summary of their thanks, and my own:

> *For much of this ordeal, Jonathan Franks has been at our side every step of the way and we would not be here today without his help. Aside from our own family, and Lina, no one has worked harder or contributed more than Jon to bring Trevor home. We're also grateful to Montel Williams for his support.*
>
> *First and foremost, we'd like to thank President Biden for his kindness, his consideration, and for making the decision to bring Trevor home. The president's action may have saved Trevor's life.*

We'd also like to thank Ambassador John Sullivan, Ryan Feeback, Anton Vozheiko, and the Moscow embassy staff for believing in Trevor's innocence and for their zealous advocacy. We'd like to thank Secretary of State Antony Blinken for his efforts and for keeping a promise to bring up Trevor and Paul Whelan in all conversations with the Russian government. Similarly, we'd like to thank National Security Advisor Jake Sullivan, Alexandra Miller of the NSC, and Victoria Bonasera (Consular Affairs). In particular, we want to thank Roger Carstens and his SPEHA team, including Fletcher Schoen, Steven Gillen, Carolee Walker, and Dustin Stewart. We can't say enough about the importance of the work they do every day for hostages and wrongful detainees.

We'd like to thank our congressman, August Pfluger, for his unwavering support; Congressman McCaul, Senator Cornyn, Congresswoman Jackson Lee, Leader McCarthy, Adam Kinzinger, Congresswoman Haley Stevens, Congressman Mike Conaway, members of the House Foreign Affairs Committee, and so many others who worked together in a bipartisan manner to bring Trevor home.

We are also grateful to Governor Bill Richardson and Mickey Bergman for traveling to Moscow in the hours before the Ukraine war broke out in an effort to win Trevor's release.

There are so many people in the local, national, and international media that we want to thank for their genuine concern for Trevor's situation. In particular, we'd like to thank ABC's Patrick Reevell and CNN's Jake Tapper. There are foreign journalists that were of great assistance to us, but we can't release their names here for fear of retaliation.

We want to thank our relatives, friends, neighbors, and strangers who supported Trevor and our family through this ter-

rible ordeal. Know that your letters, emails, signs, donations, and contacts with elected officials helped get us through this and make a difference.

Let me add my thanks to my attorneys in Russia for proving my innocence to the world—and for their patience in dealing with me and my father.

My translator, Yulia, was a kind, considerate, and dedicated friend. She saw me at my worst and was always there not only to translate, but to console and listen. Her visits were like a little bit of freedom. I can't thank her enough.

Thank you, Fred Smith, the founder and chairman of FedEx, and a decorated US Marine combat veteran, for allowing Mickey and Governor Richardson to use your personal jet to fly to Moscow for negotiations on Paul Whelan's and my behalf.

Thanks, also, to Dr. Janine von Wolfersdorff, who founded and headed an NGO now known as Life Bridge Ukraine. She got approval for my treatment by the German military as well as organized my evacuation from Ukraine, contacting Mark Neviajsky, the founder and director of an Israeli-Ukrainian organization called FRIDA, which facilitated my evacuation to the Polish border.

I also need to thank Jake Tapper and CNN for offering to drive me from Ukraine to Poland after I was injured. (I was fortunate to have set up the other arrangements, but I greatly appreciate the offer.) Jake has been a phenomenal booster and a good friend to my family and me throughout my ordeal, and afterward.

I can't give enough credit to my guys who kicked my butt around and helped get me back in shape after my ordeal in Russia. Kyle Nance, owner of the fanciest pants I've ever seen on a Marine. Cody "Cockblockrell" Cockrell, who earned his nickname on a beach that shall remain nameless, and also punched me in the face over a zebra cake. John Michael Sidwell, whom I taught everything he knows about pistols.

Seriously, without my personal Three Amigos, I would never have made it to Ukraine or, more important, back.

Jim and I would like to thank our agents, Byrd Leavell of UTA and Judy Coppage of the Coppage Company, for their efforts. Our editor at William Morrow, Mauro DiPreta, was a valuable sounding board and adviser; we truly appreciate his patience. Assistant Editor Allie Johnston was a big help smoothing some details out for us. Thanks also to the entire team for their help and continuing efforts, including William Adams, Lisa Glover, Jennifer Eck, John Simko, Tess Day, and Brian Moore for his excellent cover and persistence in the quest to get it just right.

We'd also like to thank some of the various sources who helped augment my memory, especially my parents, Lina, Jose, Yan, Jon Franks, and those whose position required anonymity or continued to be in the line of fire as we were working on this book.